Jewish Genetic Disorders

Jewish Genetic Disorders

A Layman's Guide

Ernest L. Abel

McFarland & Company, Inc., Publishers
Jefferson, North Carolina, and London

Acknowledgments: Portions of this book were read and helpful suggestions made by Drs. Melvern Ayers, Ken Ginsburg, Maureen Mayes and David Savinarch. Any errors in the text are entirely mine.

Library of Congress Cataloguing-in-Publication Data

Abel, Ernest L., 1943–
    Jewish genetic disorders : a layman's guide / Ernest L. Abel.
       p.   cm.
    Includes bibliographical references and index.
    ISBN 0-7864-0941-X (library binding : 50# alkaline paper) ∞
    1. Genetic disorders—Popular works.   2. Jews—Diseases—
Popular works.   I. Title.
RB155.5.A245   2001
616'.042'089924—dc21   2001031589

British Library cataloguing data are available

Manufactured in the United States of America

McFarland & Company, Inc., Publishers
  Box 611, Jefferson, North Carolina 28640
   www.mcfarlandpub.com

Table of Contents

Introduction

Illness is as old as mankind. Explanations for its occurrence date back to the beginnings of recorded history. In the ancient Near East, people believed illness was caused by someone's misdeeds, especially against capricious gods. Today we attribute illnesses to diseases, disorders in the structural or functional integrity of cells.

When a cell's integrity is threatened, it attempts to maintain its internal balance by summoning its reserves. If conditions exceed a cell's ability to cope with the threat, it tries to adapt. If there are no reserves (or medications) to call upon or adaptation isn't possible, cells die. When a critical number of cells in an organ die, the organs of which they are a part can no longer work properly. Eventually the organ shuts down. If a person cannot arrest the deterioration, the whole body may cease to function, and the individual dies.

Cells may become damaged as a result of conditions that originate outside the body, such as viral or bacterial infections or physical injuries, or from environmental conditions such as excessive heat or lack of water. They can also be injured by substances that we voluntarily take into our bodies, such as alcohol, cigarette smoke, and pollutants. Cells can also be injured by poisons that our bodies make because of genetic abnormalities we are born with, or because our genetic inheritance makes us more susceptible to these and other environmental factors.

In this book, the terms "disease" and "disorder" are used interchangeably, but an important distinction is made between "disease/disorder" and "illness." This is because someone may have a disorder and not have an illness. An illness is a condition in which someone is unable to perform normal daily activities. Although all illnesses stem from disorders of bodily structure or function, not every disorder results in illness. Diabetes and asthma, for instance, are disorders of the way the body works,

1

but a diabetic or an asthmatic who takes the appropriate medication can function normally most of the time. Despite the medication and sense of well being, however, the disorder is still present.

In other cases, a disorder may be present but it doesn't make its effects felt. This may be because other parts of the body are able to suppress its effects or because the condition is so mild that its effects are unnoticeable. Still other disorders have no effect unless they are confused with other disorders. Essential pentosuria, for example, is a condition in which an excessive amount of pentose sugar is excreted into urine. The disorder, which occurs almost exclusively among Jews, does not cause any illness and is not symptomatic of any other disorder.

Acquired Versus Hereditary Diseases

The causes of diseases are often divided into the categories of acquired and hereditary. Acquired diseases result from exposures to outside factors like viral infections, chemicals in the environment, physical damage, etc. Hereditary disorders are conditions that are part of our being over which we often have no control.

Distinctions between acquired and hereditary diseases, however, are overly simplistic. Certainly, there are many hereditary disorders, like Tay-Sachs, which will run their course no matter what we do. But for many diseases there is an interplay between environmental conditions and heredity. Many parents have at one time or another wondered why their kids seem to catch every cold, while someone else's kids seem to be totally immune. Two adults may live in the same neighborhood and one may become very sick because of some contaminant, while the other remains perfectly healthy. If there were no colds or contaminants, no one would get sick from them. At the same time, if heredity made everyone nonresponsive to these conditions, no one would get sick.

Somewhere in between these two ideals are different degrees of illness-causing conditions and hereditarily-determined sensitivities to those conditions. Although some hereditary conditions are influenced by environmental factors, for most of the disorders described in this book, the problem concerns an intricate bodily mechanism that does not operate properly.

What It Means to Belong to an Ethnic Group

During the late nineteenth and early twentieth centuries, anthropologists attempted to legitimate classifying people into racial groups on the basis of physical features they believed were unique to them. For many anthropologists, the physical differences they observed between people from different parts of the world were visible evidence that people could be classified in terms of distinctive, hereditary "races." They measured physical characteristics, sometimes with painstaking detail, and then grouped people with similar characteristics into racial categories, typically Caucasoid (European), Negroid (African), and Oriental/American Indian (Asian). Some anthropologists also considered Jews, especially Ashkenazi Jews, to constitute a distinctive race because they were believed to possess body features such as "Jewish noses" that were different from the noses of other Europeans.

People from the same racial group were believed to share not only the same physical but also the same biological, mental and moral characteristics. Scientists like Francis Galton, Charles Darwin's cousin, insisted the Jews were different from other people. They had, he said, a "cold, scanning gaze," a whiney voice, a hooked nose, a peculiar smell, and a neurotic disposition. Studies concentrated on showing how Jews were physically and mentally inferior to other Europeans, and many of these ideas subsequently found their way into prominent textbooks.

While the research was ostensibly intended to develop a basic understanding of the different peoples of the world, it was instead a forum for justifying the ranking of people on a hierarchy of superiority. The bias underlying all such studies was that the different races represented different stages in evolution, with black Africans on the lowest rung, white Europeans on the highest, and Jews somewhere in between. These beliefs were in large part responsible for subsequent social policies, including limiting the immigration of Jews into the United States during the 1920s.

Although race is still a socially recognized way of categorizing people, modern day anthropologists eschew this classification because physical traits like height, skin color, or noses are not discrete; they vary in a continuous manner. Just as black people differ markedly in their skin color, Jews from different parts of the world are very different in their physical features, and they cannot be distinguished from non–Jews by physical appearance alone. Incidentally, the "Jewish nose" is much more common among non–Jewish Germans.

Instead of using race as a way of categorizing different people, most anthropologists and other social and medical scientists are much more likely to describe characteristics that occur with high frequencies in certain groups as "ethnic." Anthropologists have described ethnic groups in various ways, but in general these characteristics include a highly biologically self-perpetuating group, sharing an interest in a homeland connected with a specific geographical area, a common language and traditions, including food preferences, and a common religious faith. Ethnic groups also have a membership that identifies itself and is identified by others as different from other groups. Jews themselves never spoke of themselves as a "race," but rather as a "people," a group united by the characteristics of ethnicity.

Heredity Versus Geography

The characterization of ethnicity is significant for several reasons. First, the idea of a biologically self-perpetuating group is very much in keeping with the more familiar notion of "common blood" and, more recently, genetic homogeneity. Second, it implies that while some groups may have an identity with a particular area of the world, they are not necessarily the only ones to have that claim.

In the last 30 years it has become evident that certain diseases tend to occur in some ethnic groups more than in others. However, medical researchers looking for diseases unique to a particular ethnic group have repeatedly emphasized the need to be careful in distinguishing between those diseases that are specifically associated with the group being studied and those common to the geographical area of the world a group considers its homeland. Diseases related to geography usually transcend specific ethnic differences.

At the same time, medical researchers also have to consider the historical and present-day living conditions of the ethnic groups they study. People who live in highly polluted areas, or areas where there are poor drainage and sewer systems, are likely to develop bacterial infections at a much higher rate than those living in less polluted and contaminated areas. People may become segregated in different areas because they are forced to, or because poverty prevents their escape, or because they have always lived there and have no wish to live elsewhere (although they would be happy if their part of the world were more healthy). These living conditions may account for relatively high or low frequencies of a physical characteristic or disorder associated with a particular ethnic group.

In other words, the fact that some diseases are more common among specific ethnic groups doesn't necessarily mean that they are "hereditary." A disorder could be due to some environmental factor, but because many members of an ethnic group live in the same area, a disorder might show up more often in that group simply because of increased exposure.

On the other hand, if a group remains tied to a particular geographical area for centuries and marries within its own, it may selectively adapt itself to local conditions so that those with a hereditary sensitivity die early in life, while those who are less sensitive survive and have children who are also less sensitive, thereby altering the hereditary pattern of the population as a whole.

Some Ethnic Differences in Health

Physical and physiological differences between different ethnic groups are apparent for many traits. Differences between people in skin color are obvious. Skin color varies from very dark in the equatorial parts of the world to white at its poles. These differences emerged as a result of the migrations of people from Africa many thousands of years ago and occurred because skin responds to solar radiation. Since dark skin protects the body from solar radiation, the darker the skin of someone living in Africa, the more likely that person will live to an age old enough to be able to produce children. People living in the northern parts of the Northern hemisphere are not as endangered by exposure to intense solar radiation, but they have a need for vitamin D, which solar radiation produces when it passes into the body. As a result, their skin is very pale.

People living in an area over thousands of years have developed other differences from one another as well. While there are very few illnesses that are totally "ethnic" in the sense that only people from the same ethnic background are affected by them, there are nonetheless many disorders and reactions to which people of specific ethnic backgrounds are more prone than are other groups. African Americans, for instance, are more prone to sickle cell anemia, a disorder affecting the ability of red blood cells to carry oxygen, than are Asian Americans, but they are less likely to suffer from malaria. African Americans also have higher levels of low-density lipoprotein, the "bad" kind of cholesterol, and lower amounts of high-density lipoprotein, the "good" kind of cholesterol, in their blood.

Many of these physical and physiological differences translate into increased susceptibilities to a higher occurrence of illnesses like stroke and heart disease, increased susceptibility to infections, and higher infant mortality for black people compared to whites. Other groups have their peculiar susceptibilities as well. Native Americans have a higher than normal prevalence of diabetes; Hispanic Americans have a higher than normal susceptibility to lupus, an immune disorder that affects connective tissues;

Asian Americans are prone to lactose intolerance (an inability to digest dairy products properly, resulting in stomach cramps and diarrhea); and Italian, Greek, and Middle Eastern Americans are more often affected by a blood disease called thalassemia than people whose ancestry is northern European.

Ethnic factors likewise affect responses to drugs. People of Asian ancestry are twice as sensitive as those of European ancestry to the effects of propranolol, a common medicine for controlling blood pressure, and to Valium, an antidepressant, and they are considerably more sensitive to alcohol.

Jews also have their particular susceptibilities to various illnesses. Some of these are discussed at length in this book. For now, it's worth mentioning that some disorders affect very large groups of Jews, whereas others affect much smaller groups. Oriental Jews (those from Middle Eastern areas like Iran and Iraq) and Sephardic Jews (primarily from Spain and North Africa), for instance, are much more prone to some disorders like thalassemia than are Ashkenazi Jews (who mainly come from Europe) whereas a disorder like Tay-Sachs or breast cancer primarily affects Ashkenazi Jews.

There are also a number of illnesses that occur more commonly among particular groups of Jews whose ancestry has been traced to particular parts of the world. Phenylketonuria, for instance, mainly affects Jews whose ancestral homeland for many generations was in Yemen, while Creutzfeldt-Jakob disease, which causes dementia, and cystinuria, which causes kidney stones, are relatively common among Libyan Jews but very rare among Ashkenazi Jews. These isolated relationships became especially noticeable after the state of Israel was created and massive numbers of Jewish immigrants began streaming there from other countries. However, it is still the case that, when considered as a whole, Jews from different parts of the globe are much more similar in the illnesses that affect them when compared to non–Jews.

This brings up an important point. Few of the disorders that are discussed in this book are exclusively "Jewish." Many of the same disorders, such as breast cancer and cystic fibrosis, that affect Jews affect other ethnic groups as well. However, in each of these different ethnic groups there are specific genetic variations that cause these disorders which are peculiar to them. The fact that a disorder is described in this book as "Jewish" implies that like Tay-Sachs it occurs among Jews at a much higher rate than in the general population, or that there is a peculiar genetic variant linked to the disorder which is more common among Jews.

Although there are a considerable number of disorders that definitely belong in this survey, the scientific evidence for many of them is not as strong, or some only show up in relatively few Jews. The list of "Jewish disorders" keeps changing as some of these are removed and others are added.

While ethnically-related susceptibilities and traits have been recognized for a long time, many medical scientists and communities in general have either ignored them, refused to study them, or in some cases have argued vehemently against the very existence of such associations. The reason for this reluctance is that any evidence that a disorder is ethnically related raises the specter of hereditary inferiority. Having just lived through the Holocaust, Jews are especially anxious about a recurrence of Nazi-like programs of identification and extermination that began long before the Holocaust, such as the "anthropological genetics" of the latter part of the last century and the early half of our own century. Sensitive to a replay of the past, some Jewish scholars have been concerned that any scientific evidence showing that Jews are unique in any way could lead again to their classification as a "distinct" or "separate" race. What makes this era of genetic research different from the research of the past, however, is that the criteria are clearly and narrowly stated and the conclusions medical scientists draw from those studies are tightly linked to their stated purpose.

There is, however, no guarantee that any scientific discovery may not be used for a purpose for which it was not intended. But someone who is prejudiced against another will always be able to find some reason to justify that prejudice. So while we should remain vigilant about the uses to which all scientific discoveries are put, we should not bury our heads in the sand. Ignorance is seldom bliss and attitudes have definitely changed.

While the realization that you or your children have some hereditary predisposition to an illness may not necessarily alter your probability of experiencing that illness, that awareness may prompt your family members to take precautions that lower their chances of developing the hereditary disorder. At the same time, exciting new developments are happening every day, and some diseases once thought incurable are no longer fatal. A good example is colon cancer, which affects Ashkenazi Jews at a considerably higher rate than others. Knowing this, people of Ashkenazi background should have regular medical examinations of their colons. If the cancer can be detected in its early stages, it can be removed before it invades other areas of the body.

An unexpected twist to the ongoing discovery of hereditary linkages between bodily disorders and specific groups of Jews is that in some cases these linkages enable historians to trace the migration of the Jews from their ancestral homeland throughout the Diaspora. In so doing, these studies have provided a unique insight into the origins of Jewish communities throughout the world and have shed light on the extent to which different Jewish groups share a common ancestry.

The first two chapters in this book provide the background for what we mean when we say a particular hereditary disorder is "Jewish." Chapter One provides basic information about how heredity works and particularly what genes, the units of heredity, are and what they do. It isn't necessary to know the nuts and bolts of our genetic inheritance to understand how each of the disorders discussed in this book affects the body. However, a passing familiarity with genetics will enable you not only to understand the cause of various disorders that have a hereditary basis, but also to get a better sense of what we mean when we say a disease is a "Jewish disorder." Chapter Two presents a broad overview of Jewish history and explains how and why "Jewish disorders" exist.

Understanding why some disorders are more common among Jews may at least enable some readers to answer the perennial "why me?" question. Some of the disorders that primarily affect Jews appear to have emerged as a way of protecting the population as a whole from certain diseases. Having one "dose" of a defective gene causing an illness in some way makes someone less susceptible to other illnesses. These "Faustian bargains," as they are called here, will not be a comfort if you or someone in your family is suffering from a "Jewish disorder," but they do explain why this disorder never went away.

For readers who prefer to go directly to the chapter discussing a particular disorder, there is a glossary at the end of this book that provides a brief definition of many of the concepts discussed in Chapters One and Two.

The remaining chapters examine the symptoms and causes of many of the disorders generally recognized as occurring with a greater frequency among Jews than among non–Jews. These disorders have been arbitrarily grouped on the basis of either a common causal factor or a feature they have in common.

In many cases, some other grouping would be just as reasonable. For instance, Tay-Sachs Disease is classified as a Lipid Storage/Metabolic disorder because it is caused by a dysfunction in lipid metabolism, but it could also have been placed in a section for Neurological Disorders because it has neurological consequences. Regardless of which category a disorder has been placed into, each disorder is examined in terms of subcategories: Variations (if any), Symptoms, Frequency, Cause, Faustian Bargain (although this subcategory is only included for disorders for which such a bargain has been proposed), Diagnosis, Transmission, Treatment, Prevention, Further Information (organizations that can be contacted), Screening Centers (where genetic testing facilities for the disorder are located), and References (books and scientific articles that may also be consulted for more information).

The final chapter considers some of the implications of genetic testing. One of these implications has already been mentioned with respect to identifying Jews as a distinctive people. Does the mere existence of "Jewish disorder" mean that anti–Semites will have a new biological weapon for stigmatizing Jews? Other questions concern employee relations. Are businesses likely to hire someone who is going to develop a disease? Will insurance companies refuse to insure such people, or if they do insure them, will they charge higher rates? Will immigrants have to be screened first for their gene pools before being admitted to the United States? Would you marry someone if you knew that person carried a particular gene? Although we now are able to predict with reasonable certainly who will develop a disease, why would anyone would want to know if he or she is at risk for a debilitating disorder if it is incurable?

References

Bonne-Tamir, Batsheva, and Avinoam Adam, eds. *Genetic Diversity Among Jews.* New York: Oxford University Press, 1992.

Gilman, Sander. *The Jew's Body.* New York: Routledge, 1991.

Goodman, Richard M., and Arno G. Motulsky, eds. *Genetic Diseases Among Ashkenazi Jews.* New York: Raven Press, 1979.

Lasker, Gabriel W., and Robert N. Tyzzer. *Physical Anthropology.* New York: Holt, Rinehart and Winston, 1982.

Levav, Itzhak, Robert Kohn, Jacqueline M. Golding, et al. Vulnerability of Jews to affective disorders. *American Journal of Psychiatry* 154 (1997): 941–947.

Naroll, Raoul. On ethnic unit classification. *Current Anthropology* 5 (1964): 283–312.

Neel, James V. Inferences concerning evolutionary forces from genetic data. *Israel Journal of Medical Science* 9 (1973): 1519–1531.

Polednak, Anthony P. *Racial and Ethnic Differences in Disease.* New York: Oxford University Press, 1989.

CHAPTER ONE

Basic Facts About Genetics and Genetic Diseases

A ny book that deals with diseases and genetics necessarily contains many medical terms. Since this book was written for a general audience, I have tried to minimize the use of these terms as much as possible while still retaining the important concepts inherent in them.

We begin with the smallest and most basic component in every living organism, the cell, because ultimately every disease comes down to some abnormality in our cells.

The human body contains trillions of highly specialized cells that are grouped together to form tissues like muscles and nerves. These tissues are likewise arranged in larger groupings to form specialized organs like the heart and the brain. Regardless of how specialized and complicated they are, the body's organs are essentially collections of cells working together to perform a particular function. These cells have to work efficiently and appropriately or the organ to which they belong will not be able to do its job. Just as a chain is as strong as its weakest link, an organ is as healthy as its weakest cell.

Inside a Cell

The inside of a cell is filled with a watery substance called cytoplasm and many small structures called organelles (literally, "little organs"). Each of these organelles performs a special function within the cell. Some of these organelles make a cell's energy; some synthesize proteins; some break down fat; some, like the lysosomes, contain enzymes that remove waste matter from the cell. The largest of these organelles is the nucleus. The job of orchestrating all these activities belongs to components within the nucleus, which we call genes.

Genes and Chromosomes

Genes are basic biological units that contain the instructions enabling cells to perform their various functions and are collectively arranged into chromosomes. The vast number of different things our cells do for us every moment of the day requires an equally vast but finite number of genes. Some geneticists estimate that every cell has as many as a hundred thousand different genes.

A cell's genes are positioned like beads on thread-like structures called chromosomes. Chemically, chromosomes are composed of molecules called deoxyribonucleic acid, or DNA for short. Genes are clusters of chemicals in DNA, composed of elements called bases. These elements are usually abbreviated in terms of their first letter: A (adenine), T (thymine), C (cystine), and G (guanine). The information in the book you are reading is written in a code made up of 26 different letters of the alphabet. Morse code uses dots and dashes to represent each of these letters and by grouping these dots and dashes in arrays of three or four, every letter is represented. Computer language is a binary code. Each element is a "bit" combined in groups of eight called a "byte." The genetic code is "written" using different sequences of these four bases, combined in groups of threes, a grouping called a "codon."

Structurally, chromosomes are made of two strands of DNA that twist around one another in a spiral staircase-like structure that has come to be known as the "double helix." Every base on a strand in the double helix is paired to a base on the other strand in a specific combination: A is always paired with T, and C is always paired with G. These pairs are held together by a chemical connection called a "bond" and these pairings and bonds give the double helix its form and its stability.

Except for the male sex chromosome, chromosomes come in pairs and each species has its own characteristic number of pairs. Humans have 23. To distinguish these pairs from one another, geneticists assign a specific number to each pair according to their appearance under the microscope. Twenty-two of these pairs are called autosomes. The twenty-third pair is called the sex chromosome because it alone determines gender. This is also the only chromosome in which each member in the pair may be visibly different. In females, the two chromosomes are similar and each is designated with the letter "X." In males, they are different. This is because males have one "X" chromosome and a much smaller chromosome designated by the letter "Y." In other words, females have two X chromosomes, while males have one X and one Y chromosome.

Collectively, the genes which comprise our chromosomes are referred to as the "genome" (a contraction of "gene" and "chromosome"), the "genotype," or the "genetic code." Every species has a genotype unique to that species. This is the reason dogs produce other dogs, cats produce other cats, and people produce more people. The physical features we develop as a result of our "genotypes" are called "phenotypes." Hair color, height, body build, as well as the symptoms of the "genetic diseases" discussed later on in this book, are phenotypes resulting from our unique genotypes. Although we all share many of the same genes, their expression and precise structure may vary in subtle yet discrete ways. The more closely we are related to someone, the more genes we share with that person. Brothers and sisters, for example, have many more genes in common than cousins. The only people who share exactly the same genes are identical twins.

A gene is like a sentence: it has a beginning and an end and it contains a message. The sentence may be made up of a hundred bases or several thousand. There are now "gene-sequencing machines" that are able to "read" hundreds of thousands of bases a day. Once a piece of DNA has been sequenced, it can be compared with a central bank of sequences to see if it is in any way different. The general message is always the same: make protein.

The specifics of every sequence are what make people different. In the present context, this sequence of protein production makes them either more or less likely to develop certain diseases. Some of these proteins are structural; they give parts of our body their particular shape and a supporting edifice, and they give individual cells membranes to keep their internal components intact. Some are enzymes, catalysts that enable cells to work efficiently and at lightning speed. Catalysts enable our bodies to break down food into the nutrient chemicals we need to survive, absorb those nutrients across cell membranes, put those nutrients to work, and get rid of whatever is left over. Some are regulatory proteins like hormones that enable cells and organs to communicate with one another harmoniously. Every disease described in this book occurs when genes cause cells to produce too much or too little of some protein.

These proteins are in turn made out of clusters of chemicals called amino acids, joined together in a specific order that is dictated by a particular gene. The genetic code specifies which amino acids are to be joined and where they are to appear in the chain of amino acids that make up a protein. Although every cell contains the same genes, every cell does not make the same proteins. This is because cells are specialized to perform a particular task and only certain genes are expressed for a given cell type. A protein that a muscle cell might need to enable it to contract is not needed by a nerve cell, so it isn't made. How a muscle cell "knows" to make a muscle protein and not a brain protein is still a mystery.

Since each chromosome comes in pairs and every chromosome contains the same arrangement of genes, there are two genes that could produce a cell's proteins. The only exception, as noted previously, are the XY chromosomes characteristic of males. The X chromosome is much longer than the Y. The genes on the Y chromosome have the job of making the proteins that determine the early development of the embryo and the structures that will develop into the male reproductive system. A sperm cell can contain either an X or a Y chromosome, whereas an ovum can only have an X chromosome. The male, therefore, determines the gender of a child. If an X-carrying sperm fertilizes an ovum, a girl (XX) will be born; if a Y-carrying sperm fertilizes an ovum, it will develop into a boy (XY). Because females have two X chromosomes, they have two copies of the same gene, whereas males have only one copy. As we will see in a moment, this has important implications for the development of certain diseases.

In some cases, a change in just a single base (called a "point mutation") may result in the substitution of one amino acid for another in a protein, making it nonfunctional. This in turn could result in a lifelong debilitating disease. The classic example is sickle-cell anemia, a blood disease in which the CTC (cystine-thymine-cystine) part of the gene which codes for the amino acid glutamic acid is altered to CAC (cystine-adenine-cystine), the code for the amino acid valine. As a result of this single amino acid substitution, the structure of the hemoglobin molecule in red blood cells is altered, resulting in a "sickling" of the molecule, which interferes with its ability to transport oxygen. A faulty protein due to a defect in a single gene is also the cause of many of the "Jewish diseases" discussed in this book.

Polymorphisms

To complicate matters even more, a gene can have many subtle variations, most of which still result in a gene that functions normally. These variations are called "polymorphisms." A genetic polymorphism is the occurrence in a population of two or more distinctive variants or pheno-types for the same trait, in which the least frequent form exists in at least 1 percent of the population. An example of a polymorphism is blood type. Some people are type A, some B, some AB, and some O. Every popula-tion has a certain percentage of individuals with each of these types. The highest frequency of blood group O, for example, is found among Cen-tral and South American Indians (about 90 percent) compared to 68 per-cent among people of northwest European descent and 71 percent for African Americans. These and other polymorphisms are very common, and geneticists have long wondered about the conditions that were respon-sible for their origins and continuation.

Mutations

A permanent change in the sequence of gene bases, like the one caus-ing sickle-cell anemia, is called a "mutation." Every genome contains hun-dreds of mutations. Fortunately, most of these mutations occur in regions within a gene that act as "fillers" and are therefore harmless, although they are nevertheless passed on from one generation to the next. Mutations are always occurring. Geneticists estimate every individual genome will undergo about 30 new mutations in a lifetime. Most occur spontaneously in the normal course of the hundreds of millions of cell divisions that occur throughout the body as cells duplicate themselves. Rarely do any of these mutations have consequences for our health. One reason they usually don't affect us is that they are usually repaired by other genes. There are cer-tain genetic diseases, however, where the repair mechanism is disrupted. The readiness with which this occurs may depend on the genes involved. Differences in certain genes in being able to do the repair may be what makes us either more or less predisposed to certain diseases.

When cells duplicate, the double helix making up each chromosome unravels into two separate strands. Each strand then creates a comple-mentary strand of itself by attracting bases from within the cell accord-ing to the rule that As and Ts and Gs and Cs must match. In the course of each duplication, billions of bases will have to be correctly matched. Cells contain enzymes to correct mismatches but sometimes a mismatch can escape detection. If the mutation occurs in any cells except the repro-ductive cells, it will not be passed on to the next generation. If it does occur in a sex cell, then it could be passed on and someone may inherit a mutated version of a gene sequence.

In the 1930s, geneticists discovered that errors could also be induced by external factors like X-rays. The first indication came from the lowly fruit fly—the geneticist's favorite experimental subject because they don't take up much space, reproduce in a very short time, and, it turns out, share some of the same genes as humans. In one of the first such studies, geneticists found that when fruit flies were irradiated, the gene for red eyes was altered in some of the flies so that their offspring were born with white-colored eyes, and all of their descendants also had white eyes. Subsequent studies showed that a number of chemicals called "mutagens" could also permanently alter genetic material and these alterations in some instances would pass from generation to generation.

Founders

Mutations can arise as a result of environmental exposure, but more likely they arise as a result of some error that occurs in the course of cells duplicating themselves. However, unless the mutation occurs in the sex cells, it will not be "passed on." If it does occur in the sex cells, it has the potential to affect that individual's children. In that case, the parent in whom the original mutation occurred is known as a "founder." The classic example of a founder effect in recent history is hemophilia, the uncontrollable bleeding disease that plagued many of the royal families of Europe and Russia. England's Queen Victoria was the genetic founder for the disease, since it had never occurred in her ancestors. However, several of her children and grandchildren developed it and introduced it into the royal families of Europe and Russia.

Founder effects arise among small groups of people who have their movements restricted and choose to marry or are forced to marry others from within a small group. This inbreeding maintains the founder mutation in that population. Once the group expands, the founder mutation spreads to a much larger proportion of the population and accounts for the relatively high frequency of certain diseases in those populations. Because of these founder effects, a very few individuals can have a major impact on a family, as in the case of Queen Victoria, or on a population.

Phenylketonuria, for instance, occurs very rarely among Ashkenazi or Sephardic Jews, but has a relatively high frequency among Jews from Yemen. In this latter group, the disorder is caused by a mutation that has been traced to a single Jewish inhabitant of the capital of Yemen in the early 18th century. Founder effects that are "dominant" may appear in the founder's children. If "recessive," they might not show up for many generations later.

Some mutations, on the other hand, have "survival value" because they increase resistance to disease; for example, the disorder that causes sickle-cell disease is found in regions with endemic malaria and confers resistance to that disease. Some disorders like Tay-Sachs, Niemann-Pick, Gaucher and Mucolipidosis are due to gene mutations that affect the same internal cellular component, the lysosome. While one of these conditions may have arisen as a result of a founder effect, it is much less likely that a founder effect could have given rise to four similar mutations in the same population. These kinds of genetic susceptibilities to some disorders and resistance to others are called Faustian bargains.

Dominant and Recessive Genes

Even if a mutation occurs in a gene, it usually will not result in any noticeable difference because there are usually two genes for every trait, and the normal gene generally counteracts any mutation in the altered gene. Even though genes are located at the same position on each one of the chromosomes in the pair, each gene in the pair may or may not be identical. The corresponding genes on the chromosome pair are called alleles. When both alleles are identical, the alleles are said to be homozygous. If each allele is different, the alleles are heterozygous. Homozygous genes produce exactly the same protein product; heterozygous genes do not. In the case of heterozygous genes, the gene that dominates is the one whose protein will usually be expressed.

Since every individual receives a complete set of genes from each parent, he or she has two genes for every trait (with the exception of the genes for gender). Sometimes a trait represents the blended influence of each gene. However, it is often the case that one gene is more powerful than the other and only its influence is expressed. In this situation the influential gene is said to be dominant and the noninfluential gene is said to be recessive. Eye color is an example of a phenotype which is affected by dominant and recessive genes. The gene for brown eyes is dominant; the gene for blue eyes, recessive. If you inherited the gene for brown eyes from your mother and either the gene for brown or blue eyes from your father, you would have brown eyes. Blue eyes occur only when the recessive trait for blue is inherited from *both* parents. Inheritance of shades of brown, blue and green is still a mystery.

Dominant alleles, whether they are normal or abnormal, override their opposite allele. If the dominant gene is abnormal and its opposite is normal, the abnormal condition the dominant gene codes for will more likely be expressed. If the dominant allele is normal and its opposite is abnormal, the normal condition will be expressed. A recessive allele can only produce a disorder if there is no dominant allele to override its effects. Mutations in recessive genes are only expressed when both genes in a pair have the mutation. If one of the genes is normal, it can override or compensate for the mutated gene unless the latter is dominant. One such example is Tay-Sachs Disease. In this disorder, an enzyme protein that breaks down a chemical substance in the cell, and thereby keeps it from accumulating and poisoning the cell, is missing. If an individual has one normal gene for making the enzyme and a mutated form of the gene that is unable to do so, the normal gene will be able to cause enough of the protein in each cell to be produced to keep the cell from being poisoned.

Autosomal dominant and recessive genes each have their own inheritance characteristics. In both kinds of disorder, male and female children are equally likely to be affected. In autosomal dominant disorders, however, one of the parents will usually exhibit signs of the disease and there is a 1 in 2 chance that parent's child will inherit the disease. If both parents are affected, all their children will inherit the disease.

In the case of an autosomal recessive disorder, neither parent may exhibit signs of the disease, but one or both may be "carriers," that is, they have one of the abnormal genes for the disease. If both parents are carriers, that is, both are heterozygous, they will each carry one copy of the defective gene. Their children will have a 1 in 2 chance of being a carrier and a 1 in 4 chance of inheriting both defective genes and therefore developing the disease. If one parent is a carrier and the other is not, none of their children will exhibit signs of the disease, but each child will have a 1 in 2 chance of being a carrier.

An important exception to the rule about recessive genes needing two mutated copies for their trait to be expressed is if those genes are on the X chromosome. Since a female has two X chromosomes, she can have two, one, or no copies of a defective gene. If one of the genes on her X chromosome is recessive and a mutated form of a disease-related gene, she will not have the disease herself but she will be a carrier. A male, on the other hand, will be affected and a carrier if he has only one copy of the defective recessive gene because there is no other allele to offset the defective gene's effects. As a result, males are much more likely to be affected by sex-linked diseases. The classic example again is hemophilia, which affected the males in many of the royal families of Europe and Russia and was passed down to them by England's Queen Victoria.

Genetic diseases can also arise as a result of abnormalities in either the number or structure of one or more chromosomes, which can occur during formation of sperm or eggs. In such cases, instead of each paired chromosome segregating into one cell during cell division, the two chromosome pairs stay together. Then when fertilization occurs, the newly formed cell contains either three of the same chromosomes, or only one. These kinds of accidents, however, are not passed on from generation to generation and do not occur more commonly in any group of people.

It is important to keep in mind that when geneticists say a child has a 1 in 4 or a 1 in 2 chance of inheriting a genetic disorder, these are probabilities which in practice are only found when we look at large numbers of people. When we look at an individual family, the theoretical probabilities often do not appear. For example, two couples with the same dominant mutation may each have four children. Where all of the children of one couple may inherit the dominant mutation and develop the disorder, none of the children of the other couple may do so, and therefore none of their children will develop the disorder. Every conception is a chance encounter between a sperm and an egg, and each is independent of every other such encounter.

Penetrance

Another condition to keep in mind when thinking about the odds of developing symptoms of a genetic disorder is the phenomenon of "penetrance." One of the still-unsolved mysteries of genetic diseases is that even if an individual has the defective gene which causes a disease, the disease may not be expressed—a phenomenon called "reduced penetrance." "Complete penetrance" means the effects of a gene are always expressed; "nonpenetrance" means that the defective gene is present, but its effects are not expressed, although its effects may be expressed in the next generation if the gene is inherited.

An example is a recessive mutated gene whose effects are counteracted by a normal gene. In reduced penetrance, only some of those who have the defective gene develop symptoms. This is the reason that the frequencies of many genetically related diseases are far lower than what might be expected based on their carrier rates. In other words, the fact that a woman may be found to have a genetic defect associated with a particular disease like breast cancer, for instance, does not necessarily mean she is destined to develop breast cancer. Medical researchers speculate that the reason behind reduced penetrances is that other genes or as yet unidentified environmental conditions modify the expression of many genes.

Single and Multifactorial Gene Disorders

Genetic diseases are typically divided into single and multifactorial disorders. Single gene disorders result from a mutation in a single gene, whereas multifactorial disorders are caused by a complex interplay between environmental conditions like diet or smoking. Cancer is an example of a multifactorial genetic disorder. Whereas single gene disorders are inherited in patterns that are very recognizable to geneticists, the same cannot be said for multifactorial genetic disorders.

There are two subtypes of single-gene disorders, autosomal and sex-linked. Autosomal disorders are due to mutations in genes that do not affect gender; sex-linked disorders are related to the sex chromosomes, nearly always the X chromosome.

Autosomal single gene disorders are either dominant or recessive. Recall that a dominant gene influences the characteristic of a trait, whereas a recessive gene will influence trait characteristics only if an individual has another similar recessive gene. If the dominant gene is abnormal, then a child who inherits that gene will exhibit that abnormality even though it inherits a normal or recessive gene from the other parent. In the case of a recessive gene that is abnormal, a child must inherit that gene from both parents to be affected.

Genetic Screening

It is now possible to determine if someone is a carrier for a particular mutation that causes a disease. This technology has resulted in complex and controversial questions about who should be offered such testing and when should it be done. These issues are examined in the last chapter of this book. The remaining section of this chapter deals with the basic methods used for predictive testing.

There is no way to correct or stop the inexorable deterioration associated with many of the hereditary disorders that predominantly affect people of Jewish ancestry. The only way they can be prevented from occurring is for couples at risk for conceiving an affected child not to have children, or to abort an affected child. Genetic testing for carrier status for many disorders like Tay-Sachs is now routine. For most couples, it is done prior to marriage, prior to their decision to have children, or during the first trimester of pregnancy when the possibility that a child does or does not have a particular disease can often be determined.

The oldest and still the most basic technique for identifying genetic disorders is to look at a cell's chromosomes under a microscope to determine their number and arrangements. Some chromosomal disorders are due to abnormalities in replication so that instead of the newly created cell having a pair of similar chromosomes, it has one or three. Other abnormalities are related to the actual structure of the chromosome. These kinds of abnormalities arise when breaks or translocations occur in a chromosome and parts of the chromosome are either lost or rearranged. Some of these changes result from exposure to environmental agents like ionizing radiation; others like Fanconi's Anemia and Bloom Syndrome—two "Jewish diseases"—result from a relatively high level of chromosomal instability. In some of these breaks, called "balanced translocations," a single break occurs in each chromosomal pair and the two segments switch. Although there is no net loss of genetic material, the altered sequence of genes means that the proteins, or their order, or those genes that control their expression, may be altered.

Another widely used procedure for assessing gene mutations is to determine the amount of protein present in tissues. In Tay-Sachs Disease, for instance, there is an almost total absence of an enzyme protein called hexosaminidase A. Carriers of one of the defective genes will have lower than normal levels of the enzyme but nevertheless are able to produce enough of it so that they do not experience any illness. This kind of test enables medical geneticists to identify as carriers people who have no symptoms of the disease. Related biochemical tests can identify proteins with abnormal structures. The levels of these proteins are normal, but because of their altered structures the proteins are unable to perform optimally.

Even more sophisticated techniques now enable medical geneticists to see if a gene has a mutation, even to the point of determining if a single base is missing or has been altered in a gene containing thousands of bases. The main limitation to these kinds of tests is that the specific mutation in the gene causing the disorder has to be known. Some genes, for instance, have more than a hundred different mutations and it is not feasible to look for each one, especially the mutations that are not very common.

Even if a gene has not been identified it may still be possible to predict its presence if the vicinity of the gene on a chromosome is known, and genes in the vicinity can be used as "markers" for the target gene. Since genes close to one another on a chromosome are generally linked when they are passed on together as cells divide, the marker is inherited along with the target gene. The closer a marker is to the mutation, the greater the likelihood it will be found to be associated or linked with the mutation. Detecting the presence of a marker is almost the same as detecting the gene itself. However, for this to be an effective screening test, the marker linked to the mutated gene must be close along the chromosome or must be unlike the marker linked to the normal gene. If the two markers are identical, geneticists won't be able to tell if the mutant gene is present.

There are three main uses for screening tests. One is to determine if someone is a carrier. Carrier screening for high-risk groups like Ashkenazi Jews for inherited diseases like Tay-Sachs has dramatically reduced the incidence of this disorder because carriers can either decide not to marry or not to produce children. A second reason is that if a couple do marry, they can know the odds of having a child with a certain defect. Third, if they conceive a child, they can have it tested to see if it has inherited a particular disorder. If the result is positive, then that couple will have to make the emotionally difficult decision about aborting that pregnancy.

The two procedures for determining if a child has inherited a particular genetic disorder, prior to its birth, are amniocentesis and chorionic villus sampling. In amniocentesis, a needle is inserted into a mother's abdomen between her fourteenth and eighteenth week of pregnancy, and some of the amniotic fluid surrounding the fetus is removed. This fluid contains fetal cells that can be examined for the presence of abnormal genes.

In chorionic villus sampling, or CVS, a doctor inserts a narrow tube through a woman's vagina and cervix into the placenta during her ninth to twelfth week of pregnancy, and a small number of cells are removed. As in the case of amniocentesis, these cells can then be examined for the presence of abnormal genes. A list of laboratories that perform such screening tests is provided at the end of this book.

For couples whose religious beliefs would keep them from terminating a pregnancy there is an alternative called pre-implantation diagnosis, which is performed prior to pregnancy. In this case, a woman's eggs are removed from her ovary and transferred to a laboratory dish where they can be fertilized. After the fertilized eggs begin to divide into either four or eight cells, one of the cells can be removed for genetic analyses. If these analyses indicate that the embryo has not inherited a specific defect, it can be implanted in the mother's uterus.

Modern science has also developed some methods to compensate for a genetic fault. People with Gaucher Disease, for instance, lack a particular enzyme but they can be given it intravenously, although the treatment is still very costly. In the very near future, however, medical geneticists believe they will be able to replace faulty genes with healthy ones. The basic technology has already been developed and clinical trials for some genes, like the gene for cystic fibrosis, are already underway. The major impediment for some diseases is developing what geneticists call a "vector," which is a delivery system to insert a healthy gene into the genome.

References

BOOKS

The standard reference on genetic disorders is Victor A. McKusick's *Mendelian Inheritance in Man*. This book is currently in its twelfth edition. It comes in three volumes and lists more than 9,000 different genetic diseases. This book assumes a sophisticated knowledge of medical genetics.

The standard references for Jewish genetic illnesses are Richard M. Goodman, *Genetic Disorders Among the Jewish People* (Baltimore: Johns Hopkins University Press, 1979); Richard M. Goodman and Arno G. Motulsky, eds., *Genetic Diseases Among Ashkenazi Jews* (New York: Raven Press, 1979); A. E. Mourant, *The Genetics of the Jews* (Oxford: Clarendon Press, 1978); and Batsheva Bonne-Tamir and Adam Avinoam, eds. *Genetic Diversity Among Jews: Diseases and Markers at the DNA Level* (New York: Oxford University Press, 1992). Each of these texts contains valuable information, but like McKusick's text, they assume a sophisticated knowledge of medical genetics.

JOURNAL ARTICLES AND BOOK CHAPTERS

Livshits, Gregory, R. R. Sokal and E. Kobyliansky. Genetic Affinities of Jewish Populations. *American Journal of Human Genetics* 49 (1991): 131–146.

Scriver, Charles R., S. Kaufman, R.C. Eisensmith, et al. "The hyperphenylalanemias." In: Scriver, Charles R., Arthur L. Beadet, William S. Sly, et al., eds. *The Metabolic and Molecular Bases of Inherited Disease*. New York: McGraw Hill, 1995, 1015–1075.

CHAPTER TWO

Why the Jews?

According to Jewish law, you are a Jew if your mother was Jewish, or if you converted to Judaism in the prescribed manner. People who convert to Judaism or those whose mothers converted to Judaism, however, are unlikely to carry the same kinds of genes that are associated with the "Jewish disorders" described in this book because they originated hundreds and in some cases thousands of years ago.

Present-day Jews are usually divided into three subgroups, depending on where they trace their homelands prior to the twentieth century and for many centuries before that. Ashkenazi Jews come from Western, Eastern and Central Europe, especially the countries of Germany, Poland, Romania, and Russia; Sephardic Jews mainly come from the Mediterranean, especially Spain and the North African countries of Libya and Morocco; Oriental Jews mainly come from the Middle East, especially Iraq and Iran.

Regardless of these identities, most Jews (excepting converts) attribute their origins to a single ethnic group descended from the Biblical patriarchs, beginning with Abraham. Although there was certainly intermingling with other cultures, the Jews in Biblical times were always an identifiable people who lived in their own communities apart from neighboring non–Jewish communities.

The Bible also tells us that after the Exodus from Egypt, Israel was composed of 12 tribes, and males from the tribe of Levi were entrusted with special religious obligations. Aaron, Moses' brother, was selected as the first High Priest (Cohen) from among the Levites, and his male descendants were singled out to be the hereditary High Priests, the Cohanim (plural of Cohen).

On the basis of this tradition, which continues to the present, a team of genetic anthropologists from Israel, the United States and England, headed by Dr. Karl Skorecki at the Technion Israel Institute of Technology in Haifa, examined the Y (male-determining) chromosome, which is passed from father to son, of present day Levites and Cohanim. Unlike the other 22 chromosomes, which swap genes when producing sperm and eggs (see Chapter One), the Y chromosome retains most of its genes intact, thereby maintaining the genetic identity of a male's progenitors through generations.

If the Biblical tradition were true, Skorecki believed that, even with the Diaspora, there should still be a genetic identity among Levites and Cohanim similar to the traditional heritage. To test this possibility, the genetic anthropologists compared genes from 306 Jewish males from Israel, Canada and England, 106 of whom described themselves as Cohanim. What they found was that the Levites' Y chromosomes contained too many different genes to conclude they were distinctive, but the Y chromosomes from Cohanim were very similar among Ashkenazi and Sephardic Jews, implying a common origin.

Using sophisticated models of genetic change, the scientists traced the origin of the priestly Y chromosome to some time during or shortly before the Temple period in Jewish history, about 2,000 to 3,000 years ago. These findings support the belief not only that the Cohanim are descended from an ancient priesthood, but that Jews in general share a common ancestry predating the split into Ashkenazi and Sephardic communities.

In 1991 a different team of geneticists, headed by Dr. Gregory Livshits, compared Jews from 28 different countries with one another and with their neighbors, on a number of different genetic "markers." Genetic markers are "fillers," or patches of inactive genes whose only known purpose is filling the space between active genes. Since they serve no known biological purpose, these markers usually show up randomly in the general population. However, when a group of people share identical markers, it means they share a genetic inheritance. In other words, they are descendants from the same parents or group of people.

Livshits found that certain markers appeared more commonly among Jewish populations from different areas than was true for non–Jews, regardless of where they were presently living. To Dr. Livshits, this meant that Jewish populations in various parts of the world share a common original gene pool which has undergone relatively few changes.

While population studies such as Skorecki's and Livshits' support the Biblical tradition that today's Jews come from a single historical population, which became slightly modified following the Diaspora, similar studies appear to disprove historical claims. One such study, for instance, failed to support the belief of Yemenite Jews that they were descendants of one of the ancient Israelite tribes that left the Biblical kingdom in the time of King Solomon. Genetic analyses indicated that in fact they did not differ genetically very much from Arabs, implying that they were probably descendants from Arab converts to Judaism.

The Diaspora

The earliest known Jewish settlements outside of Israel occurred in the seventh century B.C.E., when a group of Jewish mercenaries founded a colony at Elephantine in Egypt. The beginnings of the Diaspora, however, are usually traced to around 723 B.C.E., when the Jews inhabiting the kingdom of Israel were forcibly deported from their homeland by the Assyrian king, Shalmanesar, and some were made to settle, according to some historians, in Assyria and present-day Kurdistan, a mountainous area claimed by Turkey, Iraq and Iran.

Kurdistani Jews are a relatively distinctive group of Jews. In large part this is because Kurdistan is a mountainous region, isolated from the major commercial centers in the countries that it straddles. In fact, little was known about the Kurdish Jews until about 30,000 of them, virtually the entire population, emigrated to Israel. Subsequent genetic studies have shown they are a distinctive population who experience the highest rates of two blood-related disorders (glucose-6-phosphate deficiency and beta-thalassemia) of any Jewish population.

The next momentous event in Jewish history took place in 586 B.C.E., when Judea was conquered and thousands of Judeans were forcibly deported to Babylonia (modern-day Iraq) or fled to Egypt. The Jewish population in Babylonia subsequently became the center of Oriental or Babylonian Jewry, the first of the main subdivisions into which Jews are divided. Although many of the deported Jews later returned to Judea, some geneticists believe those who remained in Babylonia represent the original Jewish gene pool.

In the following centuries, the Babylonian Jewish community had its ups and downs, enjoying great freedom in some centuries and harsh restrictions in others. Many of these Jews traveled throughout the Middle East as traders or refugees, some going as far as India, where their largest settlement was in Bombay. Today, these Indian descendants of the Babylonian Jewish community are known as the Cochin Jews. Other Oriental Jews migrated to Afghanistan and areas in the Caucasus and established small communities in these regions as well.

During the Hellenistic period, after the time of Alexander the Great and during the height of the Roman Empire, Jews remaining in what would subsequently be known as Palestine, as well as those in Babylonia, took the opportunity to relocate. Many settled in Alexandria, Egypt, which became home for thousands of Jews. Jews also settled in Rome and other parts of Italy, in Greece, in areas around the Black Sea, and in the modern day countries of Romania, Hungary, Spain, and France, and in the northern part of Africa.

Strabo, the Greek geographer, said there wasn't any place in the habitable world that had not received the Jews and where they had not made their influence felt. In the year 48 C.E., the Roman Emperor Claudius conducted a census of everyone living in his empire. On the basis of those figures, historians estimate that there were about 8 million Jews in the world, with about 60 percent, or about 5.5 million, living in somewhere other than the Middle East, although Jerusalem continued to be the center of religious life for Judaism.

Toward the end of the first century C.E. Palestinian Jews revolted from Rome. In 70 C.E. they were defeated and many fled to the Jewish community in Babylonia. According to the Jewish historian Josephus, 700 Jews were brought to Rome as captives. The major dispersion of the Jews from Palestine occurred 60 years later, following the failure of a second revolt against Rome under Bar Kochba which collapsed in 135 C.E. This time the Romans were ruthless in their suppression of rebellion; Jews who were able fled to other communities in the Diaspora. For their part, the Romans renamed the country Syria-Palestina (the latter a reference to the Philistines, even though they had disappeared long ago) as a symbolic way of denying any future claim Jews in the Diaspora might have to their former homeland.

Despite the description of massive deportations, many historians believe that the migration of Jews into the Diaspora, especially where Europe is concerned, came about much less dramatically through a slow but steady movement of Jews westward into Europe beginning around the first century C.E.

During the early Christian era, Jews in the Diaspora were not subject to any persecution or segregation because of their religion, and in some countries there were even large numbers of conversions to Judaism. The first of these occurred in Ethiopia in the third century C.E. Additional conversions occurred in Yemen during the fourth century. In the fifth century, the Yemenite throne was occupied by one of these Jewish converts.

Another area into which Jews had relocated was in Khazaria, a Turkic kingdom between the Caspian and Black seas. Many Khazars, including the nobility and rulers, found Judaism appealing as a religion and adopted it, while others adopted Christianity or Islam. During the ninth century, large scale conversions to Judaism occurred among the Khazars. This encouraged even more Jews from Byzantium and Persia to settle in the country. For several centuries, Khazaria's kings, nobles, and citizenry read the Torah, wrote in Hebrew, and observed Jewish holidays.

Elsewhere, beginning in the seventh century, the Moslems conquered much of the Near East and North Africa. After that Jews in those areas were often forced to live in secluded communities among the Moslems, although there was undoubtedly some assimilation and intermarriage with neighbors.

The origins of the Ashkenazi communities in Europe are very vague. By the fourth century C.E., there were enclaves of Jews in France and Germany, living as traders and suppliers for the Roman army, but they were probably very small in number. The migration of Jews and the expansion of already-existing communities is poorly documented but appears to have continued until around the eleventh century C.E., when the first Crusades occurred. Later in that century, entire communities were exterminated as part of the Crusades. Additional mass killings occurred toward the end of thirteenth century.

Those who could escape fled eastward. Beginning in the fourteenth century, large-scale expulsions of Jews occurred throughout Western Europe, and by the fifteenth century there were hardly any Jews living in France or Germany. The vast majority of these refugees migrated to Eastern Europe, established new settlements in these lands, and began speaking a distinctive language called Yiddish, a pastiche of the languages spoken in the places where they had lived and now inhabited.

At the same time that Jews in western Europe were migrating east, Jews from Khazaria were fleeing from that country. Beginning in the eleventh century, after their kingdom was overthrown and during the following two centuries, they settled in with the Jews coming from the west. In fact, it now appears that the Khazars were the dominating influence in what came to be Ashkenazi Judaism; the medieval Jewish communities in France and Germany were relatively small compared to the Ashkenazi populations of Eastern Europe, and there is relatively little mention of their eastward migration by contemporary writers.

In another vein, linguists have pointed out that Yiddish has more affinities with the Slavo-Turkic languages and Hebrew, and with the East-Middle German dialects spoken nearer to Poland and Lithuania, than with the Rhenish-German dialect—as would be the case if the Ashkenazis originated in Khazaria. Likewise, the clothes and houses of the Ashkenazi *shtetls* more closely resembled those common in the steppe region of Khazaria than those in western Europe.

Then there is the interesting occurrence of red hair among Ashkenazi Jews. Red hair is not common in the Near East, but is believed to have been predominant among the Turkic tribes prior to their conquest by the Mongols. Finally, many of the "Jewish diseases" discussed in this book, such as Tay-Sachs, are more common among Ashkenazis whose ancestral homes are further east than west.

Leaving aside the question of the extent to which the Khazars contributed to the Ashkenazi communities that emerged in Central and Eastern Europe, the communities themselves are often subdivided into three divisions, depending on where in Eastern Europe they lived: Galitzianers in Poland and Austria; Polaks in Poland; and Litvaks in Lithuania, Latvia and Byelorussia. In most places, the Jewish communities in these countries were very small, in some cases numbering only about 50 people, although in some enclaves there may have been as many as 1,000.

In 1492, the forced expulsions that had taken place in France and Germany were matched further to the south when the Spanish monarchy declared that every Spanish Jew who did not convert to Christianity would have to leave the country. About 200,000 of these Sephardic (i.e. Spanish) Jews left and joined Jewish communities in North Arica, especially those in the cities of Tripoli and Benghazi in Libya, as well as Syria and elsewhere. Once settled in these communities, they remained relatively isolated and intermarried with one another. At the same time, many of the converted Jews who remained in Spain felt insecure and left for the South American countries of Chile and Argentina. Some of the descendants of Sephardic Jews who emigrated to Chile still remember their ancestry.

Although Jews started coming to America soon after it was settled by Europeans, the great migrations to America came mainly from the Ashkenazi communities between 1880 and 1920. In 1880, there were an estimated 250,000 Jews living in this country. During the next 40 years, massive numbers of Ashkenazi Jews, whose former homeland was Eastern Europe and the Balkans, emigrated to America, so that by 1920 the Jewish population swelled to about 3.5 million. Currently, Ashkenazi Jews comprise the largest subgroup of Jews, accounting for about 80 percent of world Jewry.

Today, Jews are free to live where they want, at least in industrialized Western countries; but like people of other ethnic backgrounds, they can often be found living in identifiable neighborhoods because they want to. This means that if a larger percentage of them develop the same disease than do non–Jews, it is either the result of being exposed to some common disease-causing agent (acquired diseases), because they share some hereditary susceptibility to that disease stemming from their bio-logical or cultural backgrounds, or because the genes they inherit destine them to develop a disease like Tay-Sachs, for which there is no cure.

Genetic Markers

Studies of "who is a Jew," from a genetics standpoint, began in the early part of the century by focusing on the genetic marker of blood type. This is because blood types are inherited; their genetic basis is very sim-ple and very well understood; and they are not modified by a person's liv-ing conditions. The blood type you are born with is the blood type you will have for your whole life.

While there are several different systems for categorizing blood types, the best known system is the ABO. The name derives from four blood types, A, B, AB and O, characterized by their reactions to chemicals that do or do not cause them to clump. The different blood types are dispersed among different populations in certain frequencies: so many people have type A, so many type B, etc.

Having a particular blood type is not helpful in telling if you belong to a particular group, but by taking groups as a whole and determining the percentages of people with each particular blood type, those groups with the same percentages should be related. By comparing the percent-ages of different blood types in one population with the percentages in another, it was therefore possible to see if they came from a common back-ground.

These kinds of studies increased as new blood typing systems were created to accommodate newly discovered differences, so that now there are six other blood types (Duffy, Kidd, Knell, Mns, P and Rh) from which to make comparisons, as well as a host of enzymes and proteins and immunological traits called histocompatibility antigens.

From a comparison of Jews on 20 of these different markers, geneti-cists have concluded that, generally speaking, Jews from any particular geo-graphical area tend to resemble one another more closely than they resemble non–Jews. Likewise, these studies support the historical argument for a Mediterranean origin of the Ashkenazi Jews and do not support the claim of a significant gene influx from non–Jewish communities. Additionally, persons in each of the main Jewish subgroups resemble members of their group more closely than they resemble Jews in the other subgroups.

More recently population geneticists have turned their focus on genetically-related diseases. The genes that are responsible for these diseases are either found in very few populations, or else they appear at relatively higher rates in some populations compared to others. Many of these diseases and their related genes are discussed at length in this book.

In general, these kinds of studies indicate that the Jews are a distinctive people who maintained their genetic identity despite extensive migrations, although among the Jews themselves there are distinct differences between the three main subgroups of Ashkenazi, Sephardic, and Oriental Jews. With the sophisticated genetic analyses that are now possible, geneticists have been able to show that, even when Jews do not differ from their non–Jewish neighbors in the frequencies with which they suffer from certain diseases, the actual genetic changes responsible for these susceptibilities are not the same. In some cases, these kinds of differences shed new light both on the ways in which Jews were affected by the Diaspora and on the Diaspora itself. At the same time, they may reveal some additional information about a person's own history, even though he or she may have no living relatives.

Why "Jewish Diseases"

Wherever they settled, Jews retained their identity. Until the latter half of this century Jews primarily lived among themselves and married within their own communities. In part their insularity was due to their political and social status. Politically, they were an identifiable minority wherever they settled outside of Israel. This made their fate and fortune dependent on the goodwill of the rulers in whatever area they lived and had the effect of making them very loyal citizens. But their dependence also forced them to rely on one another and this reduced any inward tensions that might have caused their communities to factionalize. Culturally, their adherence to their religion and their reliance on the Hebrew alphabet for their written language, regardless of what languages they spoke, helped them maintain their cultural uniqueness.

A third factor was their total inwardness. Not only were they not permitted to marry outside their religion, their dietary laws kept them from eating with non–Jews. And not only was their religion unique, they were not permitted to be present at any non–Jewish religious ceremony, so the chances of apostasy were lessened. The fact that the tradition of the Cohanim continues until today, a fact now backed by genetic evidence, indicates how strongly these factors resulted in their retention of their identity over hundreds of generations.

Also contributing to the maintenance of Jewish identity over many centuries was the backlash caused by their insularity. The self-imposed exclusivity was answered in kind by laws, adopted especially in Christian host countries, which enforced their segregation. Jews were forced to live in restricted areas called ghettos; they were required to wear badges that identified them; and they were prohibited from interacting with Christians in almost every way.

Since Jews hardly ever married outside their religion and were not permitted to travel freely outside their ghettos, their enforced "inbreeding" meant that certain biological and cultural traits were concentrated among the Jews living in each of these communities. If Jews from a particular community had an hereditary constitution which included genes that made them susceptible to certain diseases, then this gene pool would have remained confined to this community and would have intensified, since there was no possibility of dilution from outside.

Faustian Bargains

Natural or "Darwinian" selection is the process by which the frequencies of different genes change over time as a result of differences in survival and reproduction. A classic example of natural selection that has already been mentioned is skin color, which varies from very dark to white. Since dark skin protects the body from solar radiation, the darker the skin of someone living around the equator, the more likely he or she will live to be old enough to be able to produce children. People living in the far regions of the northern hemisphere are not as endangered by exposure to intense solar radiation, but they have a need for vitamin D, which the solar radiation produces when it passes into the body. As a result, their skin is very pale.

With the exception of the male-determining genes, everyone has two copies of the same gene. Some of these copies are identical; some are not. How could having a defective copy be a genetic advantage? As peculiar as this sounds to us, geneticists have found that, for a small number of genetic diseases, for both copies to be defective can be catastrophic; whereas having only one defective copy creates a "Faustian bargain" with Nature. Such people do not develop the disease for that gene because their other normal gene overrides its deleterious influence; at the same time the single defective copy prevents them from developing some other disease. If there were a selective advantage to being a carrier, says Dr. Jared Diamond, inheriting one abnormal gene for Tay-Sachs and the lysosomal diseases related to it would become "pumped up to high frequencies by selection."

This is also why sickle-cell anemia is more common among African Americans. As mentioned earlier, sickle-cell anemia is caused by an abnormality in one of the genes that governs how hemoglobin, the oxygen-carrying protein that gives blood its red color, is made. Inheriting the abnormal gene for sickle-cell anemia from both parents causes someone to develop the disease, but inheriting only one such gene protects that person from contracting malaria, one of West Africa's most devastating diseases. Individuals who inherit only one of the abnormal genes are still able to produce enough hemoglobin to transport oxygen throughout their bodies. At the same time, the abnormal hemoglobin makes them less susceptible to the parasites that cause malaria. From a population standpoint, it is obviously advantageous for everyone to have one of these abnormal genes: while 25 percent of the population has a risk of developing sickle-cell anemia, 50 percent is resistant to malaria.

The same kind of trade-off occurs with Tay-Sachs disease and diseases like cystic fibrosis. In the case of Tay-Sachs, the Faustian bargain is with tuberculosis (see the Tay-Sachs section of Chapter Five); for cystic fibrosis, the trade-off is with typhoid fever and cholera (see Chapter Nine on cystic fibrosis). Living in crowded ghettos for the last 700 years meant that over the course of many generations, people who inherited a single gene for a lysosomal disease like Tay-Sachs gained an evolutionary advantage that outweighed the personal tragedy individuals and their families experienced if they developed these diseases.

Founders

Not all of the diseases that affect Jews represent Faustian bargains. Some diseases are due to what geneticists called founder effects. As related in Chapter One, a founder is someone who develops a mutation in one or more genes and passes it on to his or her children. If people married randomly, any mutation would likely disappear from the population in a few generations. But people do not marry randomly. They usually marry others from their own country and more often from their own community and religion.

The rapidity with which a founder effect spreads through a population (a phenomenon called genetic drift) is greater in relatively small groups of people like the Jews, living in relative isolation, than in large groups because the mutation stays and remains concentrated in the community. The more isolated the community, the more likely the original founder mutation will be inherited by a lot of people. If the mutation occurs in a gene that controls a physiological function, then there is the possibility that people inheriting that gene will inherit two copies and develop a disease. In some cases, inheriting only one copy may be enough.

Dr. Neil Reish speculates that genetic drift was much more likely to occur among elite Ashkenazi Jews such as civil and business leaders, scholars and rabbis, rather than their poorer neighbors. Families in the elite group were able to provide better living conditions, and more of their children reached adulthood compared to poorer Jewish families. A mutation spread more rapidly among elites, says Reish, because members married among themselves and had many children.

As a result of selective advantage and founder effects, Jews developed disorders that other people did not. When these people fled Europe in the late nineteenth and twentieth centuries for the United States, Israel and other countries, they introduced the mutation into the Jewish population of their new homelands. The fact that most of American Jewry is Ashkenazi in origin means that their influence has had the greatest impact on their culture and health.

References

Abel, Ernest L. *The Roots of Antisemitism*. Farleigh Dickenson University Press, 1975.

Adam, A. Genetic diseases among Jews. *Israel Journal of Medical Science* 9 (1973): 1383–1392.

Cohen, T. Genetic markers in migrants to Israel. *Israel Journal of Medical Science* 7 (1971): 1509–1514.

Diamond, Jared M. Jewish Lysosomes. *Nature* 368 (1994): 291–292.

Diamond, Jared M. Who Are the Jews? *Natural History* (November 1993): 11–17.

Goodman, Richard M. "Thoughts on genetic diseases among Jewish people." In: Eriksson, A.W. et al. Ds. *Population Structure and Genetic Disorders*. London: Academic Press, 1980, pp. 337–351.

Goodman, Richard M., and A.G. Motulsky, eds. *Genetic Diseases among Ashkenazi Jews*. New York: Raven Press, 1979.

Koestler, Arthur. *The Thirteenth Tribe*. New York: Random House, 1976.

Livshits, Gregory, Robert R. Sokal, and Eugene Kobyliansky. "Genetic Affinities of Jewish Populations." *American Journal of Human Genetics* 49 (1991): 131–146.

Mourant, Arno E. *The Distribution of the Human Blood Groups*. Oxford: Blackwell, 1954.

Mourant, Arno E., Ada C. Kopec, and Kazimiera Domaniewska-Sobczak. *The ABO Blood Groups*. Oxford: Blackwell, 1958.

Mourant, Arno E., Ada C. Kopec, and Kazimiera Domaniewska-Sobczak. *The Genetics of the Jews*. Oxford: Clarendon Press, 1978.

Myrianthopoulos, Ntinos C., and S.M. Aronson. "Population Dynamics of Tay-Sachs Disease." II What confers the selective advantage upon the Jewish heterozygote? In: B.W. Volk and S.M. Aronson, eds. *Sphingolipids, Sphingolipidoses, and Allied Disorders* New York: Plenum Press, 1972, pp. 561–570.

Myrianthopoulos, Ntinos C., and S.M. Aronson. "Reproductive Fitness and Selection in Tay-Sachs Disease." In: S.M. Aronson and B.W. Volk, eds. *Inborn Disorders of Sphingolipid Metabolism* Oxford: Pergamon, 1967, pp. 431–441.

Myrianthopoulos, Ntinos C., and M. Melnick. "Tay-Sachs Disease: A Genetic-Historical View of Selective Advantage." In: M.M. Kaback, ed. *Tay-Sachs Disease: Screening and Prevention* New York: Alan R. Liss, 1977, pp. 107–110.

Neel, James V. "History and the Tay-Sachs Allele." In: Goodman, Richard M., and Arno G. Mutulsky eds. *Genetic Diseases among Ashkenazi Jews.* New York: Raven Press, 1979, 285–299.

Patai, Raphael, and J.P. Wing. *The Myth of the Jewish Race.* New York: Charles Scribner and Sons, 1975.

Polednak, Anthony P. *Racial and Ethnic Differences in Disease.* New York: Oxford University Press, 1989.

Seltzer, Robert. *Jewish People, Jewish Thought.* New York: Macmillan, 1980.

Sheba, Chaim. Gene frequencies in Jews. *Lancet* 1 (1970): 1230.

Sheba, Chaim. Jewish migration in its historical perspective. *Israel Journal of Medical Science* 7 (1971) 1333–1341.

Skorecki, Karl, Sara Selig, Shraga Blazar, et al. Y chromosomes of Jewish priests. *Nature* 385 (1997): 32.

Thomas, Mark G., Karl Skorecki, Haim Ben-Ami, et al. Origins of Old Testament priests. *Nature* 394 (1998): 138–140.

CHAPTER THREE

Blood Disorders

The adult male body contains about 5¼ quarts of blood; an adult female body has about 3½ quarts. There are three main types of cells in blood: red (erythrocytes) which carry oxygen from the lungs to all the cells of the body, white (leukocytes) which fight infection, and platelets (thrombocytes) which help the blood clot when bleeding occurs. Other substances in blood are primarily proteins and minerals. About 78 percent of blood, however, is water.

The total number of red blood cells is estimated at about 45 trillion. A tiny drop of blood from a needle prick contains about 5 million of them. Red blood cells are manufactured in the bone marrow at a rate of about 480 million every minute. Each one lives for about four months and carries oxygen to the trillions of other cells in the body. A complete circuit through the blood stream takes only about 20 seconds; during its four-month life span, each red blood cell will have made about a quarter of a million round trips, traveling a distance of about 950 miles. As a red blood cell approaches the end of its life, it returns to the bone marrow where it was formed and is consumed by another type of cell, called a phagocyte.

Red blood cells get their color from hemoglobin, a molecule made up of heme (an iron-containing part that combines with oxygen) and globin (a protein). Hemoglobin makes up nearly all of the red blood cell; the rest is water. It is hemoglobin's job to carry oxygen from the lungs to other cells and bring back carbon dioxide, a cell's waste matter, so that it can be breathed out. If the hemoglobin is deficient or abnormal (a condition known as anemia), the oxygen-carrying capacity of hemoglobin is decreased. Cells need oxygen to produce energy. Without it, they cannot perform the thousands of jobs that keep us healthy and alive.

The job of the white cells is to protect the body from infection once it has been invaded by some disease-causing agent like a bacterium or a virus. Like red blood cells, white blood cells are manufactured and stored in the bone marrow. They begin as stem cells and evolve into mature red, white or platelet cells. Once released, they live for only about four days, if they do not encounter any infection; if they do encounter an infecting agent, their lifespan is cut to a few hours at most.

There are basically two kinds of white blood cells. The type that are immediately released, and whose job it is to offer the first line of defense against invasion, are called phagocytic cells because they literally gobble up the invading cell. The second line of defense is made up of cells that form antibodies, or special proteins that latch onto invading cells and destroy them. A deficiency in white blood cells is called leukopenia.

The smallest cells in the blood are the platelets. These colorless cells cause the blood to clot when we bleed. They do this by first adhering to an injured surface, then aggregating with each other, after which they release coagulant substances, and finally they retract the blood clot. Abnormalities in any of these functions can cause extensive or prolonged bleeding, despite a normal number of platelets. Like the red and white blood cells, platelets are also formed in the bone marrow, at a rate of about 200 billion per day. A deficiency in platelets is called thrombocytopenia. A deficiency in all three types of cells is called pancytopenia or aplastic anemia.

In this chapter, we will examine several blood-related diseases that affect Jews at a disproportionately higher rate than the general population.

Gaucher Disease

Gaucher (pronounced go-shay) Disease, named after Dr. Philippe Charles Ernest Gaucher, the French physician who first described its symptoms in 1882, is the most common genetic disorder affecting Ashkenazi Jews. Although the name refers to a single disorder, it has three different variations.

VARIATIONS

The three types of Gaucher Disease are distinguished by the absence (Type I) or presence (Types 2 and 3) and severity of central nervous system disturbance. All three forms, however, involve enlargements of the spleen and liver, bone lesions, and damage to various bodily organs.

The variation that primarily affects Ashkenazi Jews is Type I, also called "non-neuropathic" or "adult" Gaucher Disease. It is called non-neuropathic because, unlike the other two forms of the disease, it does not affect the central nervous system, and adult because its symptoms don't appear until adulthood. (In some cases, symptoms do not appear until 80 or 90 years of age.)

Symptoms of Type I Gaucher Disease can be debilitating, but they are not always fully expressed, and those that are expressed may vary in intensity between, as well as within, families. The disease may be life-threatening for one sibling; for another, the symptoms may be so mild that a person wouldn't even know he or she had the disorder if it weren't for the sibling's symptoms. People with mild symptoms and asymptomatic siblings may not even be aware that they have the disease.

Type 2 Gaucher Disease, also called "Infantile" or "acute neuropathic," is less common than Type 1 but is much more serious and occurs in all ethnic groups. It is called infantile and acute neuropathic, because its symptoms appear by a child's first three months of life and include damage to the brainstem. Death often occurs by age two.

"Juvenile," "chronic neuropathic," or Type 3 Gaucher is also less common than Type 1 and doesn't begin to make its presence known until much later in childhood. Like the Type 2 form of the disease, it too mainly affects the brain, albeit a different area than in Type 2, causing incoordination, mental deterioration, and seizures; but it is not usually fatal.

FREQUENCY

Type 1 Gaucher Disease occurs in people of every ethnic background but is about 60 times more common in Ashenazi Jews compared to the general population (1 per 1,000 versus 1 per 60,000). The carrier frequency for the genetic defect causing Gaucher disease is 1 in 20 for Ashkenazi Jews. Carriers have no symptoms of the disease unless they have two defective genes.

The incidence of Types 2 and 3 Gaucher in the general population is relatively low, affecting only 1 out of every 50,000 to 60,000 births, and there is no preponderance of either of these variations among Jews.

SYMPTOMS

The most common symptom of Type I Gaucher Disease is an enlarged spleen, which usually does not cause any pain. Other symptoms include an enlarged liver, frequent nosebleeds, anemia (a deficiency in red blood cells) and a related lack of energy, an increased susceptibility to infection, and intense pain in the bones. Children with Type I Gaucher are often shorter than other children their age and may experience delayed puberty. Severity of symptoms varies between individuals; some experience only some of these symptoms, while some may have these and others.

The enlarged spleen is due to the accumulation of Gaucher cells in that organ, causing it to enlarge as much as 50 times its normal size. This gives the abdomen a distended appearance almost resembling pregnancy. The spleen not only becomes enlarged, it also becomes overly activated. This leads to numerous complications, including anemia, decreased resistance to disease, and heavy nosebleeds.

The spleen is primarily affected because its job is to remove and break down old red and white blood cells from the circulation. Ordinarily, the rate at which red cells are broken down matches the rate at which they are produced in the bone marrow. An overactive spleen breaks down blood cells at a faster rate than the matching production rate, resulting in a net loss. This excessively rapid destruction of red blood cells is called hemolytic anemia. Since red blood cells carry oxygen to all the other cells of the body, the cells of patients with Gaucher Disease do not receive enough oxygen to function properly.

As a result, the Gaucher patient feels a lack of energy, becomes easily tired and short of breath with mild exertion, and may feel his or her heart beating more rapidly than normal, because the heart has to beat more often to carry more blood to the body's cells to make up for the decreased red cells. The increased work on the heart can in turn result in heart failure, characterized by even more shortness of breath and swollen ankles. Also symptomatic of the excessive breakdown of red blood cells are jaundice, characterized by yellowing of the skin and the whites of the eyes, and an increased risk of developing gallstones, which can occur as a result of the increase in bilirubin associated with the excessive release of hemoglobin.

People with Gaucher Disease also develop more infections because an overactive spleen also destroys white blood cells at a faster rate. White blood cells are one of the body's defense mechanisms for fighting infection. With fewer white blood cells, the body is less capable of fighting off infections.

The third component of the blood adversely affected by an overactive spleen is the platelets, the blood component that forms clots. Instead of returning the platelets to the blood, the disease causes them to become sequestered in the spleen. As a result, Gaucher patients bruise easily and bleed profusely when injured. Nosebleeding is especially common in Gaucher Disease. In some cases, the bleeding is so damaging that the spleen has to be surgically removed to restore the blood's clotting ability.

Since the spleen is also a barrier to infection, its removal will result in increased susceptibility to infection.

The liver can also become enlarged as a result of the build-up of macrophages, but aside from the associated abdominal pain, this usually causes only minor problems. However, in some cases, cells in the liver die and are replaced with scar tissue. This condition is called cirrhosis, which can interfere with the ability of the liver to function properly. The risk of cirrhosis is greatly increased if the spleen has previously been removed.

The third area of the body where Gaucher cells accumulate is the marrow inside the bones. This often results in episodic pain called "bone crisis." The pain is sudden and starts as a dull ache, usually in the hips, shoulders and vertebrae, and then intensifies over the next two to three days, when it becomes so excruciating that narcotic medication may be required. The pain then slowly diminishes over the next one to two weeks. Bone crisis pain stems from the blockage of blood flow to the parts of the bone that Gaucher cells lodge in. Cut off from their normal blood flow, the bones also become brittle and more easily broken. In addition to cutting off blood flow, the accumulation of Gaucher cells in bone marrow interferes with its ability to produce new red blood cells, thereby aggravating the anemia produced by an overactive spleen.

Although the spleen, liver and bones are the main areas of the body usually affected in Gaucher Disease, Gaucher cells may also accumulate in other parts of the body. The kidneys may not function normally and the ability of the lungs to deliver oxygen to the blood may become impaired. Some people also suffer a loss of appetite; sometimes their skin may take on a yellow-brownish tone.

CAUSE

All forms of Gaucher Disease are caused by a deficiency in an enzyme called beta-glucocerebrosidase (GC), also known as beta-glucosidase. The deficiency is caused by one of several different mutations in the gene regulating the enzyme. About five of these mutations are responsible for nearly 90 percent of the disease in Ashkenazi Jews.

Glucocerebrosidase is located in the lysosome. In Type I Gaucher, it is not produced in the lysosomes of a specific cell in the body, called the macrophage. Macrophages come from bone marrow and are the body's scavenger cells. It is their job to travel through the body and literally swallow and then digest worn out and injured cells. After that, they travel to the spleen, liver and bone marrow, where they rid themselves of their waste. The site within the macrophage where this digesting process goes on is the lysosome. It does this using a number of enzymes, one of which is glucocerebrosidase. It is the job of glucocerebrosidase to break down a fatty substance called glucocerebroside (also called glucosyleramide), which is left over when cells die, into glucose and a fatty substance called ceramide.

When the macrophage's lysosome lacks this enzyme or the enzyme is not working properly, glucocerebroside accumulates in the lysosome. This accumulation causes the marcrophages to take on a characteristic bloated appearance. These bloated Gaucher cells eventually travel to the lymph nodes, spleen, liver and bone marrow, causing these organs to enlarge and become impaired. The reason macrophage cells are affected, rather than other cells in Gaucher Disease, is because they are the only cells involved in storage of glucocerebroside.

The most common gene mutation, accounting for about 75 percent of all cases among Ashkenazi Jews, is called the N370S (also called 1226G). The other mutations contributing to Gaucher Disease in Ashkenazi Jews are called L444P (also known as 1448C), the 84GG insertion (also known as 84GG), and the IVS2+1 gene. Collectively, these three mutations account for 97 percent of all cases among Ashkenazi Jews.

DIAGNOSIS

A clinical diagnosis can often be made on the basis of the disease's main symptoms of enlarged spleen and liver, tiredness, pain in the bones, skeletal weakness, excessive bruising and frequent nosebleeds. Anemia can be determined by measuring red blood cell and hemoglobin levels in the blood.

A firmer diagnosis can be made by a blood test to determine if the glucocerebrosidase enzyme is either present or at lower than normal levels. A certain diagnosis is possible through genetic testing for one of the mutated genes that cause the disease. It is also possible to detect Gaucher Disease in early pregnancy by amniocentesis or chorionic villus sampling.

TRANSMISSION

Gaucher Disease is an inherited autosomal recessive genetic defect, which means that it occurs equally in children of both sexes. Although due to a single gene defect, in Ashkenazi Jews nearly every case of Type I Gaucher is due to one of three different mutations affecting this gene. Both parents have to carry the mutation for their child to develop the disease. If neither parent carries any of the mutations for Gaucher Disease, then the children will not develop the disease nor will they be carriers themselves.

TREATMENT

In contrast to most of the other lysosomal storage diseases which are not treatable, treatments are now available for Gaucher Disease which can arrest and in many instances reverse the symptoms. If the disease is detected early, people with Type I Gaucher Disease can live relatively normal lives. However, treatment must be lifelong and is very costly. (In some cases, treatment may be covered by insurance.)

Two different kinds of therapy are now available.

Enzyme Replacement Therapy. This is now the most common form of treatment for Gaucher Disease. Since 1991, it has been possible to replace the abnormal GC enzyme that leads to Gaucher Disease with a modified form of the enzyme called Ceredase. Ceredase targets macrophage cells and enables them to break down the fatty substance, glucocerebroside, that otherwise accumulates in the cell into glucose and ceramide.

Patients are given intravenous injections of Ceredase every other week, either in their own homes or a medical facility. For most patients, Ceredase arrests and in many cases reverses the symptoms, allowing the spleen and liver to return to their normal size and bone function to be restored. To be most effective, enzyme replacement therapy needs to begin before any damage occurs to bones or bodily organs. This is why early diagnosis is so important. Enzyme replacement therapy is very expensive (about $100,000 to $400,000 each year) and has to be taken for a lifetime. The University of Pittsburgh Gaucher Disease Diagnosis and Treatment Program estimates that about 800 people around the world are currently receiving enzyme replacement therapy for Gaucher Disease.

Bone Marrow Transplantation. This procedure involves taking healthy bone marrow cells from another person and inserting them in the patient's bone marrow. When successful, the technique results in rapid reconstitution of the missing enzyme and a rapid decrease in glucocerebroside, followed by a disappearance of Gaucher cells in bone marrow within about 10 to 12 months after treatment begins.

Although it has been successfully performed in several patients, there are still several disadvantages that have to be overcome before bone marrow transplantation can become widely used. One problem is the limited number of donors. Only about 25 percent of patients with Gaucher Disease have a suitable donor. The procedure is also not without risk from fatal complications, which can occur from 10 to 25 percent of the time. Therefore, unless the disease is life threatening, the better option is still enzyme replacement therapy. A second problem is that just because normal donor cells are placed into the marrow of someone with Gaucher Disease, that does not mean that the normal cells will take. In other words, the new cells do not necessarily replace the abnormal cells in Gaucher Disease.

PREVENTION

It is now possible through gene testing to confirm if someone has the disorder or is a carrier for Gaucher Disease. The same techniques can also be used prenatally to determine if a fetus has one or more of the mutant genes. The cost of testing for the genes for Gaucher Disease, along with the genes for Tay-Sachs and Canavan Disease and cystic fibrosis, is about $300.

FOR FURTHER INFORMATION

National Gaucher Foundation
11140 Rockville Pike, Suite 350
Rockville, MD 20852-3106
TELEPHONE: 1-800-925-8885
　　　　　　1-800-428-2437
E-MAIL: ngf@gaucherdisease.org
INTERNET: www.gaucherdisease.org

Massachusetts General Hospital—
　Gaucher Treatment Program
Department of Molecular Genetics
Building 149, 13th Street
Charlestowne, MA 01219
TELEPHONE: 617-726-9329

University of Pittsburgh
Gaucher Disease Diagnosis and
　Treatment Program
E1650 Biomedical Science Tower
Pittsburg, PA 15261
TELEPHONE: 1-800-334-7980

Connecticut Children's Medical
　Center
282 Washington St.
Hartford, CT 06106
TELEPHONE: 860-545-9580

SCREENING CENTERS

Baylor College of Medicine—DNA
　Diagnostic Laboratory
Boston University School of Medi-
　cine—Center for Human Genetics
Children's Hospital and Regional
　Medical Center, Seattle
Genetics & IVF Institute
Genzyme Genetics
Jefferson Medical College
Thomas Jefferson University
Mayo Clinic
Medical Genetics Institute, S.C.
Mount Sinai School of Medicine
New York State Institute for Basic
　Research in Developmental
　Disabilities—Genetic Testing

New York University School of
　Medicine—Molecular Genetics
　Laboratory
North Shore University Hospital at
　Manhaset
SmithKline Beecham Clinical Labo-
　ratories
University of Pittsburgh Medical
　Center
Wayne State University—Biochemi-
　cal and Molecular Genetics Labo-
　ratory
Wayne State University—Harper
　Hospital
Yale University School of Medicine

REFERENCES

Beutler, Ernest, and Terri Gelbart. Glucocerebrosidase (Gaucher Disease). *Human Mutation* 8 (1996): 207–213.

Beutler, Ernest, Nicole J. Ngyen, Michael W. Henneberg, et al. Gaucher Disease: Gene Frequencies in the Ashkenazi Jewish Population. *American Journal of Human Genetics* 52 (1993): 85–88.

Diaz, Anna, Magda Montfort, Bru Cormand, et al. Gaucher Disease: The N370S mutation in Ashkenazi Jewish and Spanish patients has a common origin and arose several thousand years ago. *American Journal of Human Genetics* 64 (1999): 1233–1238.

Horowitz, Mia, Metsada Pasmanik-chor, Zvi Borochowitz, et al. Prevalence of glucocerebrosidase mutations in the Israeli Ashkenazi Jewish population. *Human Mutation* 12 (1998): 240–244.

Horowitz, Mia, Galil Tzuri, Nurit Eyal, et al. Prevalence of nine mutations among Jewish and non–Jewish Gaucher Disease patients. *American Journal of Human Genetics* 53 (1993): 921–930.

NIH Technology Assessment Panel on Gaucher Disease. Gaucher Disease: Current issues in diagnosis and treatment. *Journal of the American Medical Association* 275 (1996): 548–543.

Sidransky, E., N. Tayebi, and E.T. Ginns. Diagnosing Gaucher Disease. Early recognition, implications for treatment, and genetic counseling. *Clinical Pediatrics* 34 (1995): 365–371.

Zimran, Ari, Terri Gelbart, B. Westwood, et al. High Frequency of the Gaucher Disease Mutation at Nucleotide 1226 among Ashkenazi Jews. *American Journal of Human Genetics* 49 (1991): 855–859.

Factor XI Deficiency

Factor XI deficiency is a clotting disorder due to a deficiency in a protein produced by the liver and sent into the blood. The deficiency was first identified in a Jewish family in the United States in 1953 and was called hemophilia C to distinguish it from two other bleeding disorders, hemophilia A and B. However, unlike those two conditions, it is not associated with spontaneous bleeding and it occurs in both males and females. Because it does not occur unless someone is injured, the condition may not be recognized, especially among those who have only one defective gene for the disorder and whose bleeding is less profuse than those who are homozygous.

FREQUENCY

Factor XI is one of the most common hereditary disorders among Ashkenzi Jews with an incidence rate of about 1 in 190 for severe cases (see Symptoms) and a carrier frequency of about 8 per 100. At least four mutations in the gene responsible for the deficiency are known, but two of these variations, called Type II and III, account for 98 percent of the abnormal alleles in Ashkenazi Jews.

Excessive bleeding may also occur among Sephardic Jews, but in this case it results from a deficiency in two other clotting factors, called Factor V and Factor VIII, which are normal in Ashkenazis. Carrier frequency for the combined deficiency of factors V and VIII has been estimated at 1 in 100,000 for Sephardic and Oriental Jews.

Symptoms

Unlike hemophilia, in which bleeding often occurs spontaneously, in Factor XI deficiency bleeding does not occur unless someone has an accident, is circumcised, undergoes minor surgery, or has a tooth pulled, in which case bleeding becomes more excessive than normal and may require blood and or platelet transfusions. Women with Factor XI deficiency may be particularly affected because of their monthly menstrual periods and because of blood loss during childbirth. Many women, in fact, first become aware of their condition because of menorrhagia, an excessive loss of blood connected with their periods. Deficiencies of Factor XI, however, are not all or none. Some people have very minor coagulation problems, whereas some may bleed so profusely they require frequent transfusions. Severity may be related to whether an individual has one or both anomalous copies of the gene causing the disorder.

Cause

Clotting, also called coagulation, is a complex reaction that keeps us from losing all our blood when we are cut. The process involves different proteins acting in a programmed consecutive order. If one of these proteins does not function, clotting is severely impaired.

The first stage in the clotting process involves the adhesion of platelets to the site of injury and to each other (a process called aggregation) to arrest the first episode of bleeding. Once aggregation occurs, the platelets in the area around the injured tissues release a substance called thromboplastin, which interacts with the blood protein, Factor XI, to convert a related chemical called prothrombin into thrombin. Thrombin then causes a substance called fibrinogen to convert into fibrin, which then forms a meshwork of interlacing fibers that is a clot, preventing further blood loss. In Factor XI deficiency, the absence of the protein means that one of the steps in the formation of a clot cannot occur, resulting in excessive blood loss during injury.

The severity of the bleeding depends on whether the gene controlling Factor XI doesn't function at all, so that there is no protein, or if some is produced, whether it is functional.

Factor XI deficiency among Ashkenazi Jews is due to one of four different mutations. Recently one of these four mutations has also been detected in Jews from Iraq with the same frequency as occurs in Ashkenazi Jews, suggesting to some medical researchers that this mutation has existed among Jews since ancient times.

Since one of the mutations (Type II) occurs in both Iraqi Jews and Ashkenazi Jews, Dr. Hava Peretz at the Chaim Sheba Medical Center in Tel Aviv speculated that the mutation common to both existed from ancient times. Subsequently she found that the chromosome on which the Type II mutation occurred was identical in Ashkenazi and Iraqi Jews. Since Ashkenazi and Iraqi Jews have a similar historical background and share the same mutation, Dr. Peretz believes that this explains the occurrence of this common mutation in these two otherwise different groups of Jews. The fact that Ashkenazi Jews have another mutation (Type III) that is absent in Iraqi Jews indicates to her that in this case the mutation arose from a founder who lived at a time after the Ashkenazi Jews separated from their original roots.

Another interesting relationship also exists for Factors V and VIII among Sephardic and Oriental Jews. Although they suffer from the same abnormality, the specific genetic change is due to a different founder effect in Tunisian and non–Tunisian Jews, indicating a split between Tunisian Jews and other Sephardic and Oriental Jews.

DIAGNOSIS

Diagnosis is based on laboratory tests of the coagulation process and measurement of Factor XI levels.

TRANSMISSION

Factor XI deficiency is an autosomal recessive disease caused by one of four mutations in the gene producing Factor XI. Carriers (heterozygotes) can suffer symptoms, although not as severe as those who have two copies of the mutant gene (homozygotes). Since the mutation is recessive, both parents have to be carriers for a child to inherit the disorder.

TREATMENT

Tranexamic acid is the usual drug prescribed for excessive blood loss due to menorrhagia and for minor surgical procedures in Factor XI–deficient women. Factor XI-deficient individuals who experience considerable bleeding due to injury may require frequent transfusions of blood and platelets.

PREVENTION

Prevention of bleeding episodes depends on precautions to avoid injury. Since the aberrant gene for Factor XI is relatively common among Ashkenazi Jews, Dr. Uri Seligsohn recommends that every Ashkenazi Jew be tested for the disorder before undergoing surgery.

FOR FURTHER INFORMATION

Fanconi Anemia Research Fund
1902 Jefferson St.
Eugene, OR 97405
TELEPHONE: 541-687-4658
E-MAIL: info@fanconi.org

SCREENING CENTERS

State University of New York
  Health Science Center

REFERENCES

Asakai, Rei, Dominic W. Chung, Oscar D. Ratnoff, et al. Factor XI (plasma thromboplastin antecedent) deficiency in Ashkenazi Jews is a bleeding disorder that can result from three types of point mutations. *Proceedings National Academy of Sciences* 86 (1989): 7667–7671.

Bolton-Maggs, P.H., D.A. Patterson, R.T. Wensley, et al. Definition of the bleeding tendency in factor XI–deficient kindreds: a clinical and laboratory study. *Thrombosis and Haemostasis* 70 (1993): 68–71.

Kadir, R.A., E.L. Economides, and C.A. Lee. Factor XI deficiency in women. *American Journal of Hematology* 60 (1999): 48–54.

Nichols, W.C., U. Seligsohn, Z. Zivelin, et al. Linkage of combined factors V and VIII deficiency to chromosome 18q by homozygosity mapping. *Journal of Clinical Investigation* 99 (1997): 596–601.

Peretz, Hava, Avital Mulai, Sali Usher, et al. The two common mutations causing Factor XI deficiency in Jews stem from distinct founders: One of ancient Middle Eastern origin and another of more recent European Origin. *Blood* 90 (1997): 2654–2659.

Rosenthal, R.L., O. Dreskin, and N. Rosenthal. New haemophilia-like disease caused by deficiency of a third plasma thromboplastin factor. *Proceedings of the Society of Experimental Biology and Medicine* 82 (1953): 171–174.

Sadler, J.E. Combined factors V and VIII deficiency climbs onto the map. *Journal of Clinical Investigation* 99 (1997): 555–556.

Seligsohn, Uri. "Factor XI Deficiency in Ashkenazi Jews." In: Goodman, Richard M. and Arno G. Motulsky, eds. *Genetic Diseases Among Ashkenazi Jews*. New York: Raven Press, 1979, pp. 141–147.

Seligsohn, Uri. Factor XI deficiency. *Thrombosis and Haemostasis* 70 (1993): 68–71.

Seligsohn, Uri, A. Zivelin and E. Zwang. Combined factor V and factor VIII deficiency among non–Ashkenazi Jews. *New England Journal of Medicine* 307 (1982): 1191–1195.

Shpilberg, Ofer, Hava Peretz, Ariella Zivelin, et al. One of the two common mutations causing Factor XI deficiency in Ashkenazi Jews (Type II) is also prevalent in Iraqi Jews, who represent the ancient gene pool of Jews. *Blood* 85 (1995): 429–432.

Fanconi Anemia

Anemia literally means "lack of blood." In clinical terms, it refers to a lower-than-normal level of circulating hemoglobin. When bone marrow is unable to produce other cells as well, the condition is called aplastic anemia. Fanconi Anemia is a type of aplastic anemia named after Dr. Guido Fanconi, the Swiss pediatrician who discovered it in 1927.

Fanconi first became aware of this bone marrow disease as a result of treating two brothers for the same physical complaints of tiredness, frequent bleeding and infections. Subsequent studies found that these symptoms were caused by a failure in the bone marrow's ability to produce red and white blood cells and platelets.

FREQUENCY

Fanconi Anemia occurs in all ethnic groups, but the most common variant of the FA gene causing the disease, known as Type FAC or IVS4 + 4-T, is only found among Ashkenazi Jews. This variant accounts for about 85 percent of all cases of the disease in Ashkenazi Jews. The next most common variant is called 322delG. Although it is found in Ashkenazi Jews, it also occurs in non–Jews.

The rate of Fanconi Anemia among Ashkenazi Jews is about 2.7 per 100,000; the carrier rate is about 1 in 100. Corresponding rates in the general population are not yet known.

SYMPTOMS

Fanconi Anemia usually makes its existence known very early in life, although a few people do not become symptomatic until they reach their late teens or adulthood. Fanconi Anemia should not be confused with Fanconi Syndrome, which also appears in childhood but is primarily a kidney disease.

Although Fanconi Anemia is due to bone marrow failure, many other bodily organs become damaged as a result, and frequent infection and hospitalization are common. The average lifespan is 22 years of age; many of those who reach that age often develop various types of cancer.

One of the main general symptoms of the disorder is growth retardation. Children with Fanconi Anemia are generally smaller than normal at birth, but since there are many other reasons for low birth weight, this in itself it is not enough for a doctor to suspect that a child has Fanconi Anemia. A related symptom is failure to catch up in size to other children; but again, a failure to thrive can be due to many other factors.

The tell-tale symptoms of Fanconi Anemia begin to appear between the ages of three and 12. Children seem overly tired and more prone to catch colds and other infections than other children their age. These symptoms typically increase in severity with age and often require hospitalization. Nosebleeds and bruising also become very common.

Whereas some children with Fanconi Anemia have no visible birth defects other than smaller-than-normal growth, most have physical defects affecting the skeletal system, such as mishappen, missing, shortened, or extra thumbs, underdeveloped or missing bones in the forearm, spinal malformations, scoliosis, and abnormalities affecting the ribs and hips.

A minor but consistent symptom is a peculiar facial appearance. People with Fanconi Anemia have small heads (microcephaly)and are often mentally retarded. The ears are often misshapen, and deafness is also not uncommon. Noses are thin; eye slits (palpebral fissures) are small; and occasionally one or both eye lids droop (ptosis).

Skin discoloration is also common. This usually takes the form of a deep-sun-tanned appearance over large parts of the body, called hyperpigmentation, and pallid patches called "cafe-au-lait" spots.

Boys with Fanconi Anemia often have small testicles; girls with the same disorder, however, do not appear to have a corresponding underdevelopment of their ovaries. Although fertility is usually very low in males with Fanconi, girls with Fanconi have become pregnant and have given birth to normal children.

Other abnormalities include kidney defects such as missing, rotated, malformed, or fused kidneys, thin walls separating the chambers of the heart, and blockages in the stomach or intestine that often require surgical correction.

As if these problems were not enough, about 25 percent of those whose Fanconi Anemia is due to the type "C" gene, the "Jewish" type of the disease, develop leukemia. The most common type of leukemia, called acute myelogenous leukemia (AML), is characterized by an overproduction of immature white blood cells known as "blasts." These blasts suppress production of normal white cells so that the body loses its ability to fight infections. Once leukemia develops, few individuals live beyond their teenage years.

CAUSE

Fanconi Anemia is caused by a mutation in five known genes, known by letters A through E, and medical researchers suspect there may be three additional genes involved. The variant that primarily affects Ashkenazi Jews is Fanconi Anemia Type C.

The immediate cause of Fanconi Anemia is the inability of bone marrow to keep up with the job of turning out the hundreds of thousands of red and white blood cells and platelets each day that the body needs to function properly. When it is unable to produce sufficient red blood cells, the condition is called anemia; an inability to produce enough white blood cells is called leukopenia; and an inability to produce enough platelets is called thrombocytopenia. When marrow can't produce enough of all three types, the condition is called pancytopenia, or aplastic anemia.

In contrast to Ashkenazi Jews, the FAC mutation is not found in Iraqi Jews. This implies that the very high rate among the former is due to a founder effect which occurred relatively recently rather than prior to the time of the Babylonian deportations. Most of the Ashkenazi Jews with Factor XI Disease have ancestors who came from Russia or Poland.

DIAGNOSIS

Fanconi Anemia is often suspected on the basis of its symptoms. The diagnosis can be confirmed through a blood test in which red and white blood cells and platelets are counted. The most definitive test, however, is the chromosome breakage test. This involves exposing the white blood cells to one of two chemicals, mitomycin C or diepoxybutane. Mitomycin C and diepoxybutane cause chromosomal breakage, but normal cells are able to repair most of these breaks; cells from someone with FA are able to repair only a few. The same kind of test can be performed on fetal cells by either chorionic villus sampling or amniocentesis, and can also be performed on embryonic cells before they are implanted.

TRANSMISSION

Fanconi Anemia is an autosomal recessive genetic disease. This means that both parents have to be carriers for a child to inherit the disease. The chances of its doing so are 1 in 4.

Dr. Peter Verlander believes that a mutation with as high a frequency as FAC should be included in the routine screening for genetic diseases in the Jewish population. Verlander estimates that of the approximately 35,000 Ashkenazi Jews tested annually for the Tay-Sachs gene, about 395 will be found to be carriers for the FAC gene. Siblings of children with Fanconi should be tested, even if they are healthy, to determine if they are carriers or have the disease which has not as yet made its presence known.

TREATMENT

There is no cure for Fanconi Anemia. Treatment mainly takes the form of antibiotics to treat infection and blood transfusion to increase red cell concentrations.

Long term treatment mainly involves treatment with artificial androgens, which are male hormones. These hormones also have the effect of stimulating production of red blood cells and platelets, and in some cases they also stimulate white blood cells. However, androgen treatment is only effective in about half of all Fanconi patients. While androgen treatment can cause improvements for many years, unfortunately it loses its effectiveness in most patients after a few years.

A number of experimental treatments are now being tested. One of these involves administration of naturally occurring blood-stimulating growth factors. One such factor, known as GM-CSF, stimulates production of white blood cells.

Another treatment is bone marrow transplant. This requires removing bone marrow cells from a sibling with a particular match for the recipient. However, this treatment is very risky because it requires destruction of the recipient's own bone marrow to make room for the new marrow. It is also risky because the recipient's immune system has to be suppressed through the use of drugs, so that it will not reject the new marrow. The procedure is presently considered too risky to be done on a routine basis. However, if it can be safely done, it would constitute a cure for the disease. Another alternative is for people with Fanconi Anemia to store their own bone marrow for possible later transplant.

PREVENTION

Since cancer is a common result of Fanconi Anemia, people who have the disease should avoid exposure to agents like X-rays, chemotherapeutic drugs known to cause chromosomal damage, tobacco smoke, organic solvents like gasoline and pain thinners, weed and bug killers, and fumes from combustible materials.

FOR FURTHER INFORMATION

An international registry of FA patients and their families is located in New York City at the Rockefeller University.

International Fanconi Anemia
Registry
c/o Dr. Arleen Auerbach
Rockefeller University
1230 York Avenue
New York, NY
TELEPHONE: 212-327-7533

Fanconi Anemia Research Fund
1902 Jefferson, Suite 2
Eugene, OR 97405
TELEPHONE: 1-800-828-4891
    541-687-4658
FAX: 541-687-0548
INTERNET: www.rio.com/~fafund/
    FAHTML/FAHome

SCREENING CENTERS

All Children's Hospital of St. Petersburg
St. Children's Hospital of Pittsburgh
Genzyme Genetics
New York University School of Medicine—Molecular Genetics Laboratory

Mount Sinai School of Medicine
St. Jude Children's Research Hospital
University of Pittsburgh Medical Center

REFERENCES

Magazine Articles

    A recent article in *Business Week* (July 12, 1999, p. 94) dealt with the Frohnmayer family in Eugene, Oregon, whose children had died of the disease, and described efforts currently underway to find a cure.

Journal Articles

Alter, B.P. Fanconi's Anaemia and its variability. *British Journal of Haematology* 85 (1993): 9–13.

Auerbach, A.D., and R.G. Allen. Leukemia and preleukemia in Fanconi Anemia patients. *Cancer Genetics and Cytogenetics* 51 (1991): 1–4.

Kohli-Kumar, M., C. Morris, C. DeLaat, et al. Bone marrow transplantation in Fanconi Anemia using matched sibling donors. *Blood* 84 (1994): 2050–2054.

Seligsohn, U. High gene frequency of factor XI (PTA) deficiency in Ashkenazi Jews. *Blood* 87 (1978): 165–171.

Strathdee, C.A., A.M.V. Duncan, and M. Buchwald. Evidence for at least four Fanconi Anemia genes including FACC on chromosome 9. *Nature Genetics* 1 (1992): 196–198.

Verlander, Peter C., Athena Kaporis, Qian Liu, et al. Carrier frequency of the IVS4 + 4A—T mutation of the Fanconi Anemia gene FAC in the Ashkenazi Jewish population. *Blood* 86 (1995): 4034–4038.

Whitney, Michael A., Hiroshi Saito, Petra M. Jakobs, et al. A common mutation in the FACC gene causes Fanconi anaemia in Ashkenazi Jews. *Nature Genetics* 4 (1993): 202–205.

Glanzmann Thrombasthenia

Glanzmann Thrombasthenia is a bleeding disease resulting from an inability of blood platelets to aggregate. In contrast to Factor XI deficiency, Glanzmann is relatively rare among Ashkenazim and instead is found more often among Iraqi Jews.

SYMPTOMS

The symptoms of Glanzmann Thrombasthenia are similar to those of Factor XI deficiency, for example, life-long moderate to severe bleeding episodes, bleeding in the gums, and excessive menstrual bleeding. Bleeding episodes can be very severe, requiring blood and platelet transfusions, and can result in death if not arrested in time. An otherwise normal circumcision can become dangerous, and excessive bleeding can also be a complicating factor in abortion, giving birth, tooth extractions, and any accident.

There are two variations of the disease. People with Type I Glanzmann Thrombasthenia have little or no platelet fibrinogen and no clot retraction, whereas those with Type II have some platelet fibrinogen and some clot retraction.

FREQUENCY

Glanzmann Thrombasthenia is a relatively rare disorder but is much more common among highly inbred populations such as Iraqi Jews, Gypsies in France, and Arabs in Jordan, Israel and Saudi Arabia. The prevalence among Iraqi Jews is estimated at 1 in 7,700. Carrier frequency for the Type I mutation is estimated at about 1 in 114 and 1 in 700 for the Type II mutation.

Although Glanzmann Throbasthenia is also common among Arabs and gypsies, the mutations causing the Jewish variation of the disorder differ from those occurring in other groups.

CAUSE

Glanzmann Throbasthenia is a rare bleeding disorder in which there are a normal number of platelets, but an abnormality in their functioning causes them not to attach to one another when bleeding occurs. This abnormality is due to the absence of two proteins which stimulate formation of fibrinogen and other clotting factors (see Factor XI). This defect is in turn caused by at least one of two autosomal recessive mutations in one of two genes. Dr. Nurit Rosenberg and his colleagues at the Sheba Medical Center in Tel Aviv, who have been studying this disorder, believe it arose as a founder effect among Iraqi Jews.

TREATMENT

The main treatment for this disorder is transfusion of blood or platelets when bleeding is excessive.

PREVENTION

Prenatal diagnosis is possible for this disorder. Any Iraqi Jews who are to undergo surgery would be advised to be tested for this disorder.

REFERENCES

Rosenberg, Nurit, Rivka Yatuv, Yael Orion, et al. Glanzmann Thrombasthenia caused by an 11.2-kb deletion in the glycoprotein IIIa (beta3) is a second mutation in Iraqi Jews that stemmed from a distinct founder. *Blood* 89 (1997): 3654–3662.

Seligsohn, Rui, and Hava Peretz. Molecular genetics aspects of Factor XI deficiency and Glanzmann Thrombasthenia. *Haemostasis* 24 (1994): 81–85.

Glucose-6-Phosphate Dehydrogenase (G6PD) Deficiency

Glucose-6-phosphate dehydrogenase (G6PD) is an enzyme located in red blood cells. A deficiency in this enzyme ultimately causes a "hemolytic anemia," the term given to a decrease in red blood cells resulting when red blood cells are broken down faster than they can be replaced. Glucose-6-phosphate deficiency is the world's most common inherited disorder, one that affects between 200 and 400 million people.

VARIATIONS

Depending on the severity of the enzyme deficiency, some people with G6PD deficiency may never experience any symptoms, while others may experience excruciating pain and even death. Different ethnic groups have different mutations, but members of a particular ethnic group share the same mutation and the same set of symptoms.

FREQUENCY

While G6PD deficiency affects millions of people, there are so many different variations of the disorder that the frequency of the different forms and gene mutations among specific groups has been hard to determine. Among Sephardic Jews, the frequency of the disorder is relatively high (about 35 percent), whereas it is very rare among Ashkenazi Jews and relatively uncommon among North African Jews. The highest frequency of occurrence (70 percent among males) is found in Kurdish Jews.

SYMPTOMS

Most people with G6PD deficiency may be completely unaware of it because it is only under certain circumstances that its effects are expressed. One of these circumstances is when someone with the disease eats fava beans, which causes a severe allergic reaction. This is the reason G6PD is also known as "favism." In most cases, however, symptoms are brought on by triggering factors such as exercise, infections, or certain drugs.

The initial symptoms of G6PD deficiency are dark urine, caused by the breakdown of hemoglobin. This is followed or accompanied by fatigue and abdominal or back pain, headaches, irregular breathing, and heart palpitations. As the symptoms progress, the urine turns black. Remnants of red blood cells become sequestered in the liver and spleen and can cause them to increase in size. In general, attacks caused by drugs like primaquine last for about a week. Attacks caused by infections are generally more common than those caused by drugs.

A relatively large number of Mediterranean and Sephardic newborns with G6PD often experience neonatal jaundice at birth. Neonatal jaundice is a yellowish discoloration of the skin, whites of the eyes and mucous membranes. It is a relatively common condition in newborns, but usually-disappears. Treatment consists of placing children under special lights, called bili-lights. If jaundice persists in spite of treatment, it is usually indicative of glucose-6-phosphate dehyrogenase deficiency. The liver usually metabolizes the yellow-brown bilirubin in blood cells when they are broken down and excretes it into the bile and then into the intestine. However, in G6PD deficiency, an excess number of blood cells are destroyed, and more of the pigment is released into the blood than can be broken down. The ensuring build-up of bilirubin results in a characteristic yellowish coloring of the skin and whites of the eyes and its accumulation in various tissues. If untreated, neonatal jaundice can cause permanent brain damage—a condition called kernicterus—or death. While symptoms of G6PD can usually be attributed to its triggering conditions, jaundice still occurs for reasons yet unknown in newborn Sephardic Jews and other Mediterranean newborns.

CAUSE

Glucose-6-phosphate dehydrogenase is an enzyme in the membrane of red blood cells, which enables cells to process glucose, the cells' main source of energy. A deficiency in this enzyme usually has no effect unless certain foods or drugs are encountered, in which case the deficiency triggers a hemolytic anemia—a destruction of red blood cells faster than they can be replaced by the body, resulting in decreased oxygen transport to cells.

G6PD deficiency is an X-linked recessive disorder caused by a mutation in a single gene. Over 400 different variations in this mutation have now been identified. Most of those affected by G6PD deficiency live in the Mediterranean countries, Africa, or Southeastern Asia, or are descended from people from these parts of the world. The occurrence of these mutations is a Faustian bargain, protecting people from malaria, which is rampant in these areas.

Malaria is an infection of red blood cells caused by a parasite known as a plasmodium which is carried by the female Anopheles mosquito. When this mosquito bites someone, the parasite enters that person's blood. There are actually several types of malarial parasites. The one that causes the most severe reactions, such as chills, recurrent fever, anemia, enlarged spleen and often death, is called plasmodium falciparum. Cells that lack glucose-6-phosphate dehydrogenase do not produce a metabolite that the parasite needs to survive, and so it dies before it can multiply and cause serious illness. Someone with one of the genes for G6PD who lives in a malaria-infested area would be protected against death from malaria and would therefore have a better chance of surviving and passing the mutation on to his or her descendants.

In 1993, medical researchers at the Hadassah University in Jerusalem, led by Dr. O. Oppenheim, suggested that the high level of this disorder among Kurdish Jews predated their deportation. Malaria is not very common in Kurdistan, the researchers point out, and non–Jewish Kurds have a very low frequency of G6PD. This implies that, however the Kurdish Jews acquired it, the event was sometime before their deportation, while they were still living in Israel. The most likely area for this to have occurred was probably the Hulla valley, which has a notoriously high frequency of malaria in Israel.

Having the mutation which results in a deficiency in G6P prevents the cells from metabolizing another enzyme called glutathione. Glutathione protects membranes of red blood cells from injury by inactivating the byproducts of oxidative stress, a condition arising from a lack of oxygen when performing strenuous activities. Oxidative stress can also come from oxidant drugs like the antimalarial drug primaquine, foods like fava beans that contain vicine and isouramil, or from some infections such as viral hepatitis, typhoid fever and pneumonia.

In reacting to these conditions, hemoglobin changes its shape. Because of this structural alteration, it loses its ability to use and transport oxygen. These cells then die, and their hemoglobin is broken down into its two main components, heme and globin.

The heme is converted to bilirubin, which is then attached to albumin in the blood and carried to the liver. There it is broken down and excreted into the bile and stored in the gall bladder to be excreted into the small intestine, where it is broken down further by intestinal bacteria and gives feces its brownish color. The breakdown of red blood cells results in a condition called hemolytic anemia. Neonatal jaundice, a discoloring of the skin and sclera of the eye, occurs when there is too much bilirubin in the blood because of the rapid breakdown of blood cells, or because of liver disease or a blockage in the bile ducts.

A disorder involving the liver's inability to transport bilirubin into the bile, called Dubin-Johnson syndrome, has a relatively high incidence among Iranian Jews (1 in 1,300) compared to Sephardic (1 in 40,000) and Ashkenazi Jews (1 in 100,000). The rate among Iranian Jews is believed to be the highest in the world. Unlike glucose-6-phosphate dehydrogenase deficiency, symptoms of Dubin-Johnson do not appear until puberty or early adulthood, and the condition is rarely life-threatening. It can, however, result in gallstones, small stones made up of bilirubin, cholesterol, calcium, phosphates and bile salts that form in the gallbladder. Gallstones may not produce any symptoms or they may result in mild or severe abdominal pain, fever, chills, nausea and vomiting. Chronic severe pain, resulting from inflammation and/or obstruction of bile ducts, may necessitate surgical removal of the gallbladder.

DIAGNOSIS

Diagnosis of G6PD may be suspected on the basis of clinical signs of darkened urine, jaundice, and back or abdominal pain. Confirmation can be made by determining the presence or absence of the enzyme in the blood.

TRANSMISSION

G6PD is a recessive X-chromosome linked trait which means that the gene responsible for G6PD is located on the X-chromosome. While both males and females can have the disorder, females will only experience the disorder if they inherit the abnormal gene from each parent. Males, on the other hand, will experience symptoms if they inherit only one abnormal gene from their mothers, since they have no other X-linked gene to offset its expression. In general, the overwhelming majority of people affected by G6PD are men.

Since G6PD is a recessive X-linked trait, every daughter of an affected male will inherit the trait and be a carrier. While males can inherit it from their mothers, they cannot inherit it from their fathers. A son who has a mother who is a carrier has a 50 percent chance of inheriting the disorder. Daughters are unlikely to develop this disorder unless their parents' ancestry is Mediterranean or, in the case of Jewish ancestry, Sephardic.

TREATMENT

Treatment for neonatal jaundice consists of placing newborns under special lights, called bili-lights. Adults are treated with folic acid, nasal oxygen and bed rest, and with blood transfusion if necessary.

PREVENTION

Prevention takes the form of avoiding certain foods like fava beans and drugs characterized as oxidizing agents.

Because it is such a common disorder, mass screening of newborns in populations known for high risk is being considered. Such screening is now possible by a simple fluorescent test on a spot of dried blood.

REFERENCES

Cohen, Tirza. Genetic markers in migrants to Israel. *Israel Journal of Medical Science* 7 (1971): 1509–1514.

Cohen, Tirza. Thalassemia types among Kurdish Jews. *Israel Journal of Medical Science* 9 (1973): 11461–1463.

Horowitz, A., T. Cohen, E. Goldschmidt, et al. Thalassemia types among Kurdish Jews in Israel. *British Journal of Haematology* 12 (1966): 555–559.

Kaplan, Michael, and Ayala Abramov. Neonatal hyperbilirubinemia associated with glucose-6-phosphate dehydrogenase deficiency in Sephardic-Jewish neonates: Incidence, severity and the effect of phototherapy. *Pediatrics* 90 (1992) 401–405.

Kaplan, Michael, Hendrik J. Vreman, Cathy Hammerman, et al. Contribution of haemolysis to jaundice in Sephardic Jewish glucose-6-phosphate dehydrogenase deficient neonates. *British Journal of Haematology* 93 (1996): 822–827.

Oppenheim, Ariella, Corrine L. Jury, Deborah Rund, et al. G6PD Mediterranean accounts for the high prevalence of G6PD deficiency in Kurdish Jews. *Human Genetics* 91 (1993): 293–294.

Shani, M., U. Seligsohn, and A. Adam. The inheritance of Dubin-Johnson syndrome. *Israel Journal of Medical Science* 9 (1973): 1427–1432.

Shani, M., U. Selgisohn, E. Gilon, et al. Dubin-Johnson syndrome in Israel. I: Clinical and genetic aspects of 101 cases. *Quarterly Journal of Medicine* 39 (1970): 549–556.

Thalassemia

Thalassemia refers to a group of hereditary blood disorders affecting formation of hemoglobin, the oxygen-carrying chemical inside red blood cells. The term is derived from the Greek word for sea, referring to its high frequency among the Mediterranean populations, although it also occurs among people whose origins are in Asia, Southeast Asia and India.

The inability either to produce or make normal hemoglobin, the immediate cause of the disorder, means that red blood cells cannot carry enough oxygen to the body's cells. As a result, people with the disease develop anemia and require frequent blood transfusions.

Thalassemia is not only one of the most common hereditary blood disorders in the world, it is also one of the oldest, dating back thousands of years. In 1991, bone fragments suggestive of the disease were found in a prehistoric site near Haifa, and some anthropologists believe that some of the forms of the mutations that give rise to the disorder date back to that period.

VARIATIONS

There are two main types of thalassemia, called beta and alpha, depending on the part of hemoglobin molecule that is affected. Thalassemia occurs when one of the genes for producing the protein for one of those two parts doesn't produce enough of it. When the beta protein is involved, the condition is called beta thalassemia; a malfunctioning alpha gene results in alpha thalassemia.

Beta-Thalassemia Major, the most serious of the thalassemias, is also known as Mediterranean Anemia, Cooley's Anemia (named after pediatrician Dr. Thomas Cooley, who recognized it as a distinct disorder in 1925), or Homozygous Beta Thalassemia. It results from either the absence of both beta chains (a condition known as beta thalasemia^0) or from formation of these chains at a decreased level (known as beta thalassemia$^+$).

In Beta-Thalassemia Minor, the mutation is present in only one of the two genes' coding for the beta chain. As a result, symptoms are usually very mild if they occur at all. In some instances, a person may inherit two beta thalassemia genes, each of which produces some beta protein, but not as much as in thalassemia minor. This intermediate condition is called thalassemia intermedia.

Since there are hundreds of variations in the mutation, the severity of the disorder varies considerably. Some people may not even know they have the condition. However, it is important to know because if a person marries someone with the same disorder, their children may inherit both mutations and develop the major form of the disease.

Alpha Thalassemia results from a mutation in the genes that code for the alpha chain in the hemoglobin molecule. Like the beta variation, there are several variations in this type of thalassemia.

FREQUENCY

The thalassemias are the most common genetic disorders, with over 100 million carriers. About 120,000 people are born with one of the forms of this disorder every year. Those most likely to be carriers or sufferers are those whose ancestors came from the Mediterranean countries: Greece, Italy, the Middle East, and Turkey.

The alpha-thalassemia syndromes are very rare among people whose origins lie outside the Mediterranean region but occur relatively frequently among those whose origins are connected with this part of the world. Both the alpha and beta forms of the disorder have a relatively high occurrence among Jews of Kurdish ancestry originating from northern Iraq and Syria, eastern Turkey and western Iran and Yemen. The carrier frequencies for these two forms of the disease among Kurdish Jews are about 1 in 10 for the beta form and about 2 per 100 for the alpha type. Although some Ashkenazi Jews have a variation of one of the mutations for thalassemia, the variation is rarely expressed, whereas about 1 percent of newborn Kurdish Jews have the disease.

SYMPTOMS

If someone inherits only one of the abnormal genes for the disease, symptoms may be very mild or totally absent. If both abnormal genes are inherited, symptoms of severe anemia usually appear in infancy.

Most children with thalassemia major seem normal at birth, but two to 12 months later, symptoms of severe anemia often appear, beginning with stunted growth, jaundice (yellowing of the skin), increased infections (the most common cause of death), fussiness, listlessness, poor appetite, and vomiting. If they do not receive treatment, their bones become thin, distorted, and easily broken. Facial bones tend to assume a peculiar shape with depressed nasal bridges, prominent chins and noticeable overbites, so that children with thalassemia often look very similar. As the disease progresses, the liver and spleen become very enlarged. If they receive early blood transfusions, these children may avoid many of these symptoms or at least experience less severe forms.

When red blood cells die, the iron inside them is released and is carried to other cells, often resulting in organ damage from the excess iron levels. The liver and heart are particularly vulnerable. In general, death from this or other related effects occurs in the teenage years or early 20s, but with regular transfusions and drugs to remove iron people with the disorder can live well into adulthood.

Beta-Thalassemia Minor usually produces few clinical problems, unless stresses are made on the body in cases of illnesses or pregnancy.

CAUSE

Hemoglobin is the part of the red blood cell that gives it its color. It is also the part of the cell that carries oxygen from the lungs to all areas of the body.

In thalassemia, hemoglobin production is defective, so that it cannot carry the normal amount of oxygen that cells need to survive. To compensate for the deficient hemoglobin, the bone marrow works overtime to produce more red blood cells. The excessive demands on the bone marrow result in a thickening, which is reflected in the bone structure of the face. At the same time, the spleen increases in size because of the excessive destruction of defective red blood cells, and it too becomes overactive, destroying more blood cells.

The cause of the abnormal hemoglobin production in thalassemia is a gene mutation affecting the structure of the hemoglobin molecule. Ordinarily, a hemoglobin molecule has four protein (called globin) arms, two alpha and two beta arms. Different genes are involved in production of each arm. The most common mutations are those affecting the beta arms.

In Beta-Thalassemia Major, the mutation occurs on both copies of the genes' coding for the beta chain. The alpha thalassemias are more complicated than the beta forms, because four genes are involved in producing the alpha chain, whereas only one gene is involved in producing the beta chain. Individuals with three or fewer abnormal genes for the alpha chains usually experience only mild symptoms. Inheriting four of the defective genes nearly always results in fetal death.

A large and growing number (more than 475 to date) of different mutations affecting the beta globin gene cause thalassemia major. Every geographically distinct population has a unique mutation. People with thalassemia major are often homozygous for one of the common mutations affecting their ethnic group, or heterozygous for one of the common mutations and one of the geographically unique mutations.

DIAGNOSIS

A diagnosis can be made by examining red blood cells for a characteristic abnormal appearance and for presence or absence of hemoglobin chains and by genetic testing.

TRANSMISSION

Beta-Thalassemia Major is an autosomal recessive genetic disorder due to a mutation in a single gene. This means that if both parents are carriers (Beta-Thalassemia Minor), any one of their children has a 1 in 4 chance of developing the major form of the disorder and a 1 in 2 chance of being a carrier.

The probability that a child will inherit the alpha form of the disorder is more complicated because four different genes are involved.

Since some people with thalassemia major are now living to adulthood, they may marry and have children, although sexual maturation often does not occur in this condition. If someone who is fertile should marry someone who also has the disorder, all their children will likewise have the disorder. Their children may also develop the disorder if their spouses have the minor form. All of their children will be carriers.

TREATMENT

The most common treatments for thalassemia major are monthly blood transfusions, called hypertransfusions, to keep hemoglobin levels as close to normal as possible, and antibiotics to ward off infections. Thalassemia minor usually does not require any special treatment unless complications arise.

Although blood transfusions can replace missing hemoglobin and enable a child to develop stronger bones and grow stronger, regular blood transfusions result in an accumulation of iron in the body, which destroys various organs. To prevent this from happening, drugs known as iron chelators, such as Desferal, are given in conjunction with these transfusions. Desferal is often administered by means of a portable battery-operated pump which slowly injects the drug under the skin over a 12-hour period. The drug has to be administered for a minimum of five days a week and is typically administered in the home. Parents have to perform this task until a child is old enough to do it for him or herself.

The chelator binds excess iron before it can become deposited in the body's tissues and carries it out to the urine, where it is eliminated from the body. With regular blood transfusions and iron chelation therapy, a child with thalassemia major can live a relatively normal life, go to school, marry and have a family. However, the need for regular blood transfusions and chelation therapy are difficult for most people to deal with over a lifetime, and some may require medication for depression and complications of infection. There are also side effects associated with Desferal treatment, such as visual impairments due to cataracts, loss of color vision, and hearing losses.

Another complication that often requires treatment is an enlarged spleen due to the accumulation of dead red blood cells. If this complication arises, it usually occurs around seven years of age and often requires surgical removal of the spleen.

Although still largely experimental, bone marrow transplants have been used successfully to cure thalassemia. Another new procedure is administering blood from the umbilical cord of a newborn baby. A newborn's cells are immature and so there is a lessened likelihood that they will be rejected than is the case with bone marrow transplants.

People with thalassemia major need to restrict their intake of foods that contain relatively high levels of iron, such as meat, spinach, and certain breads and cereals.

PREVENTION

Prenatal diagnosis by amniocentesis or chorionic villus sampling is now possible at several medical centers. Asymptomatic beta thalassemia carriers can be detected by this procedure and appropriately counseled concerning the risks of conceiving a child with the disorder. Programs of public education for specific ethnic groups, population screening, genetic counseling, and prenatal diagnosis can have a major influence on reducing its occurrence.

For Further Information

Cooley's Anemia Foundation
129-09 26th Avenue, Suite 203
Flushing, NY 11354
TELEPHONE: 1-800-522-7222
                718-321-2873
FAX: 718-321-3340
INTERNET: www.thalassemia.org

Screening Centers

Applied Genetics, Inc.
Celtek Laboratories
Eastern Virginia Medical School
Emory University—Department of Pediatrics
Johns Hopkins University School of Medicine—DNA Diagnostic Laboratory
Kapiolani Health Research Institute
Mayo Clinic
New York University School of Medicine
State University of New York at Syracuse

University of California at Davis
University of California at San Francisco—Molecular Diagnostics Laboratory
University of Pennsylvania—Genetic Diagnostic Laboratory
University of Tennessee Medical Center, Biochemical and Molecular Genetics Laboratory
Wayne State University—Harper Hospital

References

Cohen, Tirza. Thalassemia types among Kurdish Jews. *Israel Journal of Medical Science* 9 (1973): 1461–1463.

Giardina, P., and M. Hilgartner. Update on Thalassemia. *Pediatric Review* 13 (1992): 55–62.

Hershkovitz, I., B. Ring, M. Speirs, et al. Possible congenital hemolytic anemia in prehistoric coastal inhabitants of Israel. *American Journal of Physical Anthropology* 85 (1991): 7–13.

Horowitz, A., Tirza Cohen, E. Goldschmidt, et al. Thalassemia types among Kurdish Jews in Israel. *British Journal of Haematology* 12 (1966): 555–559.

Rund, Deborah, Varda Oron-Karni, Ada Goldfarb, et al. Genetic analysis of Beta-Thalassemia Intermedia in Israel: Diversity of mechanisms and unpredictability of phenotype. *American Journal of Hematology* 54 (1997): 16–22.

Sancar, Gwen B., David B. Rausher, Rosalie M. Baine, et al. Alpha-Thalassemia in Ashkenazi Jews. *Annals of Internal Medicine* 98 (1983): 933–936.

Shalmon, Lea, Chava Kirschmann, and Rina Raizov. Alpha-thalassemia genes in Israel: Deletional and nondeletional mutations in patients of various origins. *Human Heredity* 46 (1996): 15–19.

CHAPTER FOUR

Cancer

Cancer is the second-leading cause of death in America (cardiovascular disease is first). The American Cancer Society estimates that about a million Americans develop some type of cancer every year and about a half million Americans die of it. This is the equivalent of about 1,375 people a day! The good news is that about half of the people who get cancer can now be cured, but this is only true for certain kinds of cancers and only if they are detected in their earliest stages.

Cancer is a general term for the uncontrolled growth and spread of abnormal cells. Cells in most areas of the body are always reproducing themselves in an orderly and controlled way by cell division when they become worn out or injured. Cancers are believed to develop when cells undergo irreversible damage to their genes. Sometimes the damage takes many years to develop; sometimes it occurs very rapidly. As the abnormal cells continue to grow, they may spread to other areas of the body. Whatever tissue they invade, they act like parasites. They sap the energy out of any organ they invade and use up all of its nutrients and oxygen. Without nutrients and oxygen the normal cells die.

No one knows whether any particular woman or man will actually develop cancer even if exposed to the same cancer-causing conditions. The current explanation for this uncertainly revolves around what is known as the "two-hit" hypothesis. Cells contain a vast number of genes whose information is coded in their sequence of DNA bases (see Chapter One). Some agents like X-rays and certain chemicals are able to enter cells and mutate, that is alter, the sequence of DNA bases. Remember that genes produce proteins. In some cases it takes no more than a single mutation in a sequence of thousands of bases to alter the information contained in that gene and therefore the protein it produces.

66

Not all mutations result in the uncontrolled growth of cells that is cancer, however. It is only when changes occur in a small set of latent genes called "proto-oncogenes" (from the Greek word for lump, "onkos") that the potential for cancer is set in motion. The first hit in the development of cancer occurs when a cancer-causing agent such as tobacco smoke alters one or more of the bases in the proto-oncogene, thereby transforming it into an oncogene. The reason tobacco smoke doesn't always cause cancer is that its cancer-causing ingredients randomly come in contact with a cell's genes and very few of them are proto-oncogenes. However, the more and the longer someone smokes, the more likely it is that a strike will occur.

Even if a proto-oncogene is converted into an oncogene, however, its actions are kept under control by another set of genes called suppressor genes. Just as oncogenes act like a car's accelerator, a cell's suppressor genes act like its brakes. The suppressor genes keep cell growth under control. Cell growth is constantly occurring as old cells wear out or are damaged and are replaced with new ones. Suppressor genes counteract any tendency toward uncontrolled growth in this process. They also counteract uncontrolled growth caused by oncogenes. If a second "hit" occurs in which a suppressor gene is mutated, then there would be no braking effect on the oncogenes and runaway cell growth can occur. In 1994 and 1995, medical researchers identified two genes, called BRCA1 and BRCA2 (short for Breast Cancer Gene), as suppressor genes for breast and ovarian cancer. These genes normally suppress tumor growth in the breast and ovary; if mutated, their restraining effect is reduced and they no longer act like a brake on cell growth, causing one or more cells to begin to grow and divide without control.

However, with the exception of sperm and ova, all cells have two copies of each gene. In the case of suppressor genes, this means that if a mutation occurs in one copy, the other will still be able to keep cell growth under control. The chances of a cancer-causing agent striking both genes is very remote. However, one of these copies may have mutated many generations before and became part of one's genetic inheritance. Then the probabilities for a cancer developing become much higher since one less "hit" is needed to knock out the braking actions of the suppressor genes.

Carcinogens (cancer-causing agents) are not the only agents that can induce cancer. Medical scientists have known for some time that the body's own hormones can also induce cancers in the breast and ovaries. The reason is that estrogen accelerates the growth of cells in tissues like the breast and ovary because they contain receptors that are particularly sensitive to its actions. The increase and subsequent decrease in estrogen levels and associated cell divisions occur regularly during each cycle from menarche to menopause. In the course of these cell divisions, there is a possibility that an error will be made in the DNA copying process (see Chapter One). The greater the number of cell divisions, the greater the possibility that one of these errors will transform a proto-oncogene into an oncogene or render a suppressor gene inoperative.

This "two hit" theory explains why breast and ovarian cancers do not usually appear until after puberty and why breast cancers occur at a much earlier age in families with a history of breast cancer. At puberty, estrogen levels rise dramatically in girls and remain high until menopause. Women with a family history of breast cancer have at least one mutation in their breast cancer suppressor genes, BRCA1 and BRCA2, so that they are at greater risk for cancer since one of these genes is already inoperative.

An abnormal growth of cells is called a tumor. A tumor is simply a lump. A tumor that remains in one place is called "benign," whereas one whose cells spread to other areas of the body are called "malignant," or "cancerous." Cancerous cells spread out from their original sites to other areas of the body by growing into them or by breaking off from the original sites and spreading to other areas.

Tumors are described according to the areas in which they originate plus the suffix "oma," and according to their "stage." For example, a benign tumor that develops in fatty tissue is called a "lipoma." Malignant tumors have the ending "oma" when they originate in a gland and "emia" when they originate in blood cells. "Leukemia" is a cancer in white blood cells.

When cancer cells spread into other areas it is called "metastasis." The original tumor is called the primary tumor; tumors arising elsewhere from these primary tumors are called "secondary" or "metastases." Metastasis usually occurs when cancer cells leave their primary site and spread to other areas through the blood circulation or through the lymphatic system, or by spreading to adjacent tissues. If they enter the lymphatic system, they are taken to the lymph nodes and often cause swelling. Enlarged lymph nodes are therefore a possible symptom of cancer.

Survival rate following treatment is closely related to a cancer's stage. A Stage One tumor is a benign tumor, one which is noninvasive and has a 99 percent 10-year survival rate associated with it. A Stage Two tumor is a small one; sometimes called "in situ," it is still a locally confined tumor whose cells have an "atypical" appearance, but those cells have not spread beyond the tumor. Treatment of this kind of tumor has a 70 percent to 90 percent 10-year survival rate. A Stage Three tumor is a much more seriously growing tumor that has spread to the lymph nodes. If treated, it is associated with a 20 percent to 50 percent 10-year survival rate. The most serious tumor is a Stage Four tumor. This is one that is large and has spread to other areas of the body. The 10-year survival rate following treatment for a Stage Four tumor is less than 5 percent.

Most cancers are believed to occur when normal cells are injured by cancer-causing agents called "carcinogens." Abnormal cell growth resulting in a cancerous tumor is called "carcinogenesis." There is no single factor or condition initiating carcinogenesis. Instead, medical researchers believe it results from a complex interplay between precipitating factors called carcinogens, hormonal conditions, stress, infections, and genetic predispositions such as those discussed in the following pages.

Among the environmental factors associated with cancer are tobacco smoke and airborne asbestos particles, which increase the possibility of developing lung cancer; too much exposure to the sun's ultraviolet rays which can cause skin cancer; and viruses like the human papilloma virus which increase the likelihood of cervical cancer in women. Diet can also increase the risk of some kinds of cancer. Regular ingestion of diets high in fat and protein increase the risk of colorectal cancer. Hormone replacement therapy in menopausal women has also been linked to breast cancer. Medical researchers have also found that the state of our immune systems affects our susceptibility to various cancers.

When a cancer does develop, the most common primary site for women is in the breast. Next comes the colon and rectum, lung and uterus. In men, the most common site is in the lung followed by the prostate, colon and rectum, and urinary tract.

Some cancers are definitely influenced by heredity. It is often the case, for instance, that two or more members of the same family in the same generation develop the same kind of cancer. Some cancers also occur more often among certain ethnic groups relative to their numbers. These genes are said to "predispose" a person to developing cancer because not everyone who has them develops cancer. In this chapter the focus is on genes that predispose Ashkenazi Jews for breast and colorectal cancer.

Breast Cancer: The BRCA1 and BRCA2 Gene Mutations

The breast is the part of a woman's body that makes milk to feed a baby. However, the breasts normally make milk only after a woman has given birth. If she does not nurse her baby, her milk-producing glands stop working and her milk dries up.

The breast is made up of glands, ducts and connective tissue, surrounded by fat. The lobes are where the milk is produced; the ducts drain the milk into the nipple. Each breast has its own nerve and blood supply. A blood vessel from the armpit supplies the outer half of the breast while a vessel from the neck area supplies the inner half. Blood from the breasts drains out through a network of veins. The breasts also contain lymphatic fluid and a network of lymphatic vessels that drain into lymph nodes. The lymph nodes filter the lymphatic fluid and destroy harmful infectious organisms before sending it back into the blood.

Breast size and shape varies considerably throughout a woman's life, mainly in response to female sex hormones. The greatest enlargement occurs at times of puberty, pregnancy and breast-feeding. In many cases, these enlargements are accompanied by the appearance of lumps and a feeling of pain, which may be mistaken for cancer, but is usually noncancerous and related to hormonal changes.

About 5 percent to 10 percent of breast cancers and about 10 percent of all ovarian cancers are due to genetic predisposition. Hispanics and Native Americans have the lowest rates of breast cancer; Caucasians and African Americans have the highest. The single most important risk factor for developing breast cancer is if a woman has a mother, sister or other close relative who has had breast or ovarian cancer. If she does, her chance of developing one of these two cancers is much higher than if none of her relatives had the disease. A second indicator is age; the older a woman, the greater her chances of developing breast cancer. Breast cancers that develop in relatively young women, on the other hand, are more likely than not to be hereditary.

Hereditary breast cancers are related to mutations in two genes. Mutations in these genes can also result in ovarian and prostate cancers, but because they were first identified in conjunction with breast cancer, they are called breast cancer genes and are called BRCA1 and BRCA2 (Breast Cancer 1 and 2 genes). Although the probability that someone has a mutation in one of these genes in the general population is about 33 per 10,000, the frequency in some ethnic groups like Icelandic and Ashkenazi women is considerably higher.

Among Ashkenazi women, for example, the population prevalence for three common mutations in these two genes may be as high as 2.5 percent, about 10 to 50 times higher than in the general population. Some medical researchers believe that a mutation in one of these two genes is the most common serious single-gene cause of disease identified thus far in any population. In addition to increasing the risk of developing breast and ovarian cancer, carriers of these two gene anomalies have been found to be four times more likely to develop colon cancer and three times more likely to develop prostate cancer in men. Other studies suggest that these gene mutations also increase the risk of developing pancreatic cancer.

FREQUENCY

The National Cancer Institute estimates that 1 in every 10 women in the United States will develop breast cancer at some point in her life, and 1 in 50 will develop it by age 50. Breast cancer now accounts for about 180,000 or 20 percent of all new cancers among women that are diagnosed each year. Although 8 out of 10 women who develop breast cancer do not die of it, breast cancer is nevertheless responsible for about 46,000 deaths a year. While breast cancer overwhelmingly occurs in women, men may also develop the disease. While there is no evidence that Jewish women develop breast or ovarian cancer more often than non–Jewish women, three gene mutations in the BRCA1 and BRCA2 genes, known to be responsible for breast cancer, occur in about 2.5 percent of the Ashkenazi Jewish population, which is about 50 times higher than in the general population.

SYMPTOMS

Breast cancers rarely produce symptoms in their earliest stages. When they do appear, more often than not, those symptoms appear in only one breast.

The first sign of breast cancer is usually the appearance of a small, hard lump or thickening inside the breast. However, most lumps in the breast are not signs of cancer. Those that are cancerous are often accompanied by other signs such as dimpling in the area of the lump, scaly skin around the nipple, nipple retraction, a clear or bloody discharge from the nipples, and swelling in the armpits.

The breasts continue to undergo growth changes throughout a woman's life and these changes are often accompanied by development of lumps, pain and discharges from the nipples. For most women, lumps are benign. Lumps detected before the age of 35 are usually overdeveloped lobular tissue called "fibroadenomas" (some grow to the size of a lemon). Lumps found between the ages of 35 and 55 are usually fluid-filled sacs, often blocked glands, called "cysts." Lumps found in the breasts of women over 55, however, are more likely to be cancerous and need to be examined immediately by a physician. However, if a woman has a mother or sister with breast cancer, she should have any lumps examined by a doctor.

CAUSE

Hereditary breast cancer, especially that related to the BRCA genes, has a different profile from non–hereditary breast cancer. For one thing, it usually occurs much earlier. About 30 percent of those women develop breast cancer before the age of 35; whereas fewer than 1 percent who develop it after the age of 75 have the hereditary form. The hereditary form is also associated with developing cancer in both breasts, and with developing cancer in the ovaries, and also with colon and prostate cancer in men.

The BRCA1 and BRCA2 genes involved in the hereditary form of breast cancer were discovered in 1994 and 1995. Subsequent studies found that a mutation in one of these two genes accounted for as much as 23 percent of all breast cancers in women with strong family histories of breast cancer. It is rare for a woman to have a mutation in both the BRCA1 and BRCA2 genes, and those who do are not more likely to develop breast cancer than women who have only one.

Because of the recent attention directed at "Jewish" mutations, there may be a mistaken impression and concern that mutations in these two genes only occur in Ashkenazi women. The fact is, however, that over 200 different mutations have now been found in these two genes in people from every ethnic background. Besides Ashkenazi Jews, other ethnic populations with high frequencies are Icelanders, the Dutch, and African Americans. However, the prevalence of specific mutations in various ethnic groups is different, suggesting that they arose from specific founders in each of these populations.

Among Ashkenazi Jewish women, there are three specific mutations that are responsible for most instances of hereditary breast and ovarian cancer. These are designated 185delAG and 5382insC in the BRCA1 gene and 6174del in the BRCA2 gene. The prevalence of the combined frequency of these mutations in the general population is 1 to 2 per 1,000. Among Ashkenazi Jews, it is 10 to 50 times higher (between 2 and 2.5 per 100). What needs to be kept in mind, however, is that these are population-based estimates. They only indicate that Ashkenazi women may be more likely to have one of these mutations; they do not mean that every Ashkenazi woman is a carrier. A 2.5 percent rate means that 2.5 out of 100 Ashkenazi women taken at random will have one of these three common mutations; the remaining 97.5 will not.

Furthermore, even if a woman is a carrier, expression and penetrance of that mutation can vary. Dr. Patricia Hartge and her colleagues at the National Cancer Institute estimated that a Ashkenazi woman with one of the three common breast cancer gene mutations had a 33 percent risk of developing breast cancer. By age 70, Ashkenazi carriers had a 56 percent chance of developing breast cancer, a 13 percent chance of developing ovarian cancer, and a 16 percent chance of developing prostate cancer in men, compared to risks of 13 percent, 1.6 percent and 3.8 percent, respectively, for noncarriers.

Interestingly, the 185delAG mutation has also been found among a number of Iraqi Jews, but not in any other non–Ashkenazi Jewish group. The Iraqi Jewish community is believed to be the oldest Jewish community outside Israel, dating back to some time after the Babylonian exile of 586 B.C.E. Dr. Dvorah Abeliovich and her coworkers at the Hebrew University in Jerusalem speculate that the mutation did not exist before the Babylonian exile and was transferred into the Iraqi Jewish community during the Middle Ages by an Ashkenazi founder who was probably a traveling merchant. Based on studies of a number of Ashkenazi families, Dr. Susan Neuhasen, a genetic epidemiologist, has traced the founder of the 185 delAG mutation back about 38 generations to around 1235 C.E.

Although mutations in the BRCA genes are associated with a high percentage of breast and ovarian cancers in Jewish women, they do not account for more than 60 percent of such cancers, indicating that breast and ovarian cancers are also caused by other genes or environmental factors that have not yet been identified.

According to the theory of cancer growth described in the introduction to this chapter, once tumor suppressor genes become inoperative, the earlier the age at which someone is exposed to a cancer promoter or the longer the duration of exposure, the more likely that person will develop cancer. In the case of breast cancer the promoter is estrogen. It is known, for instance, that the earlier a first pregnancy and the more pregnancies, the lower the risk of breast cancer because estrogen exposures are reduced. Conversely, the earlier the age of menarche and the later the age of menopause, the greater the risk because estrogen exposures are increased. Similarly, the longer postmenopausal women are on estrogen replacement therapy, the greater their risk for developing breast cancer. Obesity is another risk factor because it increases estrogen levels.

Some women may be more prone to developing cancer because of where they live, their lifestyles, or their cultures, which increase their exposures to conditions that cause hits to their genes, or raise estrogen levels.

Where a woman lives definitely affects her risk of developing breast cancer. Women living in industrialized countries, for instance, have a much higher rate of breast cancer than women in nonindustrialized countries. Women who live in Great Britain have the highest rates of breast cancer; those in Japan, the lowest. American women are in the middle. These differences were not due to inherited differences in the populations who lived in these countries. When women born in Japan move to the United States they develop risk rates more similar to American women.

Breast cancers also vary in frequency depending on where in the United States you live. Within the United States, breast cancer "hot spots" include Cape Cod, Massachusetts; Long Island, New York; Marin County, California; and Cincinnati, Ohio. Sometimes these localized links reveal hereditary associations because people who live in some communities are often ethnically related. This proved to be the case when medical researchers noticed a higher-than-normal incidence of breast cancer on Long Island, New York, where there is a relatively high concentration of Ashkenazi Jewish women.

One reason Long Island, New York, is a hot spot is believed to involve genetic susceptibilities combined with an increased level of exposure to pesticides on the island. In 1993, a year before the discovery of the BRCA1 gene, a team of medical researchers at Mt. Sinai Medical Center in New York, headed by Dr. Mary S. Wolff, measured pesticide residues in 58 women within six months of their being diagnosed with breast cancer and in a control group of healthy women. Women with breast cancer had much higher levels of DDE, a chemical formed when DDT breaks down. The researchers estimated that having these higher levels of DDE in their blood had quadrupled the risk of breast cancer. The source of the DDE was drinking water from an aquifer that had been polluted with DDT and other pesticides for many years.

DDT is one of a number of pollutants like PCBs, called "xenoestrogens" because they act like estrogen in the body. In 1997, a group of British researchers calculated that if taken for five years or more, estrogen increased the risk of breast cancer by about 35 percent. This supported the hypothesis of an increasing risk of breast cancer due to an increase in exposure to estrogens.

Lifestyle is another factor definitely related to the occurrence of breast cancer. Unlike many other diseases, however, the occurrence of breast cancer is higher among women in the upper socioeconomic groups. American women with more than 16 years of education are about twice as likely to develop breast cancer as women with less than 12 years. Women with annual family incomes greater than $50,000 are likewise almost twice as likely to develop breast cancer as those with annual incomes of less than $7,000. How a high socioeconomic status relates to an increase in cancer is still speculative, but one possibility is that well-to-do women may live in areas like Long Island that contain hidden pesticides, or their diets may increase susceptibility.

DIAGNOSIS

Some breast lumps are too small to feel, especially in their earliest stages of development, and even then it is very difficult to tell if the lump is benign or malignant. A malignant lump, however, often feels hard and has an irregular shape, whereas a benign lump often feels soft and has a round, smooth shape. Malignant tumors also often cause the skin to become dimpled as a result of pulling on the overlying skin as they move through connective tissue. In extreme cases, the skin becomes very pitted and looks like an orange peel. As the tumor moves along the ducts it may also pull on the nipple and cause it to become inverted. Although nipple inversions can occur for other reasons as well, a new inversion may be symptomatic of breast cancer.

A doctor can often tell if a tumor is likely to be benign or malignant by the way it feels. However, if it appears on a mammogram, the only way to determine for certain if it is benign or malignant, or on its way to becoming malignant, is to perform a biopsy. A biopsy is a procedure in which a needle is inserted into the lump and cells are removed, which are then examined under a microscope. If the cells are found to be cancerous, the possibility of spread to other areas can be determined by taking cells from the lymph nodes and by X-rays and blood tests.

TREATMENT

Treatment for breast cancer depends on the size of the tumor and whether it is in an early or advanced stage. Treatment for relatively small cancers that are four centimeters (two inches) or less, in their early stage that have not yet spread, usually involves surgical removal of the lump and a small amount of surrounding tissues, a procedure called a "lumpectomy," followed by radiation therapy. Often a doctor may also recommend that the lymph nodes in the armpit be removed at the same time to prevent possible spread through this area. A lumpectomy is a relatively minor procedure that can be done under a local anesthetic. The procedure leaves the basic shape of the breast intact, and a patient can return to work the following day.

If the cancer is relatively large or "aggressive" (meaning that it can spread rapidly), partial or total removal of the breast (called "mastectomy") may be recommended, along with removal of some or all of the lymph nodes in the armpit, followed by radiation therapy. In a partial mastectomy, the tumor and nearby and underlying tissue are removed. In a total mastectomy, the entire breast is removed. A mastectomy is a major operation, done in a hospital under general anesthesia. Radiation therapy or chemotherapy is then used to destroy any cancer cells that may remain or were not detected. If the cancer can be removed before its cells have spread to the lymph glands, the chances of recovery are better than 75 percent.

A cancer that has reached an advanced stage is one that has spread to the lymph nodes and likely also spread to other areas. This involves not only removal of the tumor and lymph nodes but also chemotherapy to destroy any other sites to which the cancer may have spread.

Even in the case of a small cancer that can be removed by a lumpectomy, there is always a possibility that cancer cells have spread to other areas of the breast. Therefore, to be sure a new tumor does not form, a doctor may recommend radiation or some other additional (called "adjuvant") therapy with antiestrogen drugs such as tamoxifen. Tamoxifen blocks the stimulatory effect of estrogen on breast cancer cells. Another drug used in treating breast cancer is Goserelin, which interferes with the release of hormones from the brain that influence the production of estrogen by the ovaries.

The most radical treatment is removal of the ovaries or their destruction by radiation, a procedure reported to increase the survival rate of premenopausal women with breast cancer by about 10 percent.

Chemotherapy is typically given to premenopausal women whose breast cancers have spread to their lymph nodes and beyond. The most commonly used drugs are a combination of cyclophosphamide, methotrexate or adriamycin, and fluorouracil. Treatment involves an injection or intravenous administration once a month for six months, and can usually be done without a hospital stay.

Chemotherapy has many side effects, including hair loss, nausea, loss of appetite, diarrhea, tiredness and mouth ulcers. Menstruation may be inhibited and for some women, it may also cause permanent infertility.

PREVENTION

Women most at risk for developing breast cancer are those who have one or more close relatives such as a mother or sister who have developed breast cancer before the age of 45, and have a family history of ovarian cancer. Other risk factors include menstrual periods before the age of 12, menopause after 55 years of age, not having any children, and extensive exposure to radiation, eating diets high in fat, hormone replacement therapy, and use of oral contraceptives.

While breast cancer can't be prevented, its adverse consequences can often be prevented through early detection. The three methods of early detection are breast self-examination, medical examination, and mammography. If a woman knows she has an increased risk for developing breast cancer, then she may be more likely to perform regular self-examinations of her breasts, make regular appointments for clinical checkups and mammograms, and be alert to the effects of various lifestyle choices that affect the risk of developing breast cancer.

Once a lump has formed, early detection and removal, if cancerous, is the best way of preventing its progression. The most common technique for detecting a lump before it can be felt is by a breast X-ray called a mammogram. A mammogram can detect a cancer as small as five millimeters (about one-quarter inch) whereas a lump can't be felt until it is about 20 times larger (about one-half inch). The American Cancer Society recommends that women over the age of 40 receive an annual mammogram and that women in high-risk groups (such as those whose mother or sister has had breast cancer) receive them at an earlier age. Other imaging techniques that do not use X-radiation but can also detect lumps are xero-mammography and ultrasound, which uses sound waves to determine if a lump is a fluid-filled cyst or a solid mass (they reflect sound waves differently).

The known involvement of estrogen in breast cancer raises important questions about the risks of taking oral contraceptives, which are primarily estrogen compounds, and estrogen supplements, usually in the form of Premarin, to reduce the hot flashes, decrease vaginal dryness, and counteract the increased risk of heart disease, osteoporosis (loss of calcium from bones) and colon cancer associated with menopause.

If the main reason for estrogen therapy is osteoporosis, estrogen and one of the new "designer" estrogens called raloxifene (Evista) both increase bone density by about 1 to 2 percent over several years. Although estrogen has a slight advantage over raloxifene in controlling osteoporosis, raloxifene has less risk of causing breast cancer. A California study, for instance, found that raloxifene decreased the risk of breast cancer by 76 percent in a group of older women with osteoporosis. There are also other alternatives to estrogens and raloxifene for increasing bone density, such as Fosamax and a nasal spray called Miacalcin.

Women who believe they are genetically at risk for developing breast cancer can now also be tested for the presence of abnormal BRCA1 and BRCA2 genes. The test costs about $2,400. However, genetic counselors advise Jewish women not to rush out for testing, for several reasons. One is that even if they do have these mutated genes, there is no preventative measure for women who are genetically susceptible that is any different from those currently used for all women. Another reason is that testing positive doesn't predict that a woman will develop cancer, especially if she does not have a family history of it. As a result, many genetic counselors don't recommend testing for the mutation unless a woman has a history of breast cancer in her family; and even then, the results would not necessarily mean that a woman was destined to develop breast or ovarian cancer.

The main advantage of knowing is that a woman who tests positive would likely be more motivated to give herself monthly self-exams, regular clinical breast exams and annual mammograms, beginning in her 20s, which increase the chance of early detection and, therefore, cure. Since the BRCA1 mutation is also associated with ovarian cancer, annual pelvic exams beginning in a woman's early 20s are also advised. Other preventative measures already discussed are not to postpone childbearing and to breast feed. Since oral contraceptives may increase the risk of breast cancer in women with BRCA1/BRCA2 mutations, other methods of birth control would be advisable. Similarly, post menopausal hormone replacement therapy should be given close attention.

More controversial is taking the drug tamoxifen. While tamoxifen was originally meant to be used in the treatment of breast cancer, women who were placed on tamoxifen not only had a lower risk of recurrence, they also had a lower rate of developing cancer in their other breast. As a result, tamoxifen is now being evaluated as a preventative measure for women with a higher-than-normal risk because of family history.

Even more controversial is prophylactic mastectomy and oophorectomy—removal of healthy breasts and ovaries before they develop cancer. Women whose mothers or sisters have died from breast cancer have a very high risk of developing it themselves. A study conducted at the Mayo Clinic estimated that these procedures may reduce the chance of breast cancer in women with a strong family history by about 91 percent. By removing as much breast tissue as possible, this radical procedure is meant to reduce the chance of developing cancer, but there is no certainty that in fact this will prevent its occurrence.

FOR FURTHER INFORMATION

National Alliance of Breast Cancer
Organizations
9 East 37th St.
New York, NY 10016
TELEPHONE: 212-719-0154
INTERNET: www.nabco.org
E-MAIL: NABCOinfo@aol.com

Y-Me National Organization for
Breast Cancer Information
212 West Van Buren St.
Chicago, IL 60607-3908
TELEPHONE: 1-800-221-2141
312-986-8338
INTERNET: www.y-me.org

SCREENING CENTERS

Baylor College of Medicine—DNA
Diagnostic Laboratory
Boston University School of Medicine—Center for Human Genetics
Case Western Reserve University
and University Hospitals of
Cleveland
H.A. Chapman Institute of Medical
Genetics
City of Hope National Medical
Center
Thomas Jefferson University
Kapiolani Health Research Institute
Montefiore Medical Center
Mount Sinai School of Medicine
Myriad Genetic Laboratories

Oncormed, Inc.
University of California at San Francisco—Molecular Diagnostic
Laboratory
University of Chicago
University of Pennsylvania—Genetic
Diagnostic Laboratory Cancer
University of Pittsburgh Medical
Center
University of Tennessee Medical
Center—Developmental and
Genetic Center
University of Utah
University of Vermont
Yale University School of Medicine

REFERENCES

Books
Rosenthal, M. Sara. *The Breast Sourcebook*. Los Angeles: Lowell House, 1997.

Journal Articles
Abeliovich, Dvorah, Luna Kaduri, Israela Lerer, et al. The founder mutations 185delAG and 5382insC in BRCA1 and 6174delT in BRCA2 appear in 60 percent ovarian cancer and 30 percent of early onset breast cancer patients among Ashkenazi women. *American Journal of Human Genetics* 60 (1977): 505–514.

Burke, W., M. Daly, J. Garber, et al. Recommendations for follow-up care of individuals with an inherited predisposition to cancer. BRCA1 and BRCA2. *Journal of the American Medical Association* 277 (1997): 997–1003.

Claus, E.B., N. Risch, and W.D. Thompson. Genetic analysis of breast cancer in the cancer and steroid hormone study. *American Journal of Human Genetics* 48 (1991): 232–241.

Devilee, P. BRCA1 and BRCA2 testing: Weighing the demand against the benefits. *American Journal of Human Genetics* 64 (1999): 943–948.

Easton, D.F., D. Ford, D.T. Bishop, et al. Breast and ovarian cancer incidence in BRCA I mutation carriers. *American Journal of Human Genetics* 56 (1995): 265–271.

Easton, D.F., L. Steele, P. Fields, et al. Cancer risks in two large breast cancer families linked to BRCA2 on chromosome 13q12-13. *American Journal of Human Genetics* 61 (1997): 120–128.

Feurer, E.J., L.M. Wun, C.C. Boring, et al. The lifetime risk of developing breast cancer. *Journal of the National Cancer Institute* 85 (1993): 892–896.

Ford, D., D.F. Easton, D.T. Bishop, et al. Risks of cancer in BRCA1-mutation carriers. *Lancet* 343 (1994): 692–695.

Gail, H.M., et al. Projecting individualized probabilities of developing breast cancer for white females who are being examined annually. *National Cancer Institute* 81 (1989): 1878–1886.

Goggins, M., M. Schutte, J. Lu, et al. Germline BRCA2 gene mutations in patients with apparently sporadic pancreatic carcinomas. *Cancer Research* 56 (1996): 5360–5364.

Hartge, Patricia, Jeffery P. Struewing, Sholom Wacholder, et al. The prevalence of common BRA1 and BRCA2 mutations among Ashkenazi Jews. *American Journal of Human Genetics* 64 (1999): 963–970.

Levy-Lahad, E., R. Catane, S. Eisenberg, et al. Founder BRCA1 and BRCA2 mutations in Ashkenazi Jews in Israel: Frequency and differential penetrance in ovarian cancer and in breast-ovarian cancer families. *American Journal of Human Genetics* 60 (1997): 1059–1067.

Neuhausen, Susan L., Sylvie Mazover, Lori Friedman, et al. Haplotype and phenotype analysis of six recurrent BRCA1 mutation in 61 families: Results of an international study. *American Journal of Human Genetics* 58 (1996): 271–280.

Oddoux, Carole, Jeffery P. Struewing, C. Mark Clayton, et al. The carrier frequency of the BRCA2 6174delT mutation among Ashkenazi Jewish individuals is approximately 1 percent. *Nature Genetics* 14 (1996): 188–190.

Struewing, Jeffery P., D. Abeliovich, T. Peretz, et al. The carrier frequency of the BRCA1 185delAG mutation is approximately 1 percent in Ashkenazi Jewish individuals. *Nature Genetics* 11 (1995): 198–200.

Streuwing, Jeffery P., Patricia Hartge, Sholom Wacholder, et al. The risk of cancer associated with specific mutations of BRCA1 and BRCA2 among Ashkenazi Jews. *New England Journal of Medicine* 336 (1997): 1401–1408.

Szabo, C., and M.C. King. Population genetics of BRCA1 and BRCA2. *American Journal of Human Genetics* 60 (1997): 1013–1020.

Ursin, Giske, Brian Henderson, Robert W. Haile, et al. Does oral contraceptive use increase the risk of breast cancer in women with BRCA1/BRCA2 mutations more than in other women? *Cancer Research* 57 (1997): 3678–3681.

Wolfe, M.S., P.G. Toniolo, E.W. Lee, et al. Blood levels of organochlorine residues and risk of breast cancer. *Journal of the National Cancer Institute* 85 (1993): 648–652.

Familial Colorectal Cancer: The I1307K Gene Mutation

Colorectal cancer is one of the common causes of deaths due to cancer in the United States. Every year, about 130,000 new cases are diagnosed, and about 55,000 deaths result from the disease. About 15 percent of these cases are believed to have a hereditary component. Some of these cancers are believed to be related to the BRCA1 and BRCA2 genes that also predispose people to breast cancer. Although colorectal cancer occurs among Jews disproportionately more often than among non–Jews, the increased number of occurrences is associated with a mutation in a completely different gene called APC (adenomatous polyposis coli).

VARIATIONS

There are three different types of hereditary colorectal cancer which differ in their causation. One is called "familial adenomatous polyposis" (FAP), which occurs when growths in the colon or rectum, called polyps, turn cancerous. People with this form of colorectal cancer usually develop multiple colon polyps at a very early age. This type of colorectal cancer is not more common in Jews.

The second type is called "hereditary nonpolyposis colorectal cancer." This type of cancer does not develop from polyps and is also not more common in Jews.

The third and most common (15 percent to 50 percent) of the hereditary forms of colorectal cancer is called "familial colorectal cancer." A peculiar mutation in the "colon cancer gene" known as I1307K is found in a high percentage of Jews who develop colorectal cancer.

FREQUENCY

Of the approximately 130,000 new cases that are reported each year, about 95,000 involve the colon, and as many as 20 percent are believed to have an hereditary cause.

If you have a first degree relative who has colon cancer, your risk for getting colorectal cancer doubles; if you have one of the gene mutations now known to contribute to colorectal cancer, your risk increases more than ten fold.

In Israel, Ashkenazim have the highest colorectal cancer rate of any Israeli ethnic group with a rate of about 42 cases for every 100,000 compared to a rate of 26 per 100,000 for Jews of Oriental or Sephardic descent. Ashkenazi Jews who test positive for this mutation have a 20 to 30 times increased likelihood of developing colorectal cancer in their lifetime compared to someone who tests negative.

SYMPTOMS

Symptoms of colorectal cancer resemble many of the other disorders affecting the digestive system. Blood in the stool is the most common symptom of colorectal cancer. However, blood in the stool may or may not be visible, depending on where a polyp or tumor is located. As it expands into the interior, a tumor tears and releases blood into the feces. If it is high up in the colon, the blood may mix with the feces and not be visible; the closer to the anus, the more likely it will be visible. Blood in the stool, however, can stem from many other problems, including hemorrhoids. However, if bleeding is prolonged, it can result in anemia.

Other common symptoms are a change in bowel habits, nausea, vomiting and weight loss. Since tumors grow into the interior of the colon, they can interfere with the passage of feces. This causes pressure to build up inside the colon, causing altered bowel movements and pain and swelling in the abdominal area, as well as nausea and vomiting. These symptoms usually make people lose their appetite, with the result that they lose weight and strength. Pain can also be experienced in nearby areas if the cancerous cells penetrate through the intestinal wall into adjacent organs. Urinary problems or liver pain are sometimes symptomatic of colon cancer.

CAUSES

In 1997 cancer researcher Dr. Bert Vogelstein and his colleagues at the Johns Hopkins University's Howard Hughes Medical Institute in Baltimore discovered a mutation that is relatively rare in non–Jews but is responsible for about one in four cases of hereditary colon cancer in Askenazi Jews. The discovery was not fortuitous. Since 1991, cancer researchers were aware that a stretch of DNA called the APC gene was associated with colon cancer. Once they knew where to look, Vogelstein's group examined blood and tissue samples from about 5,000 volunteers, many of them Ashkenazi Jews, and zeroed in on the chemical components of the APC gene.

They found that a single variation in the APC's chemical structure resulted in the substitution of the amino acid lysine for isoleucine in the protein made by the APC gene, and this alteration predisposed someone to familial colorectal cancer by making the cell susceptible to damage from carcinogens. The researchers found that the mutation, which they called I1307K, was present in 6 percent of healthy Ashkenazis, in 12 percent who had colorectal cancer, and in 28 percent of those who had colon cancer and at least one relative who also had the disease, but was not present in any non–Jew. In the words of the researchers, the I1307K mutation is "the most common cancer-associated mutation" in any ethnic group, occurring in 1 in every 16 Ashenazi Jews.

The researchers estimated that by the time they reached 70 years of age, 5 percent of all the Ashkenazi Jews who have the I1307K mutation in either one of their two APC genes will develop colorectal cancer, versus 3 percent of the noncarriers. Although the lifetime risk of developing colorectal cancer for an Ashkenazi Jew with the variant is about 20 to 30 percent, twice the risk for an Ashkenazi Jew who does not have the variant, the fact that healthy Ashkenazi Jews also have the I1307K gene means that, even if one tests positive, it does not mean that person has colon cancer, only that one has a predisposition. These same results have now been reported by other medical researchers who report that the I1307 mutation is unique to Ashkenazi Jews.

Until recently, medical researchers believed that nearly all colon cancers started off as precancerous growths called polyps which turned into tumors. A polyp is a clump of cells that begins to grow in the inner mucous membrane of the colon. These cells do nothing to further the digestive process and no one knows why they suddenly appear.

Although polyps increase the chances of developing colon cancer, medical researchers have discovered that a certain area of the colon can become "hypermutable," that is, very susceptible to the kinds of cellular changes associated with cancer, due to the presence of the I1307 mutation. In other words, these patches in the colon, termed "crash sites," do not have to sprout precancerous polyps to become cancerous. Such an area can be likened to an oil slick which causes cars to pile up all around.

In more traditional genetic terms, the APC gene is a tumor-suppressor gene. According to the two-hit theory of cancer formation, most people inherit two copies of a number of tumor suppressing genes. Only if both copies become dysfunctional in the same cell does a tumor develop. The first hit refers to a mutation in the gene's DNA sequence, leaving only the second copy of the gene to keep the cell from turning cancerous. If a second hit occurs, the normal copy also becomes inoperative and there is no longer any restraint in cellular proliferation.

DIAGNOSIS

The procedures for diagnosing colon cancer are the same as those for diagnosing Inflammable Bowel Disease—sigmoidoscopy, colonoscopy, barium enema X rays, and CT scan.

During a routine annual medical check up, a doctor will usually perform a digital rectal exam, in which he or she inserts a lubricated gloved finger into the rectum and feels for polyps and tumors. Since the rectum is where a substantial number of colorectal cancers develop, this exam can provide an early warning of a problem before it becomes serious.

Since colorectal tumors often cause bleeding which may not be obvious when examining feces, patients are now routinely given a special kit to take home. The kit provides a thin long stick for taking a sample of one's stool from three consecutive bowel movements, and smearing it on a sensitive card. The kit is then mailed back to the doctor or a laboratory, where it is examined for traces of blood. The presence of blood in the feces can be an early warning alerting the doctor to perform more involved tests for possible tumors.

If a tumor is discovered during a colonoscopy, it can be either partially or totally removed depending on its structure, and then examined for cancer cells. A colonoscopy will also enable a doctor to visualize any tumors that may be present and determine whether they have broken through the lining of the colon. If one has, the doctor will remove surrounding areas to see if the tumor has spread.

TREATMENT

Treatment for colon cancer depends on how far advanced the cancer has become. In cases where the cancer is detected in its earliest stages, it may be possible to remove it during a colonoscopy and its removal essentially rids the body of the cancer. If the cancer has spread into the lining of the colon or into adjacent areas, surgery will have to be performed in which the abdominal area is opened so that the doctor can see and remove the cancer and also examine nearby organs for signs that the cancer may have spread. If in fact the cancer has spread beyond the colon into other organs, the doctor may remove those areas as well.

The same procedures involved in removing part or all of the colon, which will be discussed later in this book in conjunction with Inflammatory Bowel Disease, also apply here, for example, resectioning. Unlike Inflammatory Bowel Disease, however, colostomies are not usually performed in cases of colon or rectal cancer. However, chemotherapy and or radiation is administered to patients if the cancer has perforated the colon wall or has spread to the lymph nodes.

Survival rates for colorectal cancer are relatively high. The five-year survival rate for cancers detected at an early stage before they have spread is over 90 percent. If it has spread to nearby areas, however, the rate drops to 64 percent and if it has spread to distant areas, it is only 7 percent, which is more than adequate reason for having regular preventative screenings.

PREVENTION

Medical researchers have known for some time that lifestyle contributes to colorectal cancer. For instance, in parts of the world where people eat high fiber diets and diets low in fat, colorectal cancer is almost unheard of. A diet high in fruits and vegetables is also believed to offer some protection. Likewise, people who exercise regularly get colorectal cancer less often than sedentary people. Obesity, on the other hand, increases the risk of colon cancer. Although still controversial, there is also some evidence that taking small doses of aspirin can reduce the risk of colon cancer. A well-known risk factor for colorectal cancer is Inflammatory Bowel Disease, but how this disease increases the risk of cancer is still unknown.

Since early tumors in the colon hardly ever cause discomfort, their presence remains undetected unless someone has a sigmoidoscopy or colonoscopy. The American Cancer Society and the National Cancer Institute recommend anyone 50 or over to have a sigmoidoscopy every three to five years, and colonoscopies beginning at age 40 for people who have a family history of colon cancer. Since it usually takes several years for a tumor in the colon to turn malignant, regular screening can be a very effective way of preventing this development. If everyone were regularly screened for colon cancer, most growths could be discovered and eliminated before they became fatal. However, sigmoidoscopies and colonoscopies are not procedures most people subject themselves to without reservation.

Now that a simple blood test is available for detecting the "colon cancer gene," it is possible to know if someone has an increased risk of colon cancer. At the time of this writing, however, the technique was available at only a few sites such as Johns Hopkins University in Baltimore and the Cleveland Clinic Cancer Center and costs about $230 (which does not include a $120 genetic consultation). If the test were available elsewhere, it is certain that many Jews would want to have it. The *Baltimore Sun* (Sept 1, 1997, p. 1B), for example, reported that within three days of the announcement of the test's discovery, the Johns Hopkins Oncology Center received 250 calls asking about its availability. Most of the calls came from Baltimore's Jewish community, but there were also calls from other cities as well. It is important to keep in mind, however, that this is a test indicating only if someone has an inherited susceptibility to colorectal cancer; it does not indicate whether the person being tested has polyps or cancer.

A positive blood test should certainly alert someone to have a colonoscopy, especially if they have a family history of colon cancer. The Johns Hopkins Colorectal Cancer Clinic recommends that people who test positive for the gene should start routinely having these colonoscopies at age 35, which is at least 5 to 10 years before tumors turn malignant. They also recommend that relatives of those who test positive should also be tested for the gene. However, even if someone has a negative outcome, this does not necessarily mean that they couldn't develop colon cancer from other causes.

FOR FURTHER INFORMATION

Johns Hopkins Hereditary Colorectal Cancer Program
550 North Broadway, Suite 108
Baltimore, MD 21205
TELEPHONE: 410-955-4041

National Cancer Institute
TELEPHONE: 1-800-422-6237
INTERNET: www.nci.nih.gov

Cleveland Clinic
Department of Medical Genetics
9500 Euclid Ave., Room T10
Cleveland, OH 44195
TELEPHONE: 216-445-5686
                1-800-223-2273
                (ext. 42977)

SCREENING CENTERS

Baylor College of Medicine,
  DNA Diagnostic Laboratory

Evanston Northwestern Healthcare
Montefiore Medical Center

REFERENCES

Books
Levin, Bernard. *Colorectal Cancer*. New York: Random House, 1999.
Miskovitz, Paul. *What to Do If You Get Colon Cancer*. New York: John Wiley & Sons, 1997.
World Cancer Research Fund. *Food, Nutrition and the Prevention of Cancer*. American Institute for Cancer Research. Washington, D.C.: American Institute for Cancer Research, 1997.

Journal Articles
Gruber, Stephen B., Gloria M. Petersen, Kenneth W. Kinzler, and Bert Vogelstein. Cancer, Crash Sites, and the New Genetics of Neoplasia. *Gastroenterology* 116 (1999): 210–212.
Gryfe, Robert, Nando Di Nicola, Geeta Lal, et al. Inherited colorectal polyposis and cancer risk of the APC I1307K polymorphism. *American Journal of Human Genetics* 64 (1999): 378–384.

Stern, Hartley, and Alain Lagarde. Genetics of hereditary colon cancer: a model for prevention. *Canadian Journal of Surgery* 41 (1998): 345–359.

Laken, Steven J., Gloria M. Petersen, Stephen B. Gruber, et al. Familial colorectal cancer in Ashkenazim due to a hypermutable tract in APC. *Nature Genetics* 17 (1997): 79–83.

Petrukin, L., J. Dangel, L. Vanderveer, et al. The I1307K APC mutation does not predispose to colorectal cancer in Jewish Ashkenazi breast and breast-ovarian cancer kindreds. *Cancer Research* 57 (1997): 5480–5484.

Rozen, Paul, Ruth Shomrat, Hana Strul, et al. Prevalence of the I1307K APC gene variant in Israeli Jews of Differing Ethnic Origin and Risk for Colorectal Cancer. *Gastroenterology* 116 (1999): 52–57.

Thun, M.J., M.M. Namboodiri, and C.W. Heath. Aspirin use and reduced risk of fatal colon cancer. *New England Journal of Medicine* 325 (1991): 1593–1596.

Willett, W. The search for the causes of breast and colon cancer. *Nature* 338 (1989): 389–394.

CHAPTER FIVE

Central Nervous System Disorders

The central nervous system refers to the brain and the spinal cord. Cells in this part of the body are called nerves or neurons. No one knows how many of them there are, but the smallest number is estimated at about 100 billion.

There are two main types of cells in the brain. One type is called gray matter. These are the cells where nerve signals originate and are processed. The other type is white matter. These are the cells called myelin, which insulate the grey matter nerves, enabling them to transmit their signals at faster than lightning speed. Diseases like Canavan Disease and Metachromatic Leukodystrophy are due to disorders affecting myelin.

The brain is divided into various structures, the largest of which is the cerebrum. This is the area of "higher" mental activity, where most of our thinking and planning occur. Other areas of the brain include a large structure at the back of the brain called the cerebellum, which controls balance and movement, and the thalamus and hypothalamus, which control hormonal activities and regulate a variety of ongoing functions like sleep and body temperature. The base of the brain, called the brain stem, regulates breathing, heart rate, and other basic functions, and relays signals between the brain and spinal cord.

Nerve cells are connected to one another and to cells in muscles and organs through an intricate network. The connections, however, are broken by tiny gaps called synapses. Transmission of signals across these gaps is performed by chemicals called neurotransmitters.

The central nervous system's activity is divided into voluntary and involuntary responses. Voluntary responses are those consciously controlled by the brain such as throwing a baseball, working at the computer, taking a test. With practice, many of these activities occur with minimal consciousness. Involuntary responses are divided into reflexes and autonomic activities. Reflexes occur when you involuntarily move your foot when a doctor taps your knee, or you jerk your hand away from a hot stove. These kinds of movements occur almost instantaneously because the tap or the heat, called the stimulus, goes to the spinal cord along a sensory nerve and back to the muscles in your foot or hand through a motor nerve, without having to go to the brain.

Autonomic activities regulate the body's internal environment without conscious awareness, through two sets of nerves called sympathetic and parasympathetic systems. These systems have their own pathways and act to balance one another to maintain harmony in the body. For example, the sympathetic pathway to the eyes causes the pupils to dilate while the parasympathic system causes them to constrict. Disorders like Familial Dysautonomia are due to disturbances in the autonomic nervous system.

Many of the central nervous system disorders discussed in this chapter are due to malfunctioning in a particular structure in cells called the lysosome. The lysosome, as mentioned in Chapter One, is the digestive compartment within each of our cells. Dr. Jared M. Diamond, a professor at the University of California Medical School in Los Angeles, has been particularly intrigued that Tay-Sachs and several of the other diseases discussed in this chapter are more common among Ashkenazi Jews than the general population because they all involve the lysosome.

Cells would not be able to live if they did not have some component like the lysosome. Without them, garbage from the breakdown and regeneration of cells would eventually fill the cell until there wasn't room for anything else. Ordinarily, this decayed material is disposed of by being taken into the cell's lysosomes where it is digested by a number of different enzymes that break it down into nontoxic simpler substances, which can then be either recycled and used as building blocks for renewed tissues, or passed to the blood where it will be eventually excreted by the kidneys into urine, or by the liver into stool. When the enzymes in the lysosome are missing or don't work properly, the cellular garbage accumulates in the lysosomes. As the lysosome takes up more and more of this garbage, it continues to swell in size until it occupies the entire cell; in so doing, it destroys the rest of the cell's components.

Lysosomal storage disorders like Tay-Sachs are all characterized by a missing enzyme that ordinarily removes one of these substance from the lysosome before they can accumulate and cause damage. If there is a genetic alteration in the genes that contain the instructions for making the enzymes involved in lysosomal metabolism, the metabolism cannot occur, and the cell's wastes accumulate in the lysosomes. Different diseases develop, depending on which enzyme is missing.

Dr. Diamond believes that "lightning has struck Jewish lysosomes too often to be a coincidence." The likelihood that a collection of human genetic illnesses among Ashkenazi Jews that is traceable to a defect in the same microscopic area of our cells could hardly be just a coincidence. If lightning struck your house and completely missed your neighbor's house one time, says Dr. Diamond, you might curse your bad luck; but if it struck your house eight times and missed your neighbor's each time, then perhaps you should look for something other than bad luck.

We now know that three of the most common lysosomal diseases affecting Ashkenazi Jews are due to only eight different genetic alterations in the same few genes. This makes it even more unlikely that the higher frequency of these diseases among Ashkenazi Jews is due to chance. The most likely explanation, says Dr. Diamond, is that after generations of living in particular geographical locations, differences between Jewish populations in various communities evolved which rendered those populations less likely to develop certain diseases and more likely to develop others. The best-known (although not the most common) of the "Jewish diseases" is Tay-Sachs, which primarily affects Ashkenazi Jews and hardly every affects Sephardics. The fact that Ashkenazi Jews are affected to a much greater extent by a number of diseases that hardly ever affect Sephardic Jews means that, even though they shared a common historical origin, their living conditions in the Diaspora had an impact on their bodies as well as their culture that rendered them more susceptible to these diseases and less susceptible to others.

Ataxia-telangiectasia

Ataxia is a progressive debilitating movement disorder. The ataxia part of the disorder refers to the uncoordinated movements characteristic of the disorder. The uncoordination may be due to a problem in a part of the brain called the cerebellum, which controls movement activities, or a lesion in the spinal cord, or some abnormality in sensory function, or any combination of these general problems. Ataxias can be acquired or inherited. Acquired ataxias include vitamin deficiencies, infections, and alcoholism. Hereditary ataxias are genetically determined and include a wide variety of disorders.

Telangiectasia refers to thin red "spider" veins which appear in the corners of the eyes and on the ears and cheeks following exposure to the sun. Although these spidery veins have no clinical importance, they are unusual and are the reason the disorder has this dual name.

Ataxia-telangiectasia was first described in 1926. In 1971 a review of the diagnosed cases to that time found that a relatively large proportion of patients were Jewish children of Moroccan ancestry. It is now known to be caused by one of several hundred mutations in a gene called ATM. Mutations in this gene are associated with the disorder in different ethnic groups, including Sephardic Jews.

VARIATIONS

There are several variations in the disorder. The most common features are loss of balance control, including the ability to stand, walk, and write, slurred speech, an inability to control eye movements, frequent sinus and respiratory infections, dilated blood vessels in the eyes and skin, and sensitivity to effects of radiation. A "full-blown" syndrome is not common. Instead, children typically experience some of the symptoms associated with the disorder. For example, some may have ataxia, but normal immune function. In some cases, the symptoms resemble cerebral palsy.

FREQUENCY

The prevalence of Ataxia-telangiectasia in the general population is estimated at between 1 in 40,000 and 1 in 100,000. Among Moroccan Jews, the frequency is estimated at 1 in 8,000. Other Sephardic Jews may also have a relatively high frequency. Carrier frequency is estimated at about 1 in 100 in the general U.S. population.

SYMPTOMS

The primary symptoms of Ataxia-telangiectasia are progressive deterioration in motor function, usually appearing between one and three years of age. Motor deterioration includes slurred speech, an inability to follow objects across the visual field, and jerky twitching in the face and other parts of the body ("choreoatheotosis"). Additional symptoms include frequent infections and susceptibility to cancer. The appearance of spidery veins on the cheeks, ears or corners of the eyes following exposure to sunlight is called "telangiectases."

Children with Ataxia-telangiectasia appear normal until they are about two years of age and beginning to walk and speak. Although walking is seldom delayed, soon after they do so they begin to wobble abnormally. Some children appear to improve, but around four years of age they once again begin to show signs of uncoordination which becomes progressively worse. Initially, motor coordination involves only the trunk, but this progresses to peripheral coordination as well. The same problems coordinating movement are also responsible for their slurred speech and an inability to track with the eyes objects passing across their visual field. By their eighth year their ability to use their hands for tasks like writing is impaired.

Most develop uncontrollable drooling, twitching and jerky movements. Swallowing becomes difficult and often results in choking. Growth is retarded. By 10 years of age the ability to stand is lost and they become confined to a wheelchair. At the same time, they require help to eat, dress, wash, and use the toilet.

Although motor and verbal skills make it hard for people with Ataxia-telangiectasia to complete IQ tests that are time related, intelligence for most is normal. Many have completed high school and some have earned college degrees.

Most people with Ataxia-telangiectasia have weakened immune systems and frequent sinus and lung infections which do not improve when given antibiotic drugs. In older people with the disorder, pneumonia is the major cause of death, which often occurs in their teens or 20s.

Ataxia-teleangiectasia is also associated with an increased risk of cancer, usually leukemia or lymphoma.

CAUSE

The basic cause is a mutation in the "ataxia telangiectasia mutated" (ATM) gene. Over 300 different mutations have now been identified, many of which have a distinctive effect. For instance, the 5762ins137nt mutation is associated with a slower onset and decreased severity of neurological deterioration and little risk of cancer. The mutation causing the disorder in Sephardic Jews is 103>T.

DIAGNOSIS

Clinical diagnosis is made on the basis of the common symptoms of uncoordination, slurred speech, difficulty tracking objects in the visual field, diminished deep tendon reflexes, delayed or diminished puberty, an underdeveloped thymus, and spidery blood vessels in the corners of the eyes and on the skin surface. In some cases, symptoms in young children resemble those associated with cerebral palsy. Laboratory tests include magnetic resonance imaging (MRI) which usually reveals a small cerebellum, the part of the brain which is located at the back of head and which is involved in coordination.

Other laboratory tests include an elevated serum alpha fetal protein level (above 10 ng/ml) after two years of age. Another indication is the occurrence of breaks in chromosomesolves when treated with chemicals which stimulates cell division.

A definitive test is the presence of one of the mutated genes associated with the disorder. However, because there are so many known mutations (over 300), genetic screening is not feasible unless the screening is for specific mutations.

TRANSMISSION

Ataxia-telangiectasia is an autosomal recessive disorder. Both males and females are equally affected. Children have a 1 in 4 chance of inheriting the disorder if both parents are carriers of the same mutation and a 1 in 2 chance of becoming carriers. Carriers who have only one copy of the abnormal gene have an increased risk of developing cancer.

TREATMENT

There is no cure for Ataxia-telangiectasia and no way to slow its progress. Treatment consists of early and regular physical therapy to reduce muscle contractions. Most people require a wheelchair by 10 years of age. Supportive treatment is required to help perform regular daily activities like eating and dressing.

PREVENTION

Carrier and prenatal testing are available. Regular medical visits are recommended for early detection of cancer. Since Ataxia-telangiectasia patients are very sensitive to ionizing radiation, their exposures have to be minimal.

FOR FURTHER INFORMATION

National Ataxia Foundation
2600 Fernbrook Lane, Suite 119
Minneapolis, MN 55447
TELEPHONE: 612-553-0020
FAX: 612-553-0167
INTERNET: www.ataxia.org
E-MAIL: naf@mr.net

A-T Medical Research Foundation
5241 Round Meadow Road
Hidden Hills, CA 91301
TELEPHONE: 818-704-8146

Ataxia-Telangiectasia Clinical
  Center
Johns Hopkins Hospital, Room
  CMSC 1102
Baltimore, MD 21287
TELEPHONE: 1-800-610-5691
         410-614-1922
FAX: 410-955-0229

A-T Project
3002 Enfield Road
Austin, TX 78703-3605
TELEPHONE: 512-472-3417
FAX: 512-323-5161
E-MAIL: mhoweard@atproject.org

SCREENING CENTERS

All Children's Hospital of St. Petersburg—Cytogenetics Dept.
City of Hope National Medical Center
University of California at Los Angeles Medical Center

University of Tennessee Medical Center—Developmental and Genetics Center

REFERENCES

Bundy, S. Clinical and genetic features of ataxia telangiectasia. *International Journal of Radiation Biology* 66 (1994): S23–S29.

Gatti, R. Ataxia Telangiectasia. *Dermatologic Clinics* 13 (1995): 1–6.

Levin, S., E. Gottfried, and M. Cohen. Ataxia-telangiectasia: A review, with observations on 47 Israeli cases. *Pediatrics* 6 (1977): 135.

Levin, S., and S. Perlov. Ataxia-telangiectasia in Israel. *Israel Journal of Medical Science* 7 (1971): 1535.

Canavan Disease

Canavan Disease is a disease affecting the white matter of the brain, named after Dr. Myrtelle M. Canavan, who described its symptoms in 1931. Although Canavan thought those symptoms were a variation of another disease better known at that time, in 1949 the same kind of brain damage she observed was subsequently seen in three Jewish infants. A few years later, they were documented in 48 new patients, 28 of whom were Jewish children from Vilnius, Lithuania. Medical researchers then realized that this was in fact a unique disease that primarily affected Ashkenazi Jews.

VARIATIONS

Canavan Disease is a progressive neurological disease that has three different variants. The most common variant, called "congenital," begins to appear about three to six months after birth; this condition inevitably results in early death. The second form, called "infantile," is the most common form of the disease; its symptoms usually do not appear until around six months of age. The third, "juvenile" variant, has symptoms which don't appear before the age of five.

FREQUENCY

The frequency of Canavan Disease in the general population is not known, but it is not common. Among Ashkenazi Jews, it occurs in about 1 in 6,500. Carrier frequency among Ashkenazi Jews is estimated at 1 in 40 to 60.

One reason the frequency of Canavan Disease among Ashkenazi Jews or among the general population is still largely conjecture is because until only recently medical researchers could not be certain they were dealing with Canavan Disease unless they were able to perform an autopsy on the brains of children suspected of having the disease. (When seen at autopsy, the brain has a distinctive spongy appearance characteristic of the disease.) Once the basic biochemical cause of the disease was identified, it became possible to confirm the diagnosis by analyzing blood or urine for the presence of the substance that causes the disease; the discovery of the gene involved allows medical researchers to estimate its frequency accurately, but as yet these studies have not been made.

SYMPTOMS

Children with Canavan Disease appear normal at birth and for their first few weeks they continue to develop normally. But between two to four months of age, they begin to lose muscular abilities and appear very listless. By three to six months of age, visual responsiveness begins to diminish, head size becomes enlarged (a condition called "macrocephaly") and they begin to have difficulty lifting their heads and turning over. These symptoms, which are sometimes described as "floppiness" or hypotonia, become progressively worse, turning into rigidity and spasticity. Because of the underlying muscle weakness, children with Canavan have difficulty in grasping objects and swallowing. In some cases, they have to be fed through a tube which is placed down the nose and into the throat, or directly into the stomach. Many also begin to experience seizures. They also become blind and mentally retarded, although hearing is unaffected, so that they can respond to parents or other care givers. Most children with "congenital" or "infantile" Canavan disease die in their first year of life, although some have lived for as long as 10 years; those with the juvenile form can live beyond their teens.

CAUSE

Canavan Disease results from an absence of the enzyme aspartoacylase. The job of aspartoacylase is to break down a compound called N-acetyl-aspartic acid (NAA). Although NAA is only produced in the brain, and is the second most abundant chemical in the brain after glutamate, medical researchers are still puzzled over what it does in the brain. Despite their bafflement, it is clear that the build-up of NAA attacks a substance in the brain called myelin, replacing it with microscopic fluid-filled spaces that give it a spongy-like appearance.

Myelin, a whitish substance made up of lipids and proteins, is synthesized out of a number of different chemicals in the brain, one of which is aspartoacylase. Myelin ordinarily acts like an insulation around nerves, enabling them to pass along impulses at a much faster rate than nerves that lack such insulation. In the absence of aspartoacylase, NAA accumulates in the brain. As it accumulates, it causes progressive deterioration of myelin, resulting in the distinctive spongy deterioration characteristic of the disease.

The biochemical defect causing Canavan Disease results from a mutation in a single gene. Although several different mutations have been found in this gene, two mutations called "Y231X" and "E285A" account for virtually all the cases (97 percent) of the disease in Ashkenazi Jews. Studies of the ancestors of children with this disease traced their family origin to two small communities in Eastern Europe, Vilna-Kovno in Lithuania and Volyhnia in eastern Poland.

DIAGNOSIS

A pediatrician will suspect Canavan Disease on the basis of its three tell-tale symptoms: an enlarged head, floppiness, and an infant's inability to hold its head up. Whereas confirmation of brain damage was once only possible after death, medical technology like magnetic resonance imaging now enables physicians to look inside the brain in the living for the characteristic spongy deterioration. However, the kind of brain damage associated with Canavan Disease also occurs in other diseases, so that its presence is not conclusive proof.

A more accurate diagnosis can now be made on the basis of blood and urine tests. Children with Canavan Disease have no detectable amounts of the aspartocylase enzyme in their blood and no detectable amounts of its metabolites in their urine. Although the test is useful for making a diagnosis, it is not sensitive enough as yet to be used for determining who is and who is not a carrier.

The most confident diagnosis in Ashkenazi Jews is the presence of one of the two defective genes that cause 99 percent of all cases of the disease in this group. The test for this gene defect was developed by Dr. Ruben Matalon in 1993 at the Miami Children's Hospital. The test can also be used to detect prenatally if a fetus will be affected or be a carrier for the disease. The cost for screening for these two genes, along with the mutated genes for Tay-Sachs, Gaucher, and cystic fibrosis, is about $300.

TRANSMISSION

Canavan disease in Ashkenazi Jews results from one of two genetic mutations. Since it is due to an autosomal recessive gene, both parents have to be carriers for the child to exhibit the disease. If both parents are carriers, their children have a 1 in 4 chance of inheriting the disease and a 1 in 2 chance of being a carrier. If neither parent carries the defective gene, none of their children will develop the disease and none will be carriers.

TREATMENT

There is currently no regular treatment available other than supportive care. The best parents can hope to do is to make the lives of their affected children as comfortable as possible. Children with feeding problems require the utmost patience on the part of parents. An attempt is currently underway at Thomas Jefferson University Hospital in Philadelphia to correct the disease through gene transfer. The procedure involves placing a tube under a child's scalp containing genes that brain cells need to make the missing enzyme causing Canavan. The tube has a catheter that goes into the child's brain fluids and (ideally) enters the brain cells. These tests are still in the preliminary stage and will not be perfected for many years.

PREVENTION

In light of the seriousness of this disease, the absence of any treatment, and its high incidence among Ashkenazi Jews, the American

College of Obstetricians and Gynecologists has recently recommended that all Ashkenazi Jews should be tested to determine if they are carriers for Canavan disease, preferably before they consider having children. Population screening for the disease is already available in many large cities. The purpose is to identify Jewish couples who are at risk for having a child with Canavan and are completely unaware that they are carriers.

Since the two mutations causing this disease in Ashkenazi Jews are known, carrier testing can be performed by examining cells for the presence or absence of one or both copies of the defective gene. The same method can be used prenatally to determine if a fetus is affected.

FOR FURTHER INFORMATION

Canavan Foundation
600 West 111th St.
New York, NY 10025
TELEPHONE: 212-316-6488
INTERNET: www.canvanfoundation.org

National Foundation for Jewish
  Genetic Diseases
250 Park Avenue, Suite 1000
New York, NY 10017
TELEPHONE: 212-371-1030

Connecticut Children's Medical
  Center
282 Washington St.
Hartford, CT 06106
TELEPHONE: 860-545-9580
FAX: 860-545-9590

University of Pittsburgh
Department of Human Genetics
Center for Study and Treatment of
  Jewish Genetic Diseases
Pittsburg, PA 15261
TELEPHONE: 1-800-334-7980
INTERNET: www.pitt.edu/~edugene

SCREENING CENTERS

Boston University School of Medicine—Center for Human Genetics
Duke University Medical Center—Pediatric Medical Genetics
Genetics & IVF Institute
Genzyme Genetics
Thomas Jefferson University
Johns Hopkins Medical Institute—Kennedy Krieger Institute
Massachusetts General Hospital—Neurochemistry/Amino Acid Laboratory
Medical Genetics Institute, S.C.
Mount Sinai School of Medicine

New York University School of Medicine—Molecular Genetics Laboratory of NYU Medical Center
New York University School of Medicine—Neurogenetics Laboratory
North Shore University Hospital at Manhaset
SmithKline Beecham Clinical Laboratories
University of Pittsburgh Medical Center
Wayne State University—Harper Hospital
Yale University School of Medicine

REFERENCES

Books

Bogaert, Van L., and I. Bertrand. *Spongy Degeneration of the Brain in Infancy.* Amsterdam: North Holland Publishing, 1967.

Journal Articles

Banker, B.Q., and M. Victor. "Spongy degeneration of infancy." In: Goodman, Richard E. and Arno G. Motulsky, eds. *Genetic Diseases Among Ashkenazi Jews.* New York: Raven Press, 1979, 201–216.

Elpeleg, O.N., Y. Anikster, V. Barash, et al. The frequency of the C854 mutation in the aspartocylase gene in Ashkenazi Jews in Israel. *American Journal of Human Genetics* 55 (1994): 287–288.

Elpeleg, O.N., A. Shaag, Y. Anikster, et al. Prenatal detection of Canavan disease (Aspartoacylase deficiency) by DNA analysis. *Journal of Inherited Metabolic Disease* 17 (1994): 664–666.

Kaul, R., G.P. Gao, M. Aloya, et al. Canavan disease: mutations among Jewish and non–Jewish patients. *American Journal of Human Genetics* 55 (1994): 34–41.

Kronn, David, Carole Oddoux, Justin Phillips, et al. Prevalence of Canavan disease heterozygotes in the New York Metropolitan Ashkenazi Jewish population. *American Journal of Human Genetics* 57 (1995): 1250–1252.

Matalon, Reuben, Kimberlee Michals, and Rajinder Kaul. Canavan disease: From spongy degeneration to molecular analysis. *Journal of Pediatrics* 127 (1995): 511–515.

Matalon, Reuben, Kimberlee Michals, D. Sebesta, et al. Aspartoacylase deficiency and N-acetylaspartic aciduria in patients with Canavan disease. *American Journal of Medical Genetics* 29 (1988): 463–471.

Ungar, M., and Richard M. Goodman. Spongy degeneration of the brain in Israel: A retrospective study. *Clinical Genetics* 23 (1983): 23–29.

Creutzfeldt-Jakob Disease

Creutzfeldt-Jakob Disease is a fatal neurodegenerative disease that is sometimes called "spongiform encephalopathy" because brain cells from people affected by the disease are spongelike in appearance.

FREQUENCY

Although it is very rare in Europe and North America, in the 1970s a large number of Jews who had emigrated from Libya to Israel in 1950-1951 were found to be affected by the disease. This generated a great deal of interest among medical researchers since it was the first time the disease had been found to be concentrated in an identifiable group. The worldwide frequency is estimated at 1 case per million; the frequency of the disorder among Libyan Jews is estimated at 1 in 24,000.

SYMPTOMS

Symptoms of Creutzfeldt-Jakob Disease appear around 40 years of age and typically begin with sleep disturbances, headaches, memory lapses, depression, uncoordination, general malaise and pain. These symptoms rapidly progress within weeks to involve the motor system. Gait becomes progressively unsteady and falling is common, hand movements become jerky, hands tremble, and speech problems emerge. Facial expression becomes bland. As the disease progresses, dementia worsens, and further paralysis occurs; muscles become rigid and sufferers become unable to feed and dress themselves and have to be confined to bed. In some cases, seizures may occur. Although sufferers become mute, sometimes they laugh inappropriately and uncontrollably. Death usually occurs within six months to a year after the appearance of the initial symptoms.

CAUSE

Until very recently, medical researchers believed the cause of Creutzfeldt-Jakob Disease was a virus or some other infectious agent, and that the high frequency of Creutzfeldt-Jakob Disease among Libyan Jews was due to the local custom among Jews in North Africa of eating lightly-cooked brains and eyeballs of sheep. Some of these sheep, they speculate, were infected with a disease called "scrapie."

Creutzfeldt-Jakob Disease can in fact be acquired through ingesting or exposure to infected material. This possibility has generated sensational headlines in Britain, where a form of spongiform encephalopathy called "mad cow disease" was suspected of causing Creutzfeldt-Jakob Disease in humans. The infection was believed to have originated from feeding offal from scrapie-infected sheep to cows. At the peak of the panic in 1992 and 1993, almost a 1,000 cows a week were exhibiting signs of the disease. At the same time, there was a small, but nevertheless noticeable increase in the number of people affected, which was also unusual because they were much younger than usual. Although very rare, there have also been cases in which the disease was transmitted on surgical instruments from one person to another during neurosurgeries or corneal transplants. On the other hand, there are no cases in which family members have acquired the disease through contact with another family member with the disease.

The other way is through heredity, accounting for about 15 percent of all cases. The hereditary basis is linked to a mutation in the gene that makes a class of abnormal proteins called "proteinaceious infectious particles," or "prions" for short. Prions are believed to transform normal proteins in the body into destructive proteins by altering their shape. The mutation, designated E200K, occurs in the prion gene PRNP and results from the substitution of one amino acid (lysine) for the normally occurring amino acid (glutamate). This is the most common cause of hereditary Creutzfeldt-Jakob Disease; with a penetrance of about 50 percent by age 60 and 80 percent by age 80, it accounts for 70 percent of all hereditary cases.

Although Libyan and Tunisian Jews have the highest prevalence of the E200K mutation, it has also been found in relatively high frequencies in Spain, Italy, and Chile; but it has also been found in Slovakia, Germany, Austria, and Japan. Most of those affected in Spain, Chile, and Italy shared the same 200K mutation, whereas those in the other countries had a different mutation. This suggests the E200K mutation had been carried to Spain by Libyan-Tunisian Jews and from there it was carried into Italy and Chile by Sephardic Jews expelled from Spain in 1492. After the establishment of Israel in 1948 and the independence of Libya and Tunisia in the 1950s, many of the Jews from these countries emigrated to Israel or France. Ashkenazi Jews, by contrast, did not have the mutation.

DIAGNOSIS

The diagnosis is based on the rapid appearance of symptoms in adults. There are no clinical tests that reliably confirm its presence. Since the disease is very rare, it has been mistaken for other neurological disorders. Tests such as an MRI and possibly brain biopsy may be performed to exclude these other possibilities. The only definitive test is an examination of brain tissue after death for the distinctive spongiform cell structure.

TRANSMISSION

Creutzfeldt-Jakob Disease is both a genetic and a transmissible disease. Genetically, it is an autosomal dominant disorder, which means that only one copy of defective gene need be present for it to manifest itself. The fact that it is transmissible has been shown in experiments in which tissues from the brains of affected individuals or animals have been injected into healthy animals that subsequently came down with the disease.

TREATMENT

There is no cure for this disease. Treatment consists of muscle relaxants to control muscle rigidity and antidepressant drugs to control depression. Death usually occurs within six months to a year of the appearance of symptoms.

FOR FURTHER INFORMATION

Creutzfeldt-Jakob Disease Foundation
P.O. Box 611625
Miami, FL 33261-1625
FAX: 954-436-7591
E-MAIL: crjakob@aol.com

National Organization for Rare Disorders
P.O. Box 8923
New Fairfield, CT 06812-1783
TELEPHONE: 203-746-6518
INTERNET: www.nord-rdb.com/~orphan

REFERENCES

Chapman, J., J. Ben-Israel, Y. Goldhammer, et al. The risk of developing Creutzfeldt-Jakob disease in subjects with the PRNP gene codon 200 point mutation. *Neurology* 44 (1994): 1683–1686.

Chapman, J., and A.D. Korczyn. Genetic and environmental factors determining the development of Creutzfeldt-Jakob disease in Libyan Jews. *Neuroepidemiology* 10 (1991): 228–231.

Fajdusek, D.C. The transmissible amyloidoses: genetical control of spontaneous generation of infections amyloid proteins by nucleation of configurational changes in host precursors: kur-CJD-GSS-scrapie-BSF. *European Journal of Epidemiology* 7 (1991): 567–577.

Gabizon, R., H. Rosenmann, Z. Meiner, et al. Mutation and polymorphism of the prion protein gene in Libyan Jews with Creutzfeldt-Jakob disease (CJD). *American Journal of Human Genetics* 53 (1993): 828–835.

Gabizon, R., M. Halimi, and Z. Meiner. Genetics and biochemistry of Creutzfeldt-Jakob disease in Libyan Jews. *Biomedicine and Pharmacotherapy* 48 (1994): 385–399.

Korczyn, Ad. Neurologic genetic diseases of Jewish people. *Biomedicine and Pharmacotherapy* 48 (1994): 391–397.

Lee, Hee S., Nyamkhishig Sambuughin, Larisa Cevenakova, et al. Ancestral origins and worldwide distribution of the PRNP 200K mutation causing familial Creutzfeldt-Jakob disease. *American Journal of Human Genetics* 64 (1999): 1063–1070.

Meiner, Zeev, Ruth Gabizon, and Stanley B. Prusiner. Familial Creutzfeldt-Jakob Disease: codon 200 prion disease in Libyan Jews. *Medicine* 76 (1997): 227–137.

Will, R.G., J.W. Ironside, M. Zeidler, et al. A new variant of Creutzfeldt-Jakob disease in the UK. *Lancet* 347 (1996): 921–925.

Familial Dysautonomia aka
Riley-Day Syndrome

Familial Dysautonomia is one of a group of rare genetic disorders that result from arrested maturation of sensory nerves and the autonomic nervous system (dysautonomia literally means "dysfunction of the autonomic nervous system"). The autonomic nervous system is that part of the nervous system that manages most of our internal body activities, for example, blood pressure, digestion, hormonal, urinary and bowel function, internal body temperature regulation, breathing, swallowing, metabolism, making tears, as well as our physiological reactions to stress. Nearly all of these activities are reflex-like reactions, accomplished without our awareness unless something goes wrong.

While there are several kinds of genetically-related dysautonomias such as Parkinson's disease and peripheral autonomic disorders like Guillain Barre syndrome, they each have disturbed sensory and autonomic functions in common. The type of dysautonomia that occurs almost exclusively in Ashkenazi Jews is called "Familial Dysautonomia" or "Riley-Day Syndrome," after Drs. Conrad Riley and Richard Day, who identified the disorder in 1949. In 1967 medical researchers documented 200 cases of the disorder in 164 families. Except for two, all of them were of Ashkenazi Jewish ancestry. In most cases, family origins have been traced to southeastern Central Europe, especially Romania, Galicia, and the Ukraine.

FREQUENCY

Familial Dysautonomia is the most common and widely recognized congenital sensory disorder among Ashkenazi Jews. In the United States, its frequency of occurrence among Ashkenazi Jews is estimated at about 1 in 3,600 births. The carrier frequency is estimated at 1 in 30, similar to the carrier frequency for Tay-Sachs. In Israel, the disorder has rarely been found in Sephardic or Oriental Jews.

SYMPTOMS

When in 1949 Drs. Riley and Day first described the disorder that now bears their name, they said that the "symptoms [were] so puzzling as to defy exact diagnosis yet so similar as to constitute a clinical entity." The five children that suffered from the symptoms that so puzzled all had an "undue" reaction to mild anxiety, sweated and salivated excessively, had red blotches on the skin, and had brief periods of very high blood pressure. Several other of their symptoms were also very unusual. One was a "diminished production of tears," another was decreased tendon reflexes, and a third was an abnormal indifference to pain. In fact, when Drs. Riley and Day immersed the feet of two of the children in ice water, the children didn't complain. The fourth characteristic that united these five children was that they all had Ashkenazi origins.

Symptoms of Familial Dysautonomia begin to occur soon after birth. Infants have an abnormal suck and uncoordinated swallowing so that food often goes into the lungs, where it causes repeated bouts of pneumonia due to the food-related infections. Vomiting is also very common and because swallowing is often misdirected, vomited material also gets into the lungs. Excessive drooling is common. Since feeding problems result in less than normal eating, infants gain less weight and their growth is stunted.

People with Familial Dysautonomia have little or no taste sensitivity, except for sour tasting substances, due to the absence of taste buds, called fungiform papillae, on their tongues. They also do not feel hot or cold or pain. As a result, they often burn and bruise themselves, don't seem to learn to avoid objects, and don't react to broken bones. Curvature of the spine occurs in nearly all cases by 13 years of age. Because of an inability to control body temperature, bouts of fever appear suddenly and subside just as suddenly as they appear.

The most distinctive characteristic of Familial Dysautonomia is an inability to make tears. Tears are produced by lacrimal glands located above the upper eyelids. We usually associate tears with crying, but they also act to lubricate the surface of the eye and wash away dust. Without tears, the eyes become very dry. Tears also contain an antiseptic which helps to fight infectious substances that may come in contact with them.

About 50 percent of people with Familial Dysautonomia react to emotional stress or infections with a pattern of reactions called the "dysautonomia crisis," which includes a large increase in heart rate and blood pressure, excessive sweating, skin blotches, episodic vomiting, and personality changes. Other common features of Familial Dysautonomia are breath-holding, stomach pains, diarrhea and constipation, motor incoordination, decreased blood pressure when standing up after sitting or lying down, difficulty controlling body temperature, blotched skin patches, and convulsions. Although intelligence is normal and many people with Familial Dysautonomia have completed college if treated early in life, they often have speech problems and are uncoordinated.

DIAGNOSIS

Diagnosis of Familial Dysautonomia is based on a pattern of clinical symptoms that includes absence of overflow tears, missing fungiform papillae on the tip of the tongue, scoliosis (curvature of the spine) and decreased or absent deep tendon reflex. Two laboratory tests are also diagnostic. One involves injecting histamine under the skin. Most people feel intense pain and develop redness in the area of injection; children with Familial Dysautonomia have little pain and no redness. In the methacholine test, a drop of methacholine is placed into the corner of the eye. This causes the pupil to constrict in Familial Dysautonomia but has no noticeable effect on a normal pupil. The reaction indicates absence of activity in the autonomic nervous system.

CAUSE

Familial Dysautonomia is due to a genetic defect that results in incomplete development of sensory and autonomic nerves. Although the exact identity of the gene has not yet been identified, medical researchers at the Hadassah University Hospital in Jerusalem have identified what they called "markers" flanking the gene, which they have labeled "DYS." These markers have enabled them to identify more than 98 percent of all FD patients.

While the actual biochemical causes are not known, Familial Dysautonomia is believed to be caused by an absence of a substance called nerve growth factor (NGF) during fetal development. Familial Dysautonomia is also characterized by a marked reduction in the number of nonmyelinated and myelinated nerves involved in sensory function and a decrease in the terminals for many of autonomic nerves in the skin and other parts of the body.

TRANSMISSION

Familial Dysautonomia is an autosomal recessive disorder that affects both males and females but only occurs in people of Ashkenazi Jewish descent. The probability of a child developing this disorder is 1 in 4 if both parents are carriers. If only one parent has this mutation, the disorder will not be inherited but a child has a 1 in 2 chance of being a carrier. The chance of not being affected and not being a carrier is 1 in 4.

TREATMENT

Before 1960, about half of all children with the disease died before they reached their fifth birthday. As a result of various surgical treatments now available, about half now live to at least 30 years of age.

Treatments for children consist of applying artificial tear drops to keep eyes moist, special feeding procedures to help them swallow, speech therapy, physical therapy, and drugs for regulating blood pressure. Since children with Familial Dysautonomia do not feel pain, they have to be closely supervised to avoid injuring themselves.

The primary surgical treatments are gastronomy and fundoplication. In a gastronomy, an opening is permanently made into the stomach so that a tube can be inserted, usually at night, to provide the nutrients and calories that would otherwise be taken into the body if swallowing were normal. Fundoplication is usually an accompanying surgical procedure that tightens the stomach to lower the risk of vomiting and then breathing the vomitus into the lungs.

In addition to surgical treatment, patients are also given drugs like diazepam and chloral hydrate to control vomiting, and other drugs are given to control blood pressure. Extra fluids and salt are also prescribed to help regulate blood pressure, and physical therapy is recommended for improving the function of the leg muscles.

PREVENTION

Prenatal diagnosis and carrier identification are available.

FOR FURTHER INFORMATION

Dysautonomia Foundation, Inc.
20 East 46th St.
New York, NY 10017
TELEPHONE: 212-949-6644
FAX: 212-682-7625

National Foundation for Jewish
 Genetic Diseases
250 Park Ave.
New York, NY 10017
TELEPHONE: 212-371-1030

Familial Dysautonomia Treatment
 and Evaluation Center
New York University Medical Center
c/o Dr. Felicia B. Axelrod
530 First Avenue, Suite 3A
New York, NY, 10016
TELEPHONE: 212-263-7225
INTERNET: www.Med.nyu.edu/fd/
 fdcenter.html

SCREENING CENTERS

Mount Sinai Medical Center—
 Molecular Diagnosis Laboratory

NYU School of Medicine—
 Molecular Genetics Laboratory

REFERENCES

Axelrod, Felicia B. Familial dysautonomia: a 47-year perspective. How technology confirms clinical acumen. *Journal of Pediatrics* 132 (1998): S2–S5.
Blumenfeld, Anat, Susan A. Slaugenhaupt, Felicia Axelrod, et al. Localization

of the gene for familial dysautonomia on Chromosome 9 and definition of DNA markers for genetic diagnosis. *Nature Genetics* 4 (1993): 160–164.

Blumenfeld, Anat, Susan A. Slaugenhaupt, Christopher B. Liebert, et al. Precise genetic mapping and haplotype analysis of the familial dysautonomia gene on human chromosome 9q31. *American Journal of Human Genetics* 64 (1999): 1110–1118.

Brunt, P.W., and V.A. McKusick. Familial dysautonomia: A report of genetic and clinical studies with a review of the literature. *Medicine* 49 (1970): 343–349.

Maayan, Ch., E. Kaplan, Sh. Schachar, et al. Incidence of familial dysautonomia in Israel 1977–1981. *Clinical Genetics* 32 (1987): 106–108.

Moses, S.W., Y. Rotem, N. Jogoda, et al. A clinical, genetic, and biochemical study of familial dysautonomia in Israel. *Israel Journal of Medical Science* 3 (1967): 358–362.

Oddoux, C., E. Reich, F. Axelrod, et al. Prenatal diagnostic testing for familial dysautonomia using linked genetic markers. *Prenatal Diagnosis* 15 (1995): 817–826.

Riley, Conrad M., Richard L. Day, David McL. Greeley. Central autonomic dysfunction with defective lacrimation. *Pediatrics* 3 (1949): 468–477.

Welton, W., D. Clayson, F.B. Axelrod, et al. Intellectual development and familial dysautonomia. *Pediatrics* 63 (1979): 708–712.

Hunter Syndrome

Hunter Syndrome is one of a group of eight rare lysosomal storage disorders known as the mucopolysaccharidoses designated by different numbers. Hunter Syndrome is otherwise known as mucopolysaccharidosis II. Each of the mucopolysacchardisoses has its own characteristic symptoms and enzyme deficiency. In the case of Hunter Syndrome, the deficiency involves the lysosomal enzyme, iduronate-e-sulfatase (IDS). Although relatively rare, it has been found to be more common among Jews in Israel, especially Ashkenazi.

VARIATIONS

There are two main subtypes. In the severe form of the disorder, people are mentally retarded, many bodily organs become enlarged, and subjects usually die before the age of 15. In the milder form, intelligence is normal, growth is less than normal, and life expectancy is between 20 and 60 years of age. The severe form is about three times more common than the mild form.

SYMPTOMS

The main symptoms of the severe form of Hunter Syndrome are a characteristic facial appearance, skeletal abnormalities, dwarfism, deafness, retinal degeneration, stiff joints, increased liver size, recurrent infections of the upper respiratory tract. Major cause of death is damage to the heart.

Children with Hunter Syndrome appear normal at birth and have normal growth and intellectual development. Symptoms of the severe form of the disorder usually appear between two and five years of age and take the form of stunted growth, declining motor skills, loss of bowel control and diarrhea. At the same time their faces take on a characteristic coarseness consisting of excessive hairiness, protruding tongue, small deformed and widely spaced teeth, thick ear lobes, and persistent runny nose. They also begin to develop recurrent respiratory infections, partial deafness, pebbly-appearing skin rashes, especially in the area of the upper arms, and hernias. Mental retardation and failing vision become progressive.

FREQUENCY

The worldwide prevalence for the disorder is estimated at 1 in 150,000 live births. The disorder occurs primarily in females and its prevalence in Ashkenazi Jews in Israel is estimated at 1 in 67,500 births.

CAUSE

The absence of lysosomal iduronate-2-sulfatase results from one of several mutations on the X chromosome. The most common is known as 1246 C—>T. As a result of the deficiency, cells cannot break down mucopolysaccharides and these accumulate in cells, especially those in the brain and liver.

DIAGNOSIS

Diagnosis is based levels of iduronate sulfate sulfatase levels in blood and on the presence of cells having bloated lysosomes containing storage material called "metachromatic granules" which react characteristically to certain stains.

TRANSMISSION

Hunter Syndrome is an X-linked disorder. This means that the gene defect is located on the X chromosome. Because females have two X chromosomes, females rarely develop the disorder but can be carriers, whereas all males who inherit a single copy for the abnormal gene inherit it from their carrier mothers and will experience the disorder.

TREATMENT

There is no treatment for this disorder.

PREVENTION

Prenatal diagnosis is possible by measuring iduronate sulfate sulfatase levels in maternal blood. In pregnancies in which the fetus is not affected by Hunter Syndrome, enzyme levels rise constantly during pregnancy by six to 10 weeks of pregnancy, whereas in pregnancies in which the fetus is affected, no change in enzyme levels occurs in maternal blood.

FOR FURTHER INFORMATION

National MPS Society
102 Aspen Drive
Downingtown, PA 19335
TELEPHONE: 610-942-0100
FAX: 610-942-7188
E-MAIL: info@mpssociety.org

SCREENING CENTERS

John F. Kennedy Institute

Wayne State University—
Biochemical and Molecular
Genetics Laboratory

REFERENCES

Ben Simon-Schiff, E., G. Bach, J.J. Hopwood, et al. Mutational analysis of Jewish Hunter patients in Israel. *Human Mutation* 4 (1994): 263–270.
Ben Simon-Schiff, E., J. Zlotogora, D. Abelivoich, et al. Hunter syndrome among Jews in Israel. *Biomedical Pharmacotherapeutics* 48 (1994): 381–384.
Neufeld, E.F., and J. Muenzer. "The Mucooplysaccharidosis." In: Scriver, Charles R., Arthur L. Beaudent, William S. Sly, et al., eds. *The Metabolic and Molecular Bases of Inherited Disease.* New York: McGraw-Hill, 1995.
Schaap, T., and G. Bach. Incidence of mucopolysaccharidosis in Israel. Is Hunter disease a "Jewish disease"? *Human Genetics* 56 (1980): 221–223.
Zlotogora, J., and G. Bach. Heterozygote detection in Hunter syndrome. *American Journal of Medical Genetics* 17 (1984): 661–665.
Zlotogora, J., T. Schaap, M. Ziegler, et al. Hunter syndrome among Ashkenazi Jews in Israel; evidence for prenatal selection favoring the Hunter allele. *Human Genetics* 71 (1985): 329–332.
Zlotogora, J., T. Schaap, M. Ziegler, et al. Hunter syndrome in Jews in Israel:

Further evidence for prenatal selection favoring the Hunter allele. *Human Genetics* 86 (1991): 531–536.

Metachromatic Leukodystrophy

The leukodystrophies, which include Canavan Disease and Metachromatic Leukodystrophy, are progressive neurological disorders that affect the brain, spinal cord and peripheral nerves. Metachromatic comes from "meta" (beside) and "chroma" (color); leukodystrophy comes from the Greek words "leuko" (white) and "dystrophy" (irregular development). The "white" in this disorder refers to myelin, the whitish lipid coat that insulates nerves so that nerve impulses can be transmitted more efficiently. Myelin is composed of many different chemicals; each of the leukodystrophies affects only one of these substances.

Metachromatic Leukodystrophy is a rare lysosomal storage disease resulting from a deficiency in the lysosomal enzyme arylsulfatase A, which ordinarily breaks down a component in myelin called cerebroside sulfate. As a result of the deficiency, cerebroside sulfate builds up in the brain and peripheral nerves, as well as the kidneys and other visceral organs.

FREQUENCY

The worldwide frequency is estimated at between 1 in 40,000 and 1 in 130,000 live births.

Metachromatic Leukodystrophy has a peculiarly high incidence among Habbanite Jews. The Habbanites are a very small Jewish community that inhabited the city of Habban in southwest Saudi Arabia. In 1950, the entire community of 345 people migrated to Israel, where it retained its social exclusivity. The community currently numbers about 1,500 people. Although they lived very close to the Jewish community in Yemen, the Habbanites remained relatively isolated from it. As a result, the disorder is rare among Yemenite Jews (although some cases have been noted) but relatively common among the Habbanites, with an incidence of 1 in 75 and a carrier frequency estimated at 17 per 100 for the late-infantile form. By contrast, the disorder is very rare among Ashkenazi Jews (1 in 600,000).

VARIATIONS

There are several different subtypes of the disorder which are designated by their biochemical abnormality and in terms of their age of onset: late-infantile, juvenile and adult.

SYMPTOMS

The late-infantile form usually appears in the second year of life and results in death one to seven years later. The juvenile form appears between four and 12 years, whereas the adult form may appear any time after late adolescence.

Children with the infantile form appear normal at birth. Around one year of age, muscle tone decreases, arms and legs become floppy, and speech deteriorates. Deterioration in motor skills becomes progressively worse, resulting in an inability to move, to speak, and to swallow, so that tube feeding becomes necessary. Motor deterioration becomes progressively worse, resulting in paralysis and an inability to sit. Other effects include blindness and seizures.

In the juvenile form of the disorder, disturbances are similar to the infantile form but the progression is slower. The adult form is characterized by behavioral disturbances.

CAUSE

Metachromatic Leukodystrophy results from a deficiency in the lysosomal enzyme, arylsulfatase A, its "activator protein" called saposin B, and or one or more related enzymes related to arylsufatase A, due to a mutation in a gene called ASA. The deficiency results in the accumulation of cerebroside sulfate (also called galactosyl sulfatide) which makes up about 3 to 4 percent of the myelin membranes in the central nervous system and accumulates in the liver, kidneys, testes and gallbladder. The accumulation destroys certain cells in the central and peripheral nervous system called oligodendroglial and Schwann cells, resulting in a demyelination and neurodegeneration due to the attendant decrease in the efficiency of conducting nerve impulses to the muscles, internal organs and skin. The different variants are due to differences in the amount of the enzyme or its activator, which are in turn related to whether an individual has one or both mutations, as well as to the different mutations in the ASA gene. There are also some individuals who have low levels of the enzyme but are nevertheless healthy. This condition is known as ASA pseudodeficiency. The genetic abnormality affecting Habbanite Jews has been traced to a single couple who lived in Habban at the beginning of the 19th century. Interestingly, the few cases of this disorder among

Yemenite Jews resulted from the relatively few intermarriages between the two communities.

DIAGNOSIS

A diagnosis can be made by measuring levels of arylsulfatase A in blood, which are lower than normal, and levels of sulfatides in urine, which are greatly elevated in the disorder. If cells are placed under a microscope, they have a characteristic spherical granular appearance and an altered color (called metachromatic) when treated with a specific stain.

TRANSMISSION

Metachromatic Leukodystrophy is an autosomal recessive disorder. This means both parents are carriers and each child has 1 in 4 chance of developing the disorder and a 1 in 2 chance of becoming a carrier.

TREATMENT

There are no traditional treatments for this disorder. Bone marrow transplants have been found to slow the progression of symptoms in the adult form, but since the effects of bone marrow transplant may not be seen for many months, this treatment is unable to arrest the very rapid progression associated with the late-infantile form.

PREVENTION

Prevention depends on early identification of carriers and prenatal diagnosis, which in turn depends on measuring levels of arylsulfatase A.

Since Habbanites are very orthodox, they do not consider abortion of affected fetuses as an option.

FOR FURTHER INFORMATION

United Leukodystrophy Foundation
2304 Highland Dr.
Sycamore, IL 60178
TELEPHONE: 1-800-728-5483
FAX: 815-895-2432

REFERENCES

Gieselmann, V., A. Polten, J. Kreysing, et al. Molecular genetics of metachromatic leukodystrophy. *Developmental Neuroscience* 13 (1991): 222–227.

Kafert, S., U. Heinisch, J. Zlotogora, et al. A missense mutation P136L in the aryl sulfatase A gene causes instability and loss of activity of the mutant enzyme. *Human Genetics* 95 (1995): 201–204.

Zlotogora, J., G. Bach, Y. Barak, et al. Metachromatic leukodystrophy in the Habbanite Jews: high frequency in a genetic isolate and screening for heterozygotes. *American Journal of Human Genetics* 32 (1980): 663–669

Zlotogora, J., G. Bach, C. Bosenberg, et al. Molecular basis of late infantile metachromatic leukodystrophy in the Habbanite Jews. *Human Mutation* 5 (1995): 137–143.

Zlotogora, J., V. Gieselman, K. Von Figura, et al. Late infantile metachromatic leukodystrophy in Israel. *Biomedicine and Pharmacotherapeutics* 48 (1994): 347–350.

Mucolipidosis Type IV

Mucolipidosis IV is a relatively uncommon lysosomal storage disorder whose main symptoms are mental and motor retardation and corneal opacity. The disease mainly affects Ashkenazi Jews and was first described in a seven-month-old Ashkenazi boy in 1974 by Dr. E.R. Berman at the Hadassah University Hospital in Jerusalem. It is related to Tay-Sachs and other Jewish genetic diseases in that it involves a cell's lysosomes. The term "mucolipidosis" comes from the presence of characteristic storage bodies called cytoplasmic inclusions that accumulate inside cells, resembling those found in other lipid storage diseases like Tay-Sachs. The term itself comes from the "muco" part of the first disorder and the "lipid" of the second.

FREQUENCY

To date less than 100 people with Mucolipidosis IV have been identified, but most of them are Ashkenazi Jews. Its estimated prevalence is 1 in 30,000; carrier frequency has been estimated at 1 in 50.

SYMPTOMS

The main symptoms of Mucolipidosis IV are severe mental and motor retardation and corneal clouding. Symptoms begin to appear during the first year of life. Although they have normal birth weights, by their third month of life children with the disorder begin to exhibit a characteristic cloudiness in their corneas which limits their vision, although some do not develop cloudiness until five years of age. Corneal clouding in infants is very unusual and it is this symptom which first alerted Dr. Berman to the existence of the disorder.

Children with Mucolipidosis IV never learn to speak normally and they are able to learn only a few words. They are also unable to feed themselves. Crawling and walking skills are delayed. Although they may learn to walk, they need support when doing so. Other characteristic symptoms affecting the eyes are strabismus ("crossed-eyes"), puffy eyelids, photophobia (avoidance of light), and retinal degeneration which initially causes poor vision and often leads to blindness in later years.

Another main symptom is a delay in their ability to sit upright alone; many Mucolipidosis IV children never gain the ability to walk. Other motor skills are likewise impaired. Many also do not speak or only utter a few words and do not respond to spoken commands, although hearing is normal. Growth is below normal. Mild mental retardation is apparent in the first year and progresses to severe mental retardation in the second and third years.

CAUSE

The specific genetic defects and the related biochemical changes resulting in Mucolipidosis IV are still unknown, but it is known to be due to a defect in a gene located on chromosome 19, and this genetic defect results in an abnormality in the enzymes in cellular lysosomes that break down phospholipids and gangioliosides.

DIAGNOSIS

The diagnosis of the disease is based on both the clinical symptoms of corneal clouding, growth retardation, mild retardation, the presence of abnormal storage bodies in cells which can be seen using very sophisticated microscopes, and the absence of enlargement of the various organs of the body or signs of skeletal damage. What makes this disease unique compared to other lysosomal storage diseases is that some people with Mucolipidosis IV do not develop more severe symptoms with time and some even show mild improvement

TRANSMISSION

Mucolipidosis IV is an autosomal recessive disease which means that it occurs equally in children of both sexes. It also means that both parents have to be carriers for their children to develop the disease. Children conceived by two such carrier parents have a 1 in 4 chance of being affected and a 1 in 2 chance of being carriers. If neither parent is a carrier, none of their children will develop the disease and none will become carriers.

TREATMENT

There is no cure for this disease. The only treatment is supportive care such as physical and speech therapy.

PREVENTION

Prenatal diagnosis is now possible and is based on observing the telltale storage bodies in fetal cells obtained through amniocentesis. However, detection of the characteristic storage bodies requires considerable expertise and is not widely available.

FOR FURTHER INFORMATION

ML4 Foundation
719 East 17th St.
Brooklyn, NY 11230
E-MAIL: ML4www@aol.com
INTERNET: www.ml4.org

National MPS Society
17 Kraemer St.
Hicksville, NY 11801
TELEPHONE: 610-942-0100
INTERNET: www.mpssocity.com

REFERENCES

Amir, Naomi, Joel Zlotogora, and Gideon Bach. Mucolipidosis type IV: Clinical spectrum and natural history. *Pediatrics* 79 (1987): 953–958.

Bach, Gideon, Joel Zlotogora and Marcia Ziegler. "Lysosomal storage disorders among Jews." In: Bonne-Tamir, Batsheva, and Avinoam Adam, eds. *Genetic Diversity Among Jews. Diseases and Markers at the DNA Level.* New York: Oxford University Press, 1992, 301–304.

Berman, E.R., N. Livni, E. Shapira, et al. Congenital corneal clouding with abnormal systemic storage bodies: A new variant of mucolipidosis. *Journal of Pediatrics* 84 (1974): 519–526.

Reis, S., R. Sheffer, L. Merin, et al. Mucolipidosis IV, a mild form with late onset. *American Journal of Medical Genetics* 47 (1993): 392–394.

Slaugenhaupt, Susan A., James S. Acierno, Lisa Anne Helbling, et al. Mapping of the Mucolipidosis Type IV gene to Chromosome 19p and definition of founder haplotypes. *American Journal of Human Genetics* 65 (1999): 773–778.

Zeigler, M., R. Bargal, V. Suri, et al. Mucolipidosis type IV: Accumulation of phospholipids and gangliosides in cultured amniotic cells. A tool for prenatal diagnosis. *Prenatal Diagnosis* 12 (1992): 1037–1042.

Niemann-Pick Disease

Niemann-Pick Disease is a progressive neurological disorder associated with a missing enzyme, sphingomyelinase. Absence of this enzyme results in storage of abnormally high levels of sphingomyelin and cholesterol in various parts of the body, especially the brain. The disease is named after two physicians. Dr. Albert Niemann was a German pediatrician who in 1914 first described its characteristic symptoms in an 18-month-old Jewish girl. The girl had an enlarged spleen, swelling, and pigmented skin and died a few months after he examined her. Although the girl's symptoms resembled Gaucher Disease, Niemann believed it was either a variation of Gaucher or some other disorder because of the child's death soon thereafter. In 1927 Dr. Ludwick Pick was reviewing the cases of a number of other children with similar symptoms. He recognized that all the cases resembled one another, and subsequently the disorder was called Niemann-Pick Disease. In 1966 the biochemical basis of the disease was finally determined.

VARIATIONS

There are five different subtypes of Niemann-Pick Disease which are designated in terms of their alphabetical suffix. All are autosomal recessive genetic diseases. The two subtypes that occur more commonly among Ashkenazi Jews are Types A and B, and each of these is subdivided into acute, subacute, and chronic, according to the age at which symptoms appear and their severity.

Type A is a fatal disorder that develops in infancy and is characterized by increased size of the liver and spleen, failure to thrive, and rapid neurological deterioration and death by two to three years of age. The child originally described by Dr. Niemann had the Type A form. Types B, C and D have effects similar to Type A except there are no associated neurological effects. Most cases come to medical attention because of the increased liver and spleen size, and most people with this form of the disorder live until adulthood.

FREQUENCY

The frequency of Type A Niemann-Pick among Ashkenazi Jews is estimated at 1 in 40,000 and accounts for about 75 percent of all cases of the disorder; Type B Niemann-Pick is estimated at 1 in 80,000 among Ashkenazi Jews. These frequencies are believed to be about 10 times higher than that found in the general population. Carrier frequencies for

Types A and B among Ashkenazi Jews is estimated at 1 in 70 to 100. The other forms of the disease are rarely found in Ashkenazi Jews.

SYMPTOMS

Type A "acute" or "infantile" Niemann-Pick Disease, the type that mainly affects Ashkenazi Jews, is a rapidly progressive disease affecting the central nervous system. Its main symptoms are an inability to roll over, sit or stand, due to decreasing muscle strength; increasing visual and hearing loss resulting in blindness and deafness; seizures; wasting due to eating difficulties; enlarged spleen, liver and lymph glands; and a yellowish-brown skin.

Most children with Niemann-Pick appear normal at birth but symptoms become readily apparent by three to six months of age. The first such symptoms are feeding difficulties and frequently vomiting, which become progressively worse. The inability to eat properly results in retarded growth and an emaciated appearance. An enlarged spleen and liver appear by about six months of age, making the abdomen appear very distended. About half the children develop a cherry-red spot on the retinas of their eyes similar to that seen in Tay-Sachs. Skin lesions on the face and other areas of the body and thickening of the skin are common, and the skin becomes brownish-yellow in appearance. Infections are common. Between six and 12 months of age there are progressive deterioration of motor and mental abilities and recurrent infections. Death occurs between two to four years of age.

Type B Niemann-Pick Disease is much milder than the Type A form and does not have a neurological component, so the feeding and vomiting problems are not part of the disease. The development of the enlarged spleen and liver, however, are seen in childhood and these are usually the symptoms that lead to the identification of the syndrome in children. During adolescence infections in the respiratory system, especially the lungs, become common. However, if these symptoms are promptly attended to they can be controlled, and people with the disease can live into their 50s.

Type C Niemann-Pick Disease affects all ethnic populations but appears to be somewhat more common among French-Canadians living in Nova Scotia and Spanish-Americans. Symptoms include loss of speech, clumsiness, and seizures. The disease becomes progressively worse with age. Death occurs between five and 15 years of age. Type D is only found among French-Canadians in Nova Scotia. Type E is a late onset variation of Type C.

CAUSE

Both Type A and Type B Niemann-Pick diseases are due to a mutation occurring in one of three genes.

The biochemical consequence of the mutation is a deficiency in an enzyme called sphingomyelinase which ordinarily breaks down the lipid sphingomyelin and cholesterol. Infants with Type A Niemann-Pick have no sphingomyelinase; those with type B have levels 5 to 10 percent below normal.

Sphingomyelin is present in both the spleen and liver, as well as the brain and lymph nodes. The enlargement of the spleen and liver are due to its accumulation in those organs. The accumulation of the lipid in brain cells destroys them, resulting in mental retardation and severe neurological disturbances.

Twelve mutations in the gene (ASM) that causes Types A and B Niemann-Pick Disease have been identified. Three of these mutations, R496L, L302P, and fsP330, account for about 90 percent of the mutated genes in Type A in Ashkenazi Jews; one mutation, deltaR608, is associated with Type B form of the disorder in Askenazis.

DIAGNOSIS

Niemann-Pick Disease is usually suspected in infants on the basis of the increased liver and spleen size, deafness and blindness, and related feeding problems. The diagnosis can be confirmed by examining blood or any other cells for sphingomyelinase levels, which are generally about 5 percent of normal, and for sphingomyelin and cholesterol levels, which are increased. Cells have a characteristic fat-filled foam-like appearance called a "Niemann-Pick cell." A diagnosis for both Types A and B Niemann-Pick can also be confirmed through biochemical testing for the presence of sphingomyelinase in skin or white blood cells and by genetic screening for the defective gene. Prenatal diagnosis to determine if an infant has the gene defect is also possible, as is screening to determine if someone is a carrier.

TRANSMISSION

Each of the three types of Niemann-Pick Disease are automsomal recessive diseases, which means that both sexes are equally affected. A child born to parents who are both carriers has a 1 in 4 chance of developing the disease and a 1 in 2 chance of becoming a carrier.

TREATMENT

There is no cure for this disease. Type A is fatal and death usually occurs by three years of age. Treatment consists primarily in making the child as comfortable as possible. Medical researchers at Mount Sinai School of Medicine are currently testing the possibility that enzyme, gene replacement therapy and bone marrow transplantation may provide a viable treatment.

PREVENTION

Since carrier status can be determined, prospective parents can be screened to determine if they are at risk for having a child with the disease. Prenatal diagnosis is also possible to determine if a fetus has the disease.

FOR FURTHER INFORMATION

Center for Jewish Genetic Diseases
c/o Dr. R.J. Desnick
Mount Sinai Medical Center
Fifth Avenue at 100th Street
New York, NY 10029
TELEPHONE: 212-241-6944

National Niemann-Pick Disease
  Foundation
3734 E. Olive Ave.
Gilbert, AZ 85234
TELEPHONE: 602-497-6638
INTERNET: www.nnpdf.org

National Foundation for Jewish
  Genetic Disease
250 Park Ave., Suite 1000

New York, NY 10017
TELEPHONE: 212-371-1030
University of Pittsburgh
Center for the Study and Treatment
  of Jewish Genetic Diseases
Pittsburgh, PA
TELEPHONE: 1-800-334-7980
INTERNET: www.pitt.edu/~edugene

Connecticut Children's Medical
  Center
282 Washington St.
Hartford, CT 06106
TELEPHONE: 860-545-9580
FAX: 860-545-9590

SCREENING CENTERS

Baylor College of Medicine—DNA
  Diagnostic Laboratory
Genzyme Genetics
Jefferson Medical College
Mount Sinai Medical Center—

Molecular Diagnosis Laboratory
New York Institute for Basic
  Research in Developmental Disabilities—Genetic Testing

New York University School of
  Medicine—Molecular Genetics
  Laboratory
Thomas Jefferson University, Lyso-
  somal Diseases Testing Laboratory

Wayne State University—Biochemical and Molecular Genetics Laboratory

REFERENCES

Levran, Orna, R.J. Desnick, and E.H. Schuchman. Type A Niemann-Pick dis-
  ease: a frameshift mutation in the acid sphingomyelinase gene (fsP330)
  occurs in Ashkenazi Jewish patients. *Human Mutation* 2 (1993): 317–319.
Goodman, Richard M. *Genetic Disorders Among the Jewish People*. Baltimore: Johns
  Hopkins University Press, 1979, 96–100.
Schuchman, Edward H., and Robert J. Desnick. "Niemann-Pick disease types
  A and B: Acid sphingomyelinase deficiencies." In: Scriver, Charles R., Arthur
  L. Beaudet, William S. Sly, eds. *The Metabolic and Molecular Bases of Inher-
  ited Disease*. New York: McGraw-Hill, 1995, 2601–2619.

Primary Torsion Dystonia

Primary torsion dystonia is a movement disorder characterized by
sustained, involuntary contractions or spasms of opposing muscles which
can cause abnormal, long-lasting, painful twisting and repetitive movements and postures in various parts of the body.

Primary torsion dystonia was first described clinically in 1908 by a
psychiatrist who observed the condition in three Jewish siblings, two
brothers and a sister, hospitalized because of a peculiar twisting of their
limbs. The psychiatrist thought the condition was due to "hysteria," a psychiatric catch-all term for anything psychiatrists didn't understand, and
suggested there might be a genetic basis for the disorder. One of the brothers subsequently committed suicide; the other brother was eventually dis-
charged from the hospital and later married and had a son and daughter
with the same disorder. The sister died of the disease.

Three years later two other psychiatrists observed the disorder in
a number of Jews and suggested it was probably genetically determined.

VARIATIONS

There are several variations of the disease that differ primarily in the
age in which symptoms first occur, the affected areas of the body, and the
cause. While each variation is relatively rare in the general population,
one of these variations, known as "idiopathic torsion dystonia," occurs in

a relatively high rate among Ashkenazi Jews from Eastern Europe. The reason it is called "idiopathic" is that while its genetic basis is known, the biochemical changes resulting from that genetic source that produce the condition have not been identified.

Idiopathic torsion dystonia is the result of a single genetic defect which was discovered in 1997. It differs from the other forms of dystonia in being caused by a defect in this particular gene, known as DYT1, its early age of onset (around 12 years of age), and its occurrence primarily in Ashkenazi Jews. The other variations are called adult-onset dystonia and secondary dystonia. The former occurs after age 21, and usually between 30 and 50 years of age, and is not caused by a mutation in the DYT1 gene. Nongenetic dystonia can result from damage at birth or from other nongenetic factors such as an accident, drugs, or infection to a part of the brain that controls movement called the basal ganglia.

Idiopathic torsion dystonia is a puzzling disorder because even if two or more people in the same family have the defective gene that causes it, the severity of its symptoms among different family members can vary widely.

SYMPTOMS

Symptoms of idiopathic torsion dystonia usually appear in early childhood, always before the age of 10. If symptoms do not appear by 30 years of age, they will rarely appear at a later age.

The first symptoms usually begin in a leg or arm and then spread to other limbs. Symptoms beginning in the legs usually occur first around age nine, whereas those first occurring in the arms begin around 15 years of age. In the case of the leg symptoms, a child will be running when suddenly his or her feet with invert, making the child run on a foot's outer edge. Once symptoms begin to appear, there is a rapid progression to other areas of the body which twist uncontrollably into unnatural positions—an arm or leg will twist in spasms, then the twisting spreads to other limbs and then to the trunk. Walking becomes almost impossible, and other limbs become fixed in a twisted position. As more and more voluntary control is lost, children are unable to get out of bed without help, they cannot dress themselves, and they are unable to feed themselves. However, their intelligence remains unaffected and their sensory functions remain intact. The main psychological problem associated with the disorder is depression.

Dystonia may also affect only one part of the body, in which case it is called "focal" or "segmental" dystonia. Focal dystonia tends to develop later in age than general dystonia. Among the most common symptoms of focal dystonia are abnormal contractions in the muscles of the head and neck (called "cervical dystonia"), which cause the head to assume very unusual positions and or to turn uncontrollably, which can be very painful. "Oromandibular dystonia" refers to abnormal contractions in the muscles of the jaw or face, causing the jaw to remain open or clamped shut, and the mouth and tongue to be uncontrollable so that speaking and swallowing are impaired. "Spasmodic dysphonia" results from contractions in the vocal cords, making it difficult to speak. "Blepharomatic dystonia" is an involuntary contraction of the eyelids which keep the eyes closed so that the individual becomes functionally blind. "Occupational" dystonia refers to contraction of muscles in the hand when attempting to write or perform other activities involving the hand or fingers ("writer's cramp"). In some cases the fingers contract or extend uncontrollably.

Frequency

The fact that this disease occurs more commonly in Ashkenazi Jewish families was recognized at the turn of the century when several medical reports noted its occurrence in siblings and in parents and their children from the same families. However, it was not until 1967 that medical researchers became fully aware that the disorder occurs about five times more often in Ashkenazi Jews than in the general population or in Sephardic Jews.

The Dystonia Medical Research Foundation in Chicago estimates that about 300,000 people in North America suffer from some form of torsion dystonia. The frequency of idiopathic torsion dystonia among Ashkenazi Jews is about 1 in 15,000 compared to between 1.6 and 3.4 per 100,000 for non–Jews. Carrier frequency is estimated at 1 in 1000 for Ashkenazi Jews. Idiopathic dystonia is a "reduced penetrance" genetic disorder, since symptoms occur in only about 30 to 50 percent of those with the mutation.

Cause

Idiopathic torsion dystonia is unique among genetic diseases affecting Jews in that it is an autosomal dominant disorder and there is only one known mutation responsible for the disorder. The mutation in the DYT1 gene is believed to be due to a founder effect originating in Poland.

When diseases are caused by dominant genes, medical geneticists are often able to trace the sufferer's family tree. This is what happened when Professor Neil Risch studied several unrelated Ashkenazi families in North America and Europe who carried the gene for idiopathic torsion dystonia. Despite being unrelated, 94 percent of the families he studied had an identical pattern of genetic markers neighboring the DYT1 gene.

The fact that more than 90 percent of unrelated North American and European Ashkenazi Jews shared identical markers, along with the same abnormal gene for ITD, indicated to Risch that the mutation is due to a founder effect. Rish was able to pin down its origins by asking patients about their grandparents and great grandparents. More than two-thirds of the oldest ITD carriers came from Lithuania and Byelarus. On this basis, Risch believes the original mutation arose in a Jewish ancestor of these people who lived in Lithuania, Latvia, Russia, Poland, or Ukraine at least 350 years ago around the time of violent pogroms. Those who escaped death fled west to Central and Western Europe and even farther west to North America, creating the core of American Jewry. This common heritage explains the presence of the unique markers in the genomes of these Ashkenazi Jews.

However, primary torsion dystonia has also been found in Sephardic and Oriental Jews, although to a much lesser extent.

TRANSMISSION

Although the genetic basis of the disease has been clarified, medical researchers still do not know the abnormal biochemical cause of primary dystonia. Since a single gene mutation is responsible, medical researchers believe that "torsinA," the protein made by this gene, is in some as yet unknown way important to normal functioning of the body.

TorsinA is in fact a member of a very unusual set of proteins called "heat shock" or "stress" proteins. These proteins are found in many species of animals besides humans and are known to protect cells from stress. The defective mutation prevents its production; in so doing, it somehow interferes with the way nerve cells that control muscle actions function, resulting in their involuntary contraction.

DIAGNOSIS

There are no known biochemical or pathological changes associated with idiopathic torsion dystonia. Diagnosis is first suspected on the basis of the symptoms of the disease and can now be confirmed by testing for the presence of the mutation in the DYT1 gene.

SYMPTOMS

Since idiopathic torsion dystonia is a dominant gene disorder, only one copy (allele) is necessary for its symptoms to develop. This means that a child has a 1 in 2 chance of inheriting the defective gene if one of his or her parents is a carrier. However, the gene mutation has a relatively low penetrance of around 30 percent to 50 percent, so only about a third to a half of the people who have the defective gene actually develop symptoms.

TREATMENT

There is no cure for primary torsion dystonia, but there are several drugs that relieve some of the symptoms and, in some cases, its disability. The most frequently prescribed medicines are muscle relaxants like Valium, antiepileptics like Tegretol, and a class of drugs called anticholinergics like Artane, that block the transmission of impulses from nerves to muscles.

For those whose dystonia is confined to only one or two parts of the body, injection of botulinum toxin into contracting muscles weakens those muscles so that they can be straightened. Botulinum toxin is a nerve poison that acts like an anticholinergic to block impulses from nerves to muscles.

In some case, neurosurgery has been used to relieve very twisted limbs that are unresponsive to drug treatment.

PREVENTION

In 1997 the DYT1 gene responsible for the symptoms of primary dystonia was identified. This discovery means that it is likely that the biochemical correlates will soon be identified. Genetic screening tests for detecting carriers and also for prenatal diagnosis are now possible.

FOR FURTHER INFORMATION

Dystonia Medical Research Foundation
One East Wacker Drive, Suite 2430
Chicago, IL 60601-1905
TELEPHONE: 1-800-377-3978
    312-755-0198
FAX: 312-803-0138
E-MAIL: dystonia@dystonia-foundation.org
INTERNET: www.dystonia-foundation.org

Dystonia Research Center
c/o Dr. Stanley Fahn
Columbia Presbyterian Medical Center
710 West 168th St.
New York, NY 10032
TELEPHONE: 212-305-5295

SCREENING CENTERS

Athena Diagnostics, Inc.
Worchester, MA

Massachusetts General Hospital
Neurogenetics DNA Diagnostic
Laboratory

REFERENCES

Almasy, L., Susan Bressman, and Deborah de Leon. Ethnic variation in the clinical expression of idiopathic torsion dystonia. *Movement Disorders* 12 (1997): 715–721.

Alter, M., E. Kahana, and S. Feldman. Differences in torsion among Israeli ethnic groups. *Advances in Neurology* 14 (1976): 115–120.

Augood, S.J., J.B. Penney, I.K. Friberg, et al. Expression of the early onset torsion dystonia gene (DYT1) in human brain. *Annals of Neurology* 43 (1998): 669–673.

Bressman, Susan B., Deborah de Leon, Patricia I. Kramer, et al. Dystonia in Ashkenazi Jews: clinical characterization of a founder mutation. *Annals of Neurology* 36 (1994): 771–777.

Bressman, Susan B., Deborah de Leon, D. Raymond, et al. Secondary dystonia and the DYT1 gene. *Neurology* 48 (1997): 1571–1577.

Comella, Cynthia L. "Idiopathic Dystonia." In: James M. Gilchrist, ed. *Prognosis in Neurology*. Boston: Butterworth-Heinemann, 1998, 161–165.

Eldridge, R. The torsion dystonias: literature review: genetic and clinical studies. *Neurology* 20 (1970): 1–78.

Eldridge, R., A. Harlen, I.S. Cooper, et al. Superior intelligence in recessively inherited torsion dystonia. *Lancet* 1 (1970): 65–67.

Jarman, Paul R., and Thomas T. Warner. The dystonias. *Journal of Medical Genetics* 35 (1998): 314–318.

Korczyn, Amos D. "Genetics of idiopathic torsion dystonia in Ashkenazi Jews." In: Bonne-tamir, Batsheva, and Avinoam Adam, eds. *Genetic Diversity Among Jews. Diseases and Markers at the DNA Level*. New York: Oxford University Press, 1992, 194–201.

Orzelius, Laurie P., J.W. Hewet, et al. The early onset torsion dystonia gene (DYT1) encodes an ATP-binding protein. *Nature Genetics* 17 (1997): 40–48.

Risch, Neal, Deborah De Leon, L. Ozelius, et al. Genetic analysis of idiopathic torsion dystonia in Ashkenazi Jews and their recent descent from a small founder population. *Nature Genetics* 9 (1995): 152–159.

Tsui, J.K.C. Botulinum toxin as a therapeutic agent. *Pharmacology and Therapy* 72 (1996): 13–24.

Valente, E.M., S. Povey, T.T. Warner, et al. Detailed haplotype analysis in Ashkenazi Jewish and non–Jewish British dystonic patients carrying the GAG deletion in the DYT1 gene: evidence for a limited number of founder mutations. *Annals of Human Genetics* 63 (1999): 1–8.

Warner, T.T., and P. Jarman. The molecular genetics of the dystonias. *Journal of Neurology and Psychiatry* 64 (1998): 427–429.

Zilber, N., A.D. Korcyn, E. Kahana, et al. Inheritance of idiopathic torsion dystonia among Jews. *Journal of Medical Genetics* 21 (1984): 13–26.

Tay-Sachs Disease

In 1881 Dr. William Tay, a British ophthalmologist, was called upon to examine a 12-month-old infant who had unusual retinal damage. When he examined the girl he saw a cherry-red spot in the macular area of her eye and noted that the girl also had "very little power holding its head up or moving its limbs." Somewhat later he noted the same disorder in two more children from the same family.

Six years later, in 1887, Dr. Bernard Sachs, a New York neurologist, independently described a similar occurrence in a girl who "as it grew older, gave no signs of increasing mental vigor." After treating eight such children with the same retinal damage and progressive neurological deterioration, all of whom were Jewish, Sachs concluded the disease primarily affected Ashkenazi Jewish children.

Tay-Sachs Disease (also called GM2-Gangliosidosis and Hexosaminidase A Deficiency, based on the biochemical effects that characterize the disease) is now the best-known of all the diseases primarily affecting Jews, although it occurs much less frequently than Gaucher Disease.

VARIATIONS

As is the case with Gaucher Disease, there are several forms of Tay-Sachs Disease, called "infantile," "late-infantile" or "juvenile," "chronic," and "adult." The variations that primarily affect Ashkenazi Jews are the "infantile" and the "adult" forms of the disease.

Although not exclusively a Jewish disease, infantile Tay-Sachs is about 100 times more common among Ashkenazi Jews than any other ethnic group. Infantile Tay-Sachs appears early in infancy and is always fatal. The juvenile form begins to appear around two to five years of age and, although milder, is also fatal, with death occurring around 15 years of age. The chronic form appears around age five but is much milder than the infantile and juvenile forms, with relatively little impact on intelligence, hearing or sight. Adult Tay-Sachs appears around 20 years of age and resembles the chronic form in its symptoms.

While each of these forms is due to a deficiency in the same enzyme, they differ in the extent of the deficiency. In the classical infantile form, the enzyme that causes the disease is completely absent, whereas in the other forms it is present, although at much lower levels than normal. For instance, in the adult form levels are 2 to 4 percent the normal level.

FREQUENCY

Infantile Tay-Sachs occurs about once in every 3,600 births among American Ashkenazi Jews, a rate that is about 100 times higher than that in non–Jews. The carrier frequency for the abnormal gene resulting in the disease among Ashkenazi Jews is about 10 times higher among Ashkenazi Jews than among Sephardic Jews and non–Jewish Americans (1 in 30 versus 1 in 300).

The highest rates of infantile Tay-Sachs among Ashkenazi Jews occurs among those whose heritage lies in Middle European countries like Austria, Hungary and Czechoslovakia; lower frequencies (although still much higher than in non–Ashkenazis) are encountered among Ashkenazis with ancestries in western Europe. Jews from the Poland-Russia provinces of Grodno, Suwalki, Kovno, Latvia, and neighboring Byelorussia have intermediate frequencies.

The frequency of late onset Tay-Sachs among Ashenazi Jews is less common than the infantile form and is estimated at 1 in 67,000 in the United States and about 1 in 14,000 in Israel.

CAUSE

Like Gaucher, Tay-Sachs Disease results from a deficiency in an enzyme in the lysosome, in this case, beta-hexosaminidase. Beta-hexosaminidase has two separate parts, or subunits as they are known, called alpha ("A") and beta ("B"). The mutation causing Tay-Sachs affects the alpha subunit of the enzyme (usually abbreviated as Hex-A). Another related mutation affects a part of the enzyme called an "activator" so that, although it is present in normal amounts, the activator abnormality renders Hex-A less functional.

The job of the hexosaminidase is to break down a lipid (fatty) substance called GM^2 ganglioside from worn-out nerve cells. GM^2 ganglioside is a normal component of cell membranes and is not related to the amount or kind of fat we eat. When nerve cells wear out, their membrane components like GM^2 ganglioside are removed and their component parts are eliminated or recycled. If they are not broken down, as in the case of Tay-Sachs, they accumulate in the lysosmes of nerve cells. The lysosomes continue to swell in size until they eventually fill the entire nerve cell and in so doing destroy the cell's other components. The result is a progressive deterioration of the brain's nerve cells to the point that the brain cannot function.

The reason the brain is affected so seriously is that it has the highest concentration of GM^2 ganglioside of any organ in the body. Since brain cells cannot be restored once they are killed, mental deterioration is progressive, until death results when the brain is no longer able to control breathing or regulate heart beat.

Hex-A is either not produced or is produced at very low levels in Tay-Sachs Disease because of a mutation in a single gene. Although several different mutations of this gene have now been found, nearly all instances (95–98 percent) of infantile Tay-Sachs in Ashkenazi Jews result from one of three mutations called +TATC1277, +1 IVS 12, and +1 IVS 9. Children with the acute infantile form have mutations in both genes that normally produce Hex-A. As a result, they do not produce any. Adult onset Tay-Sachs is associated with a mutation called Gly269Ser. Individuals with the adult or other forms of the disorder usually have a mutation in one of the Hex A genes and an allele that produces some Hex-A enzyme.

There is also a mutation called a Hex-A pseudodeficiency. People with this condition have a partial deficiency or very low level of Hex-A due to a disease-related mutation and another type of mutation, but they do not have any neurological abnormalities. Individuals with this condition are designated "pseudodeficient" or "Hex-A minus, normal."

A relatively high frequency of Tay-Sachs has also been found in non–Jewish populations who live in relatively isolated communities such as eastern Quebec, Japan, Switzerland, and among the Pennsylvania Dutch and the Louisiana Cajuns. However, the mutation causing the disease in these populations is different from that which causes it in Ashkenazi Jews.

FAUSTIAN BARGAIN

Geneticists have been hard-pressed to find an explanation for the high incidence of a tragic disease like Tay-Sachs among Ashkenazi Jews. Some time before the Holocaust, a study of Jewish and non–Jewish garment workers in Warsaw provided the answer. The study compared rates of tuberculosis among the two groups and found the Jewish workers had a 16 percent rate of death from tuberculosis compared to 32 percent for the non–Jewish workers. Since both groups had similar living standards and were at similar risk for the disease, the difference implied that the Jews had a greater resistance to the disease. The explanation for this difference was subsequently attributed to the living conditions European Jews experienced over many generations of ghetto life.

When the Jews were herded into urban ghettos in Eastern Europe around the 13th century C.E., they became much more susceptible than their rural gentile neighbors to tuberculosis because of their close confinement. Tuberculosis is a contagious disease that killed many people. Wealthy people were able to leave the crowded cities for homes in the countryside and escape its devastating effects, but those less fortunate could not escape; Jews living in ghettos had no option at all.

Since tuberculosis was a regularly occurring disease in a small community where there was no possibility of escape, a "weeding out" process occurred. Those whose heredity made them susceptible to tuberculosis died, often before they had children, whereas those whose heredity made them less susceptible survived and had children. Their children were less susceptible and had children of their own, and on and on. By chance, the hereditary protection that made them less susceptible to tuberculosis made them more susceptible to Tay-Sachs. However, to develop Tay-Sachs, they had to inherit two copies of the abnormal gene; if they inherited only one, they would not develop Tay-Sachs, but the single copy gave them resistance to tuberculosis.

Since a child has a 1 in 4 chance of inheriting a defective Tay-Sachs gene from both parents if they are both carriers, for every child who developed Tay-Sachs due to marriage of two carriers, two nonaffected carriers would be born. As a result, Jews with this mutation were able to survive in a tuberculosis-infested environment much better than those who did not possess the altered gene.

Because of the resistance to tuberculosis which being a carrier gave them, the carriers were not only able to survive, but their descendants were also more likely to survive and reproduce. After many generations of living under these conditions, the percentage of Eastern European Jews who were carriers greatly increased relative to those who were not, including their rural gentile neighbors.

Symptoms of Infantile Tay-Sachs

Infantile Tay-Sachs is a rapidly progressive fatal neurological disease characterized by increasing weakness and loss of motor skills. Although a child may seem perfectly normal at birth, the effects of the disease begin to be seen around three to six months of age.

The first signs are apathy; the child seems to take little interest in anything and seems slightly weaker than expected. He or she also has difficulty eating, has an exaggerated startle response to loud noises, has overly responsive reflexes, and is unable to focus his or her eyes, which often roll about from side to side. A cherry-red spot with a white halo, characteristic of the disease, is observable if the interior of the eye is examined. The spot is not an abnormality itself, but is the color of the blood vessels which would otherwise be covered by cells that are missing. The halo is due to fatty cells which are very dense in this part of the retina.

Around six months of age, profound muscle weakness begins to set in. Previously learned motor skills are lost and no new abilities are gained. Muscle weakness affects all parts of the body so that the infant lies on its back and never rolls over on its own. Because of its weakness, the infant is also unable to lift its head. Visual attentiveness is absent so that the child does not pay attention to whatever passes his or her line of vision. Infants may close their hands if a finger is extended into a palm, but they quickly drop any object placed there. They do not play with any toy. Although they can hear, they do not distinguish voices and have no preference for any caregiver.

Around eight months deterioration becomes very rapid. By 12 months of age, children with Tay-Sachs are almost totally unable to control their movements, and their bodies become rigid and convulsions become more common and more severe. Although attracted by light and able to track objects that cross their vision, between 12 and 18 months of age they become blind and deaf. During this period the body takes on a frog-like posture; the child drools uncontrollably and has episodes of abnormal laughter.

By 18 months of age the child's head begins to become enlarged, and paralysis sets in. The enlargement is due to the accumulation of the lipid ganglioside responsible for the disorder, which can occupy as much as 10 percent of the dry weight of the brain. Convulsions and spasticity become more frequent and these episodes are often followed by frequent episodes of pneumonia. A generally vegetative state continues to develop in which the child cannot eat on its own, breathing becomes very irregular, and urination occurs only once or twice a day until death occurs around four years of age, usually as a result of pneumonia.

Symptoms of juvenile Tay-Sachs usually begin to show themselves between the ages of two and five. These symptoms are similar to those in the infantile form, although the progression is much slower. The first signs are usually uncoordination. Speech is progressively impaired and, although visual abilities are not impaired in the earlier years, they progressively deteriorate to blindness by about age 10. Unlike the infantile form of the disorder, however, the cherry spot in the eye is not always present. By age 10, the child enters into a vegetative condition. Death usually occurs at about 15 years of age, usually as a result of infection.

Symptoms of chronic Tay-Sachs appear around five years of age and are much milder than the infantile and juvenile conditions. Sight, hearing, and mental abilities are usually not affected. The most common symptoms are weakness in the muscles, making it very hard to get up from a chair, walk up or down the stairs, or run and jump. Children with this form of Tay-Sachs frequently fall down due to lack of coordination.

All three of these forms of Tay-Sachs result from the same Hex-A enzyme defect; but whereas the enzyme is almost completely absent in the infantile form (0.1 percent), and present but in very reduced amounts in the late-infantile form (0.5 percent), it is present but at low levels in the adult form (2 to 4 percent). People with levels of 10 percent or more have no symptoms.

SYMPTOMS OF ADULT TAY-SACHS

Adult or late onset Tay-Sachs was the latest form of the disease to be discovered and is the rarest form. It is also due to a decrease to about 5 percent of normal levels of Hex-A, resulting in a slow but regular accumulation of GM2 ganglioside. Like the other forms of Tay-Sachs, it is found mainly but not exclusively among Jews of Ashkenazi ancestry.

Symptoms of late onset Tay-Sachs come on gradually and take the form of muscle weakness so that it is difficult to walk and go up and down stairs. Muscle cramping, especially in the legs, is not uncommon, nor are muscle twitching and hand tremors. Speech becomes slurred, often beginning in the teen years or early 20s. Disturbances in mood and especially depression are common. The gradual onset of these symptoms was the reason it took so long for the adult form of the disease to be discovered. Since they appeared so gradually, no one connected them with the infantile form until recently.

Late onset Tay-Sachs also differs from the other forms in the wide variability of its symptoms, even among siblings. In looking back over their lives, people with late onset Tay-Sachs remember being clumsy children, frequently spilling milk or other liquids when they were pouring, always dropping toys and frequently falling down when they played. When they reach adolescence or adulthood, their clumsiness and uncoordination become more serious and they may break their legs or suffer other injuries from falling.

In addition to the problems already mentioned, psychiataric problems are also common (about 40 percent) in late onset Tay-Sachs, and seizures are also not uncommon. The most frequent psychiatric symptoms are depression and psychotic episodes in which the sufferer loses contact with reality. A feeling of isolation and loneliness is common. Interacting with others becomes more difficult. Career plans have to be put on hold as the individual has to learn to deal with his or her disabilities Psychiatric symptoms are generally treated with antipsychotic or antidepressant drugs, although in some instances depression may actually worsen as a result of drug treatment. Seizures are treated with anticonvulsant drugs. Since it has not been studied much, doctors are still uncertain about the rate with which its symptoms progress or whether life expectancy is shortened.

Adult Tay-Sachs was only identified in the 1970s and its symptoms are not widely known, even by doctors. As a result, those symptoms may be misdiagnosed as schizophrenia, muscular dystrophy or multiple sclerosis.

DIAGNOSIS

The symptoms of infantile Tay-Sachs are readily apparent from the pattern of apathy and muscle weakness, exaggerated startle response, visual problems, and a cherry-red spot on the retina. (A cherry red spot, however, is also associated with several other disorders such as infantile Gaucher Disease and Niemann-Pick IA). Certainty is provided by a laboratory test on either blood, urine, saliva, or skin that measures the amount of Hexosaminidase A and B. In Tay-Sachs, Hex-A activity is totally or almost totally absent whereas Hex-B activity is normal or even elevated. Genetic testing for the presence of one of the mutated genes known to cause the disease can confirm the enzyme results but is more often used to identify carriers and for prenatal testing.

The enzyme test has been available to prospective parents since 1970 and it is estimated that about a million people have been tested. The cost for gene sampling for the three mutations in the Tay-Sachs gene, along with testing for the mutations in cystic fibrosis, Canavan and Gaucher Disease is about $300; the cost for gene sampling and biochemical testing for the Hex-A enzyme is about $350.

The diagnosis of adult Tay-Sachs is much more difficult since its symptoms are not as easily recognized. Misdiagnoses as muscular dystrophy, multiple sclerosis, or Lou Gehrig's Disease (amyotrophic lateral sclerosis) are not uncommon. A correct diagnosis can be made by enzyme or gene testing.

Prenatal diagnosis is possible by examining amniotic cells for one of the mutations. Since in some cases carriers may lack the enzyme yet still not have the disease, the test also needs to be done to determine the levels of this enzyme in each parent before a conclusive prenatal diagnosis can be made.

TRANSMISSION

Tay-Sachs is an inherited autosomal recessive genetic defect, which means that it occurs equally in children of both sexes. Although due to a single gene defect, in Ashkenazi Jews over 90 percent of all cases of Tay-Sachs are due to one of three different mutations affecting this gene. Both parents have to carry the mutation for their child to develop the disease. If neither parent carries any of the mutations for Tay-Sachs Disease, then their children will not develop the disease nor will they be carriers themselves.

A child whose parents are both carriers of the defective gene has a 1 in 4 chance of inheriting both defective genes and developing the disease. If only one parent has the defective gene, a child will not develop the disease, but will have a 1 in 2 chance of inheriting the defective gene and therefore becoming a carrier.

TREATMENT

There is no cure for this disease. Treatment for infantile Tay-Sachs is mainly supportive and includes maintaining adequate nutrition by tube feedings and nutritional supplements, postural drainage to remove secretions in the throat, laxatives to relieve constipation, antiseizure medication, and skin care to prevent bed sores. Infants require constant physical care which is sometimes beyond the abilities of parents, resulting in the need to hire skilled home care workers or placement of the child in a special care facility.

Beyond relieving the infant's distress, the parents of a child with Tay-Sachs are also often in need of supportive treatment for any feelings of guilt they may have about their child's disease. Parents may also experience considerable stress due to the financial burden of caring for their child's illness.

Treatment of the adult form of Tay-Sachs primarily consists of drug therapy for seizures, using anticonvulsant medication such as Tegretol, and antidepressant or antipsychotic drugs for these respective mental disorders. However, these medications often do not control these conditions because they inhibit Hex-A enzyme activity.

Although enzyme replacement therapy and bone marrow transplants have been attempted, neither has been successful for replacing diminished Hex-A enzyme activity.

PREVENTION

Since carriers of the abnormal gene for Tay-Sachs are perfectly normal, they will probably not be aware that their children could develop

Tay-Sachs unless they are screened for the presence or absence of the abnormal gene.

Because Tay-Sachs is a severe disease which is incurable and has a high incidence among Ashkenzi Jews, the American College of Obstetrics and Gynecology and the American College of Medical Genetics both recommend screening for Ashkenazi Jews who are of reproductive age.

Screening for Tay-Sachs among Jewish communities in North America began in the 1970s and has been implemented by other communities around the world. The purpose is to identify Jewish couples who are at risk for conceiving a child with Tay-Sachs and are unaware that they are carriers. In this way couples who are both carriers, but unaware of their carrier status, can become aware of the risks of having children who might inherit the disease.

Almost a million Jews have been screened around the world since the universal program began. About 36,000 individuals and about 1,000 couples tested positive, none of whom had previously had a child with Tay-Sachs.

Montreal, Canada, has had an education and screening program in place for populations at high risk for genetic diseases like Tay-Sachs since 1972. Between 1972 and 1992, almost 15,000 Ashkenazi Jewish high school students were screened and 521 Hex-A-deficient carriers were identified (carrier frequency of about 1 in 28). The program reached 89 percent of the Jewish population and achieved 67 percent voluntary participation. As a result, the incidence of Tay-Sachs decreased by about 95 percent, a decline attributed to the program's effectiveness. Virtually all carriers identified through the high school program remembered their status and had their marriage partners tested if they did not know their status, whereas prior to the program's initiation, screening only occurred if someone in one of the prospective couple's family had been affected.

A similar program called Dor Yeshorim has been available to ultra-orthodox Jewish communities, which have very restrictive laws against prenatal diagnosis and abortion. In these communities marriages are arranged through a matchmaker ("shadchen"). Every participant is screened for carrier status prior to any introductions and results are sent to a main office where they are examined to make sure that no two carriers are matched. In this way the community avoids conflicts with religious restrictions against abortion, prevents the birth of children with the disease, and maintains anonymity with respect to carrier status, thereby also avoiding possible stigma.

It is also possible to determine if a child will develop Tay-Sachs before he or she is born by examining sample cells using amniocentesis or chorionic villus sampling. If the unborn baby has Hex-A enzyme in its cells, it will not develop Tay-Sachs. However, sometimes enzyme testing does not give a definitive answer. If the results are uncertain, genetic testing can determine if the baby has the gene mutation that causes the disease. The cost of testing for the abnormal genes for Tay-Sachs, as well as those for Gaucher and Canavan Disease and cystic fibrosis, is about $300.

FOR FURTHER INFORMATION

National Tay-Sachs and Allied Diseases Association
2001 Beacon St., Suite 204
Brookline, MA 02146
TELEPHONE: 1-800-906-8723
    617-277-4463
FAX: 617-277-0134
E-MAIL: NTSAD-boston@
  worldnet.att.net
INTERNET: www.ntsad.org

March of Dimes Birth Defects
Foundation
1275 Mamaroneck Ave.
White Plains, NY 10605
TELEPHONE: 888-663-4637

Connecticut Children's Medical
Center
282 Washington St.
Hartford, CT 06106
TELEPHONE: 860-545-9580
FAX: 860-545-9590

Late Onset Tay-Sachs Foundation
1303 Paper Mill Road
Erdenheim, PA 19038
TELEPHONE: 1-800-672-2022
    215-836-2368
FAX: 215-836-5438
E-MAIL: mpf@bellatlantic.net
INTERNET: www.neuro-oas.mgh.
  harvard.edu/lots/main.html

SCREENING CENTERS

Boston University School of Medicine—Center for Human Genetics
Children's Medical Center at Stony Brook
Children's Hospital National Medical Center
Children's Hospital San Diego
Eastern Virginia Medical School
Genetics & IVF Institute
Genzyme Genetics
Thomas Jefferson University Medical Genetics Institute, S.C.
Mount Sinai School of Medicine
New York State Institute for Basic Research in Developmental Disabilities—Genetic Testing

New York University School of Medicine—Molecular Genetics Laboratory of NYU Medical Center
North Shore University Hospital at Manhaset
Oregon Health Sciences University—DNA Diagnostic Laboratory
Quest Diagnostics, Inc.
SmithKline Beecham Clinical Laboratories
University of Pittsburgh Medical Center
Wayne State University—Biochemical and Molecular Genetics Laboratory

REFERENCES

Books

Kaback, M.M., D.L. Rimoin, J.S. O'Brien. *Tay-Sachs Disease: Screening and Prevention*. New York: Alan R. Liss, 1977.

Milunsky, A. *Genetic Disorders of the Fetus: Diagnosis, Prevention, Treatment*. Baltimore: Johns Hopkins University Press, 1992.

Milunsky, A. *Heredity and Your Family's Health*. Baltimore: Johns Hopkins University Press, 1992.

Motulsky, A.G. "Possible selective effects of urbanization on Ashkenazi Jews." In: Goodman, Richard M., and Arno G. Motulsky. *Genetic Diseases Among Ashkenazi Jews*. New York: Raven Press, 1979, 301–314.

National Tay-Sachs and Allied Diseases Association. *A Genetics Primer for Understanding Tay-Sachs and the Allied Diseases*. Brookline, MA: National Tay-Sachs and Allied Diseases Association, 1995.

Vinken, P.J., and G.W. Bruyn, eds. *Handbook of Clinical Neurology* 10 (1970): 556–587.

Journal Articles

Barnes, D., V.P. Misra, E.P. Young, et al. An adult onset hexosaminidase A deficiency syndrome with sensory neuropathy and internuclear ophthalmoplegia. *Journal of Neurology, Neurosurgery and Psychiatry* 54 (1991): 1112–1113.

DeMarchi, Jean M., C. Thomas Caskey, and C. Sue Richards. Population-specific screening by mutation analysis for diseases frequent in Ashkenazi Jews. *Human Mutation* 8 (1996): 116–125.

Diamond, Jared M. Tay-Sachs carriers and tuberculosis resistance. *Nature* 331 (1988): 666.

Gravel, R.A., J.T.R. Larke, Michael M. Kaback, et al. "The GM2 Gangliosidoses." In: *The Metabolic and Molecular Bases of Inherited Disease*. New York: McGraw Hill.

Kaback, Michael, J. Lim-Steele, D. Dabholkar, et al. Tay-Sachs Disease—Carrier Screening, Prenatal Diagnosis, and the Molecular Era. An International Perspective, 1970 to 1993. *Journal of the American Medical Association* 270 (1993): 2307–2315.

Kaufman, Michael J., Grinshpun-Cohen, M. Karpati, et al. Tay-Sachs Disease and HEXA mutations among Moroccan Jews. *Human Mutation* 10 (1997): 295–300.

Loeslag, J.H., and S.R. Schach. Tay-Sachs disease and the role of reproductive compensation in the maintenance of ethnic variations in the incidence of autosomal recessive disease. *Annals of Human Genetics* 48 (1984): 275–284.

Michael, J.J., A. Capua, C. Clow, et al. Twenty-year outcome analysis of genetic screening programs for Tay-Sachs and beta-thalassemia disease carriers in high schools. *American Journal of Human Genetics* 59 (1996): 793–798.

Navon, Ruth, Edwin H. Kolodny, Hiroshi Mitsumoto, et al. Ashkenazi–Jewish and non–Jewish Adult GM2 Gangliosidosis patients share a common genetic defect. *American Journal of Human Genetics* 46 (1990): 817–821.

Neufeld, E.F. Natural history and inherited disorders of a lysosomal enzyme, beta-hexosaminidase. *Journal of Biological Chemistry* 264 (1989): 10927–10930.

O'Brien, J.S., S. Okada, D.L. Fillerup, et al. Tay-Sachs disease: prenatal diagnosis. *Science* 172 (1971): 61–64.

Petersen, Gloria M., Jerome I. Rotter, Rita M. Cantor, et al. The Tay-Sachs disease gene in North American Jewish populations: geographic variations and origin. *American Journal of Human Genetics* 35 (1983) 1258–1269.

Spyropoulos, B., P.B. Moens, J. Davidson, et al. Heterozygote advantage in Tay-Sachs carriers? *American Journal of Human Genetics* 33 (1981): 375–380.

CHAPTER SIX

Connective Tissue Disorders

Connective tissue refers to cartilage, a cushioning tissue at the edge of bones that reduces the friction between them when they are moved, and the ligaments that provide strength and stability around the joints between bones. Disorders affecting the joints can result in crippling disability. Arthritis is the general term for a group of related disorders characterized by inflammation in one or more joints.

Familial Mediterranean Fever

Familial Mediterranean Fever is the most common inherited disease affecting Sephardic Jews. It also relatively common in three other Mediterranean populations: Armenians, Arabs, and Turks. Although once thought to be rare among Ashkenazi Jews, new research indicates that one in five Ashkenazi Jews may be a carrier for a mild form of the disease.

VARIATIONS

Although once thought to primarily affect Sephardic Jews, the disorder is now known to appear in Ashkenazi Jews. However, the disorder does not appear to be as severe in Ashkenazis and they do not develop the related kidney problems encountered by Sephardic Jews with the disorder.

FREQUENCY

About 1 in every 500 Sephardic Jews has some form of the disorder and about one in every five is a carrier. Prevalence rates vary with country of origin. Among Iraqi and Turkish Jews, prevalence rate is 1 in 1,000; among Algerian, Tunisian and Moroccan Jews, the rate is 1 in 700. The highest rate, 1 in 250, occurs in Libyan Jews.

Although Familial Mediterranean Fever was not believed to be very common among Ashkenazi Jews, Dr. Ivona Aksentijevich and her colleagues at the National Institute of Arthritis and Musculoskeletal and Skin Diseases found that Ashkenazi Jews had the same carrier frequency for the disorder as Sephardic Jews, that is, 1 in 5. However, each group carries a different form of the mutation. The Ashkenazi mutation results in a much milder form of the disease that occurs in about 1 in 100 Ashkenazi Jews. The fact that the symptoms are much milder among Askenazi Jews is the reason why it was previously considered mainly Sephardic.

SYMPTOMS

Symptoms of FMF begin in early childhood, often around the age of two. In nearly every instance, those who have the disorder experience its symptoms by the age of 30. The most common complaint is a recurring attack of fever lasting from 12 to 72 hours. While these fever episodes may be the only symptom of the disease, more often than not people with MFM also experience other symptoms along with the fever including stomach, joint and chest pain.

Stomach pains take the form of a dull ache or intense pain which gets worse during the attack. In some cases the fever and stomach pain have been mistaken for appendicitis, and many sufferers have had their appendices removed, although the appendix is not affected by the disease.

Joint pain is episodic and causes a temporary arthritis, or inflammation in the joint. Typically pain in the form of tenderness and immobility is felt in the large joints, the knees, ankles, hips, shoulders, and elbows. Attacks often last as long as a week. In severe cases the inflammation results in a narrowing of the joint space and loss of bone tissue characteristic of osteoporosis.

Another common symptom is pain in the lining of the lungs (pleurisy).

Intervals between attacks range from a few days to several months. In some instances, the attacks are brought on by strenuous exercise or emotional stress. The most serious consequence of the disease is kidney failure. In its earliest stages, a protein called amyloid often builds up in the kidneys and keeps them from recirculating protein back into the blood. Instead, protein is passed into urine and builds up in the kidneys, causing them to stop working, a medical emergency requiring dialysis.

CAUSE

Familial Mediterranean Fever is an autosomal recessive disorder occurring in a gene known as MEFV. The mutation results in production of a protein called "pyrin" (also called "marenostrin") which produces an inflammation response and related fever.

Sixteen specific mutations are known to occur in this gene. The two most common are M694V and V726A. About 90 percent of Sephardic Jews are carriers of the M694V mutation. Familial Mediterranean Fever also occurs with a relatively high frequency among Sicilians, Arabs and Armenians. The high frequency of mutations in these populations, all of whom have a Mediterranean descent in common, suggest some evolutionary advantage which remains to be identified. Alternatively, it may be due to a founder effect introduced by some trader into Sicily, whose historic position as a crossroads of Mediterranean commerce made it a center for people from many of the surrounding countries.

DIAGNOSIS

There is no biochemical diagnostic test for FMF.

Diagnosis is currently based on the symptoms of brief, recurrent bouts of fever accompanied by pain in the stomach, chest or joints, the absence of other causal conditions, and family and ethnic history. Since the gene causing MFM has now been discovered, this discovery will undoubtedly result in a blood test for its detection.

TREATMENT

Fever attacks and related amyloidosis can be prevented in nearly all patients by daily taking the drug colchicine. Although colchicine treatment has been used successfully since 1973, medical researchers are still uncertain about how it prevents the fever or formation of amyloid protein. The two effects are not due to the same biochemical factors since colchine prevents amyloid formation in all patients, but does not prove equally effective in preventing the fever attacks.

Colchicine, however, has important side effects. In men it damages sperm production, leading to infertility, although infertility itself can be caused by FMF. In pregnant women colchicine can cause miscarriages and birth defects. However, if colchicine treatment is stopped, the fever attacks and amyloidosis production may become even more intense.

TRANSMISSION

FMF is an autosomal recessive disease. This means both parents have to be carriers for the child to exhibit the disease. If both parents are carriers, their children have a 1 in 4 chance of inheriting the disease and a 1 in 2 chance of being a carrier. If neither parent carries the defective gene, none of their children will develop the disease and none will be carriers.

PREVENTION

Since the gene causing the disease has now been identified, it is possible to determine who is a carrier.

FOR FURTHER INFORMATION

Sheba Medical Center
Institute for Medical Research
c/o Drs. Deborah Zemer or Avi Livneh Heller
Hashomer, Israel
FAX: 972-3-530-7002

SCREENING CENTERS

Boston University School of Medicine, Center for Human Genetics
Cedars-Sinai Medical Center

University of California Los Angeles, Diagnostic Molecular Pathology Laboratory

REFERENCES

Aksentijevich, Ivona, Yelizaveta Torosyan, Jonathan Samuels, et al. Mutation and haplotype studies of Familial Mediterranean Fever reveal new ancestral relationships and evidence for a high carrier frequency with reduced penetrance in the Ashkenazi population. *American Journal of Human Genetics* 64 (1999): 949–962.

Dewalle, M., C. Domingo, M. Rozenbaum, et al. Phenotype-genotype correlation in Jewish patients suffering from Familial Mediterranean Fever (FMF). *European Journal of Human Genetics* 6 (1998): 95–97.

Dupont, Madeleine, Christiane Dross, Nizar Smaoui, et al. Genotypic diagnosis of Familial Mediterranean Fever (FMF) using new microsatellite markers: example of two extensive non–Ashkenazi Jewish pedigrees. *Journal of Medical Genetics* 34 (1997): 375–381.

Heller, H., E. Sohar and L. Sherf. Familial Mediterranean Fever (FMF). *Archives of Internal Medicine* 102 (1958): 50–71.

Koopman, William J. *Arthritis and Allied Conditions.* Baltimore: Williams & Wilkins, 1997, 1280–1287.

McKusick, Victor A. "Nonhomogeneous distribution of recessive diseases." In: Goodman, Richard M. and Arno G. Motusky, eds. *Genetic Diseases Among Ashkenazi Jews.* New York: Raven Press, 1979, 280–284.

Samuels, J., I. Aksentijevich, Y. Torosyan, et al. Familial Mediterranean Fever at the millennium. Clinical spectrum, ancient mutations, and a survey of 100 American referrals to the National Institutes of Health. *Medicine* 77 (1998): 268–297.

Zemer, Deborah, Mordechai Pras, Ezra Sohar, et al. Colchicine in the prevention and treatment of the amyloidosis of Familial Mediterranean Fever. *New England Journal of Medicine* 314 (1986): 1001–1005.

CHAPTER SEVEN

Gastrointestinal Disorders

The gastrointestinal tract is the passageway that runs through the body from the mouth to the anus and is the part of the body where food is broken down, its nutrients are absorbed, and its unusable portion is processed for elimination. This digestive process begins in the mouth. As soon as we begin to chew we begin shredding our food. At the same time, the salivary glands in our mouths secrete enzymes that begin lubricating our food and converting it into its more simple components. When swallowed, food passes through the esophagus into the stomach, where it is broken down by various enzymes and acids into its chemical components. Fats are broken down into fatty acids and glycerin; proteins are broken down into amino acids; starches are converted into sugars. The process takes about two to five hours depending on how much and the kind of food we've eaten.

After the stomach has done its job, it propels its contents into a 20-foot-long compartment of the gastrointestinal tract called the small intestine or bowel. The lining of the bowel contains three layers called the mucosa, submucosa, and the serosa. The job of the small intestine is to continue the digestive process begun in the stomach. Digestive enzymes are secreted into the interior along with enzymes from other organs of the body like the pancreas and liver, and then the chemicals into which food has been broken down are absorbed through the lining into the blood.

Whatever is left behind is propelled as waste into the next compartment, called the large intestine or colon. The colon is about one-quarter the size of the bowel, about five feet in length, but it is much wider, which is why it is called "large" compared to the longer bowel. Most of the water and salt remaining in the waste is absorbed through the lining of the colon, while bacteria act on what remains to convert it into feces. The feces are then passed through to the rectum, where they are stored until eliminated from the body.

Generally we are totally unaware of what is going on in our digestive systems, except when we experience discomfort—perhaps because of the acids in the stomach going back up into the esophagus, a sensation known as "heartburn" because the discomfort is felt close to the heart; or because of something happening in our intestines, which can be nothing more serious than the occasional bout of diarrhea or constipation; or because of something much more serious like Ulcerative Colitis or Crohn's Disease.

Inflammatory Bowel Disease: Ulcerative Colitis and Crohn's Disease

Inflammatory Bowel Disease (IBD) refers to a pair of chronic digestive system disorders called Ulcerative Colitis and Crohn's Disease. Together, these two diseases affect about 300,000 Americans.

Ulcerative Colitis and Crohn's Disease are inflammations of parts of the digestive system. Although very similar in some ways, they are in fact two different disorders. In Ulcerative Colitis, the inflammation is localized in the colon and rectum, whereas in Crohn's Disease the entire length of the digestive system from the mouth to the anus can become inflamed. A second difference is that in Ulcerative Colitis, the inflammation is confined to the inner surface of the digestive tract, whereas in Crohn's Disease the inflammation penetrates into the deeper layers.

Symptoms of Ulcerative Colitis have been documented as early as the time of the Romans, but the condition didn't receive its current medical designation until 1875. Subsequent studies found that Ashkenazi Jews were disproportionately affected by the disorder. Crohn's Disease may have been recognized in the 1700s, but it wasn't known by that term until 1932 when Dr. Burrill Crohn described its symptoms in a series of 14 patients, all of whom were Jewish. Years later Dr. Crohn was asked whether, when he first began studying the disorder that bears his name, he thought it was only a coincidence that most of the patients he and other doctors were treating had names like Crohn, Ginzburg and Oppenheimer. Crohn said that by 1939 he recognized that it was a Jewish disease and joked with his colleagues about whether the cause was Jewish mothers, Jewish food, or Jewish genes.

FREQUENCY

Although the frequency of these disorders differs in different parts of the world, whenever Jews and non–Jews from the same area are compared, Ulcerative Colitis and Crohn's Disease are typically found to be about two to four times more common in the Jewish community. A second peculiar aspect of these disorders is that, whereas women are affected by Ulcerative Colitis much more than men, they are hardly ever affected by Crohn's.

The frequency of Ulcerative Colitis in the general American population is about 3.4 cases per 100,000 for men and 4.1 cases per 100,000 for women. The rate of Ulcerative Colitis among Ashkenazi men is about three times higher at 9.3 cases per 100,000 and four times higher for Ashkenazi women (16.9 cases per 100,000).

The same imbalance between Jewish and non–Jewish men is true for Crohn's Disease. The frequency of the disorder in the general male population in the United States is about 2.4 compared to 7.2 per 100,000 for Jewish men. However, Jewish women are much less prone to suffer from Crohn's. Whereas the frequency of the disorder among the general female population in the United States is about 1.3 cases per 100,000, the frequency among Ashkenazi women is less than 1 case per 100,000. No one has yet explained why Jewish women experience such high rates of Ulcerative Colitis and such low rates of Crohn's Disease.

Where someone lives is a definite factor affecting the rates for Ulcerative Colitis and Crohn's Disease. In the Northern Hemisphere, the farther north one lives, the greater the risk. The province of Manitoba, Canada, for instance, has one of the highest incidence rates. When adjusted for age and gender, the incidence is 14.3 cases per 100,000 for Ulcerative Colitis and 14.6 per 100,000 for Crohn's Disease. In Malmo, Sweden, the incidence of Crohn's Disease among Jews is about 25 per 100,000 compared to 5 per 100,000 for non–Jews; in Tel Aviv, the incidence is a little more than 1 case per 100,000.

Ashkenazi Jews are also much more likely to suffer from these two disorders than are other Jews. In Israel, the incidence of Ulcerative Colitis among Ashkenazi Jews is almost twice what it is in Sephardic and Oriental Jews.

To determine where these disorders may have originated in the Jewish population, Dr. Marie-Paul Roth and her colleagues at the Cedars-Sinai Medical Center in Los Angeles obtained the family histories of 233 Jewish patients with IBD in Los Angeles, and they compared those histories with a group of Jews who did not have these disorders. Roth found that Ashkenazi Jews who developed Ulcerative Colitis or Crohn's Disease were more likely to have had ancestors who lived in middle Europe rather than Poland or Russia. The fact that Ashkenazi Jews are not uniformly affected indicated that there were some peculiar conditions in middle Europe that acted on their genetic predisposition to cause them to develop the disease, compared to Ashkenazi Jews in other communities.

SYMPTOMS

The most common symptoms of both Ulcerative Colitis and Crohn's Disease are bloody diarrhea, severe abdominal pain, fever, fatigue, loss of appetite, weight loss, and anemia. Although rectal bleeding may occur in both conditions, it is more common in Ulcerative Colitis than in Crohn's Disease. The bloody diarrhea and cramp-like pain result from a combination of obstruction of the bowel, which causes bacteria to flourish and food absorption to be inhibited, and bleeding from both the ulcerated lining, which exudes blood and pus, along with possible tearing of the anal tissues. The blood loss may so severe that anemia (low red blood cell concentration) may occur.

Symptoms of Ulcerative Colitis usually begin to be experienced between the ages of 20 and 35 and usually begin in the rectum and then extend into the colon. Attacks are sporadic; there are periods when sufferers are symptom-free and times when they experience bloody diarrhea and extreme pain in the area of the colon. In Ulcerative Colitis, the colon may become very dilated, resulting in toxic megacolon, a serious condition in which the inflammation spreads from the inner layer of the colon into its other layers. This causes the colon to be paralyzed and perforated. Toxic megacolon can also occur with Crohn's Disease but is more common with Ulcerative Colitis. Toxic megacolin is a life threatening condition that requires immediate hospitalization.

Crohn's Disease is usually not experienced until the 30s. In its early stages, Crohn's Disease begins with an ulcer, an erosion of the lining of the digestive tract. If the inflammatory ulcer penetrates further, it can cause a fistula to develop. A fistula is a tube-like structure in the lining which results in stool from the digestive system spilling out into nearby organs like the bladder or into the abdominal cavity, causing infection which in turn causes fever and abdominal pain. Fistulas are common in Crohn's Disease but not very common in Ulcerative Colitis. The pain associated with the disorder is due to either the inflammation, which irritates the nerves and muscles in the intestine, a perforation in the wall of the digestive system, and or the abscesses caused by the spillage of stool into the abdominal cavity.

The main symptoms of Crohn's Disease—in addition to diarrhea or constipation, fever, poor appetite, vomiting, and weight loss—are abdominal pain, usually in the lower right area of the abdomen (which may be mistaken for an attack of appendicitis), and pain during defecation. Other related complications include joint pain (arthritis) due to inflammation in the joints; conjunctivitis (an inflammation in the eyes); a reddening of the skin due to inflammation, called erthema nodosum; and hepatitis (an inflammation in the liver). If the ducts draining the liver become obstructed, the malfunction can cause infection and liver failure. The explanation for these related symptoms is still unknown, but they are undoubtedly related to the same abnormal inflammatory response that occurs in the digestive tract.

The severity of these symptoms varies widely. Some may experience very mild symptoms; for others, the pain may be excruciating. For some, symptoms come on gradually; others experience sudden attacks. Some people experience pain in one particular area; others in an entirely different part of the digestive system. In many cases, the pain may be felt at a distance from the actual site of inflammation, a condition called "referred pain."

While appropriate treatment has enabled many people with Ulcerative Colitis and Crohn's to live relatively normal lives, for others complications may develop which require hospitalization. One such complication is cancer.

Colon and rectal cancer related to either Ulcerative Colitis or Crohn's occur more commonly (5 to 10 percent higher rate) if the disease begins at a relatively early age or has been present for more than 10 years. Experiencing these disorder for more than 30 years increases the risk to between 15 and 40 percent. However, the increased risk depends on which part of the colon is affected. If it is primarily confined to the rectum or lower colon, the risk of cancer is not increased.

CAUSE

Although Ulcerative Colitis and Crohn's Disease stem from an inflammation in the lining of the digestive system, no one knows what causes the inflammation. For most people, food or bacteria in the intestine do not trigger an immune response; for patients with Ulcerative Colitis or Crohn's Disease, the immune system reacts to food or other substances in the digestive system with an inflammatory response and ulcerations. Although diet can affect symptoms, diet is not the cause of the abnormal inflammatory response.

Many medical researchers believe that the two disorders have a genetic component. Not only are these disorders more common among Jews, but both run in families, Crohn's Disease more so than Ulcerative Colitis. About 20 percent of people with Crohn's have a family member who also has the disease.

FAUSTIAN BARGAIN

The likelihood that IBD has a strong genetic component which is relatively common, yet makes someone susceptible to it, has puzzled medical researchers. It is certainly not a new mutation since it would have to be occurring at a much higher rate to keep pace with an increased mortality and decreased reproduction rate.

It also does not appear to be due to a founder effect. A founder effect, you may recall, alludes to the appearance of a mutation in an individual (the founder) which is transmitted to his or her children. These children in turn pass it on to their children, and if the ethnic community in which they live is closely knit, the mutation is inherited by more and more individuals, resulting in a relatively high frequency in that community. Medical geneticists believe IBD is very unlikely to be due to a founder effect because of its very high frequency, which exceeds the possibility of a founder-like inheritance.

The alternative is some Faustian bargain. Some medical geneticists speculate that the selective advantage in IBD was a response to an unsanitary world which took the form of a protective immune response to substances that came in contact with the lining of the digestive system. A selective advantage of this sort may explain the relatively high frequency of IBD among Ashkenazi compared to Sephhardic Jews. Since IBD is much less common among Sephardim, the selective advantage must have arisen after the emergence of the Christian and Muslim divisions in Europe. In middle and eastern Europe, which were Christian, the ancestors of modern Ashkenazi Jewry were often forced to live in overcrowded ghettos with their resultant sanitation problems. The ancestors of modern day Sephardic Jewry lived in the Mediterranean, which was Muslim-controlled, and so they were less subject to ghetto urbanization and its ill effects. Once the ghetto restrictions were eased and the Ashkenazi Jews were allowed to leave, many relocated to the east, settling in Poland, the Ukraine and Russia, thereby dispersing the genetic variant.

DIAGNOSIS

IBD is sometimes misdiagnosed since its symptoms occur in many other conditions. Two other digestive system diseases that are sometimes confused with IBD are "irritable bowel syndrome" and diverticulosis. Irritable bowel syndrome resembles IBD in having many symptoms in common, such as diarrhea and abdominal pain. But it differs in that the diarrhea is not bloody; it is not associated with other tell-tale symptoms such as fever; and it is not due to inflammation of the lining of the digestive tract. (Actually, the cause of irritable bowel syndrome is still a mystery, but it seems that to some extent the cause lies somewhere other than the digestive system itself.) Diverticulitis occurs when a small sac in the inner layer of the colon bulges through a weak point in the muscle wall. The sac is called a diverticulum and when it becomes infected, the condition is called diverticulitis. If the sacs become inflamed, they can burst and spill bacteria into the abdominal cavity. Like IBD, diverticulitis can cause diarrhea, nausea, vomiting, and abdominal pain. If uncontrolled, the ruptured contents can also cause peritonitis and death.

Attacks of IBD can also be mistaken for appendicitis. Since the terminal part of the bowel (an area called the "ileum") is one of the most common sites affected by Crohn's Disease, attacks are sometimes mistaken for acute appendicitis because the appendix is also located on the right side of the abdomen.

The tell-tale symptoms of bloody diarrhea, abdominal pain, fever and weight loss are the obvious diagnostic signals for IBD. If the symptoms are experienced in the area of the colon and or the rectum, a doctor will usually suspect Ulcerative Colitis. If the symptoms are experienced higher up the digestive tract, he or she may suspect the symptoms are due to Crohn's Disease rather than Ulcerative Colitis.

Since there are many diseases that have the same symptoms as Ulcerative Colitis and Crohn's Disease, they can easily be confused with one another. The next step in making a diagnosis to determine the cause is usually a sigmoidoscopy.

A sigmoidoscope is a slender, flexible tube, about two feet long, with a tiny video camera in it. The night before the procedure, a patient will be asked to self-administer two enemas to flush the interior of the rectum and to refrain from eating after midnight. In the doctor's office a tube, the sigmoidoscope, is inserted through the anus into the rectum and lower part of the colon. The procedure is relatively painless, does not require sedation, is usually done in the doctor's office, and takes only a few minutes. The only discomfort is a brief painful sensation of bloating that lasts for only a few seconds when the doctor fills the cavity with gas so that he or she can get a better look at the lining. The cost of the procedure is about $200, which is usually covered by most medical insurance.

A similar test, called a colonoscopy, enables a doctor to view almost the entire colon. The colonoscope is a longer (about six feet) flexible tube than the sigmoidoscope and is about the width of your small finger. The tube contains a similar tiny video camera, but it also allows the doctor to send some other instruments through it, such as a wire loop that lets him or her cut a polyp with an electrical current.

Like a sigmoidoscopy, a colonoscopy can be performed in the doctor's office, but some doctors prefer to do it in a hospital. Also like a sigmoidoscopy, a patient will be asked to self-administer an enema, but for a colonoscopy the patient will be told not to eat supper and to drink a special fluid beforehand beginning around 5:00 P.M., every 15 minutes for about four hours, to help clean out the colon.

The procedure is slightly more involved than a sigmoidoscopy. For one thing, a colonoscopy takes about 30 to 60 minutes and requires the patient to be sedated (often with Valium or Demerol) so that he or she is relaxed but still conscious. Because of the sedation, the procedure itself is usually painless or at most slightly discomforting. The more experienced the doctor, the less discomforting the procedure. The cost is about $1,000 (also covered by medical insurance). Afterwards, many patients feel cramps for several hours, the after-effects of the air that was put into the colon. This subsides as the patient passes gas.

An additional test that may be given to determine the extent of the disease is a barium enema X-ray. After a patient has taken an enema, the doctor inserts an inert material containing barium into the rectum and colon through a tube and X-ray pictures are taken. To examine the upper area of the gastrointestinal tract, a patient will be asked to drink a solution containing barium. In both types of X-ray, the barium enables the doctor to visualize the inflammation or ulceration in the digestive tract. In the case of the barium drink, the X-ray enables the doctor to look at areas higher up than those that can be viewed by a colonoscope. Barium X-rays usually cost around $300.

Still other tests that may be performed include a CT (short for computerized axial tomography) scan to enable the doctor to detect abscesses that might not be visible by these other procedures. These and some similar procedures may also be performed to determine or rule out the presence of colon cancer (see "Colorectal Cancer").

Additional tests usually involve a blood test to determine if the red cell count is down (anemia) due to excessive blood loss due to the diarrhea, and simultaneously to see if the white blood cell count is increased (an immune response), since such an increase occurs as a result of inflammation in the body. A stool sample may also be examined for the presence of blood.

TREATMENT

There is no cure for either Ulcerative Colitis or Crohn's Disease. While symptoms can often be controlled with medication, severe complications usually involve surgery to cut away the diseased areas.

For some people, the symptoms of IBD are so mild they do not need treatment. Likewise, people whose symptoms are in remission do not need any special treatment. For those who suffer periodic outbreaks there are a number of drugs that provide some relief from its symptoms. Most of these drugs suppress the body's immune system so that it does not react with an inflammatory response.

The most commonly used drugs for treating IBD affecting the immune system are related to aspirin, which reduces inflammation. One of these drugs is Sulfasalazine (trade name: Azulfidine). Sulfasalazine is mainly effective in reducing inflammation in the colon and is less effective in reducing inflammation in the small intestine. However, Sulfasalazine has some unpleasant side effects such as headache, nausea, vomiting, and diarrhea.

Other drugs related to Sulfasalazine which are more effective for inflammation in the small bowel and whose side effects are not as unpleasant are Asacol, Dipentum and Pentasa. If the disorder is mainly confined to the lower colon or rectum, an enema containing another of this family of drugs (Rowasa) may provide relief.

The second class of immune suppressants are the corticosteroids such as prednisone. If used for a long time, however, corticosteroids can cause very serious side effects including diabetes, destruction of bone cells resulting in bone thinning and damage to the large joints, muscle wasting, and infections. Patients who do not respond to the aspirin-like drugs or the corticosteroids may be given stronger immunosuppressants such as 6-mercaptopurine (Purinethol) or azathioprine (Imuran). These drugs have also been found to be effective in healing fistulas. However, these drugs also have important side effects including increased risk of infection, interference with the ability of bone marrow to manufacture red blood cells, and inflammation of the pancreas.

In August 1998 the United States Food and Drug Administration approved a radical genetically manipulated drug called infliximab (trade name Remicade) for treating Crohn's Disease. Made from a combined mouse antibody and a human antibody, Remicade attacks a protein called tumor necrosis factor alpha, that induces inflammation and promotes fistulas. In clinical trials with the drug, Remicade reduced the symptoms of moderate to severe Crohn's Disease in 40 percent of a group of patients who did not respond well to the usual steroid or immunosupressants used to treat the disease. Patients who reacted positively began to show improvements within two to four weeks after a single dose of the drug. The drug also initially reduced the number of fistulas but that effect did not last for more than five months. Side effects of the drug included temporary chest pains, chills, and low blood pressure, which were attributed to the intravenous injections, and in some cases serious infections, which were able to be successfully treated with antibiotics. Remicade, however, is not cheap. The cost per treatment is about $2,000. Also, Remicade's effects only last for about three to four months and then it has to be taken again. However, each time it is taken, symptoms are relieved for a much shorter time because the body makes antibodies to the drug. After a year of taking the drug, it becomes relatively ineffective. And in some patients, the drug can actually make the obstruction of the bowel worse.

An altogether different kind of drug which is much cheaper and easier to use has given relief to others. Like many treatments, this one came out of left field and has surprised medical researchers since it's nothing other than the medical bugaboo, nicotine.

Doctors have known for some time that smokers hardly ever get Ulcerative Colitis. The only people who are usually affected are non-smokers and people who have stopped smoking. Dr. Rupert Pullan, a physician at the University Hospital of Wales in Cardiff, realized that this was a relationship worth exploring, so he gave one group of volunteers who had Ulcerative Colitis nicotine patches and another group nicotine-free patches. After six weeks of wearing the patches, the symptoms disappeared in about half his patients. Many of the nonsmokers and former smokers complained about side effects like nausea and sleep problems, but these were minor compared to their colitis symptoms. Three years later, Dr. William Sandborn at the Mayo Clinic in Rochester, Minnesota, found that 39 percent of those on nicotine patches felt a significant improvement in their symptoms.

Like any drug, nicotine may have some benefits, but there is also a paradox connected with smoking and presumably with nicotine. While smokers rarely suffer from Ulcerative Colitis, the risk of developing Crohn's Disease is five times higher among smokers compared to non-smokers.

There are also some nondrug treatments that may help reduce the severity and frequency of IBD attacks. Again, the advice here goes contrary to the advice given to otherwise normal people. Instead of increasing their fiber content, people with IBD need to watch their fiber intake. Fiber does not bring on an attack of IBD, but it can make the diarrhea worse when it does occur, and if the bowel has become obstructed, the added bulk from fiber can make passage very painful. Other foods to avoid are dairy products, especially those high in lactose. Some sufferers may also have to take their food in the form of liquid diet until the attacks subside. In some cases, if a person's intestines become very inflammed, he or she may have to be periodically fed intravenously.

For patients who lose weight a doctor may recommend nutritional supplements, especially for children whose growth may be affected because they eat less. Anti-diarrheal drugs like Lomotil and Immodium can help reduce the diarrheal symptoms and antispasmotic drugs can relieve the cramps.

For about 30 percent of colitis sufferers, the pain and complications of Ulcerative Colitis are so grave that they have to have their colons removed. Since the disease is restricted to the colon, this eliminates the disease forever.

About 60 percent of people with Crohn's Disease require surgery to either remove blockages in the bowel that have narrowed because of the build-up of ulcerated scar tissue, repair perforated areas, remove fistulas ("fistulectomy"), and or drain abscesses. (If narrowing has occurred because of inflammation, it may possibly be reduced by anti-inflammatory drug treatment.) Unlike Ulcerative Colitis, however, attacks of Crohn's Disease may recur in a part of the digestive tract that was formerly healthy. About 50 percent of all patients who have surgery for Crohn's Disease have recurrent attacks within five years.

In some instances, the diseased area may be small enough that it can be cut away and the healthy sections of the intestine joined together. Since the colon is very elastic, it can be stretched after parts have been removed, and the ends can be joined together. In some instances, however, the entire colon and the rectum are removed and the ileum, the end part of the small intestine, is channeled into a small opening in the abdominal wall, called a stoma, so that it can drain into a plastic bag that is periodically emptied into a toilet by the patient. However, it is not uncommon for the bag to overflow or to come loose during physical exertion.

An alternative to the "ileostomy" is the " J-pouch." The pouch procedure was invented in 1969 by a Swedish surgeon, Dr. Nils Kock. Instead of draining the ileum to the outside, Kock formed a pouch from the patient's intestine underneath the skin at the site of the stoma. Then he fashioned a valve that would keep the stoma closed until the patient stuck a tube into the pouch to drain out the contents. The operation proved a huge success for about half the patients who received it; the other half experienced various problems such as valve slippages and leaking.

Currently surgeons use a variation of this procedure in which the small bowel and the mucous membrane of the rectum are removed, but the rectal sphincter muscle is left intact. This muscle is connected directly to the lower end of the small intestine, which is reshaped into a pouch that acts like the rectum to store feces. This has now become the preferred operation for young Ulcerative Colitis patients who require surgery, but it can't be used by the thousands of ileostomy patients who have had their anuses removed or for those with diseased rectums.

PREVENTION

Since the causes of Ulcerative Colitis and Crohn's Disease are unknown, there is little in the way of prevention. Some studies suggest that a high meat and fat diet might be a contributing factor. Other studies suggest it is due to some virus or bacterial infection. While the immune system is certainly involved, the exact nature of this involvement is still a mystery.

FOR FURTHER INFORMATION

Crohn's and Colitis Foundation of
America
386 Park Avenue South, 17th Floor
New York, NY 10016-8804
TELEPHONE: 1-800-932-2423
212-685-3440
FAX: 212-79-4098
INTERNET: www.ccystic fibrosisa.org

Gastro-Intestinal Research Foundation of Chicago
70 East Lake Street, Suite 1015
Chicago, IL 60601-5907
TELEPHONE: 312-332-1350
INTERNET: homepage.inter
access.com/~ring/girf

Intestinal Disease Foundation
1323 Forbes Avenue, Suite 200
Pittsburgh, PA 15219
TELEPHONE: 412-261-5888

National Digestive Diseases Information Clearing House
2 Information Way
Bethesda, MD 20892
TELEPHONE: 301-654-3810

Pediatric Crohn's and Colitis Association
P.O. Box 18
Newton, MA 02168-0002
TELEPHONE: 617-290-0902

REFERENCES

Books
Hanauer, Stephen. *Inflammatory Bowel Disease: A Guide for Patients & Their Families*. Lippincott-Raven, 1997.
Saibil, Fred. *Crohn's Disease & Ulcerative Colitis*. Firefly Books, 1997.

Steiner-Grossman, Penny, Peter Banks, and Daniel H. Present. *The New People … not Patients—A Source Book for Living with Inflammatory Bowel Disease.* Kendall/Hunt, 1992.

Thompson, W. Grant. *The Angry Gut—Coping with Colitis and Crohn's Disease.* New York: Plenum Press, 1993.

Journal Articles

Bernstein, Charles N., James F. Blanchard, Patricia Rawsthorne, et al. Epidemiology of Crohn's Disease and Ulcerative Colitis in a central Canadian Province: a population-based study. *American Journal of Epidemiology* 149 (1999): 916–924.

Jacobsohn, Warren Z., and Y. Levine. Incidence and prevalence of ulcerative colitis in the Jewish population of Jerusalem. *Israel Journal of Medical Sciences* 22 (1986): 559–563.

Janowitz, Henry D. Conversation with Burrill B. Crohn, Leon Ginzburg, and Gordon Oppenhemier. "63 Years After the Discovery of Crohn's Disease." In: Cosimo Prantera and Burton I. Korelitz, eds. *Crohn's Disease.* New York: Marcel Dekker, 1–9.

Roth, Marie-Paule, G.M. Petersen, C. McElree, et al. Geographic Origins of Jewish Patients with Inflammatory Bowel Disease. *Gastroenterology* 97 (1989): 900–904.

Tilat, T., A. Grossman, Z. Fireman, et al. Inflammatory bowel disease in Jews. *Frontiers in Gastrointestinal Research* 11 (1986): 135–140.

Yang, Huiying, and Jerome I. Rotter. "Genetic aspects of idiopathic inflammatory bowel disease." In: R. Mcconnell, P. Rozen, M. Langman, et al., eds. *The Genetics and Epidemiology of Inflammatory Bowel Disease.* Basel, Switzerland: Karger, 301–331.

Lactose Intolerance

The inability to digest milk products, called lactose intolerance, is one of the most common disorders in the world. In fact, there are more people in the world who experience some discomfort when they consume milk products than people who don't. In a sense, this means that the ability to do so is a disorder rather than vice versa.

Lactose intolerance refers to an inability or decreased ability to digest milk sugar, lactose, as a result of a deficiency in the intestinal enzyme, lactase. Since lactose is found not only in dairy products like milk, butter, cheese, and ice cream, but also in other foods like cakes and many sauces, the inability to digest this enzyme produces the recognizable symptoms of the disorder.

FREQUENCY

People of Asian ancestry are the most likely to be lactose intolerant. In the United Sates, between 60 and 90 percent of all Native Americans are lactose intolerant compared to about 70 percent of African Americans, about 50 percent of Latinos, and less than 10 percent of Caucasians. The low frequency among Caucasians in the United States is due to the predominance of people whose ancestry is in Northern and Western Europe and England, where the frequency is relatively low.

The frequency of lactose intolerance among Jews is about 60 percent. Among the different Jewish groups, Yemenites have the lowest frequency (about 44 percent), followed by Sephardic Jews (62 percent), Ashkenazis (80 percent) and Oriental Jews, for example, Iraqis (85 percent).

SYMPTOMS

The main symptoms of lactose intolerance are stomach cramps, bloating, flatulence, and diarrhea. In some people these symptoms are relatively mild; one of the first physicians to describe the effect personally suffered from it, but expressed a certain amount of satisfaction over the laxative effect of drinking milk in the morning. Others, however, may experience considerable discomfort. Some people may be very sensitive and will develop symptoms after consuming the smallest amounts of milk products; others develop symptoms only after consuming relatively large amounts. This is not, however, a life-threatening disorder. In most cases, symptoms do not develop until late adolescence.

CAUSE

Most infants have lactase in their small intestines. This enables them to break down lactose, the sugar contained in milk. When they get a little older, the lactase begins to disappear and by their fourth year, many have almost none.

When lactose is not broken down in the intestine, it attracts water into the intestine, resulting in bloating. The lactose is then fermented into lactic acid, hydrogen and carbon dioxide, which causes abdominal pain and diarrhea.

Societies that rely on dairy products for much of their food have a higher proportion of people with this enzyme than those that don't. Adults in those societies are much more lactose tolerant than people who do not practice dairying. From an evolutionary standpoint, a genetic variant that enables those who possess it to use a nutrient better than those who don't will be advantageous if that nutrient is beneficial to our well being. Those who possess that variant will be healthier, will live longer, and will be more likely to have children than those who don't. One such advantage is that by breaking down lactose, lactase enhances calcium absorption, which in turn facilitates absorption of vitamin D, the absence of which results in rickets and osteomalacia. Vitamin D, it is true, can also be taken into the body through sunlight. However, in the northern countries, where there is a relatively higher level of dairying than in the latter countries, there is much less sunlight than in the latter countries. In other words, in the Mediterranean, people were able to get vitamin D from their environment, whereas in northern Europe they had to rely on some other source, in this case dairy products. The reason lactase is present in very young children is that, until only recently, infants relied on breast milk (which is high in lactose) and therefore had to have lactase to survive.

Inherited variations are present in all populations. The ability to produce lactase after childhood may have resulted from a "weeding out" process that established the lactase variant in some populations. In other words, people who relied on milk for their vitamin D had a variant that allowed them to benefit from or not become sick from milk. They survived longer and had more children than those that didn't, and selective evolution occurred.

DIAGNOSIS

The clearest indication is an absence of symptoms when foods containing lactose are eliminated from the diet.

In the lactose-tolerance test two clinical indicators, which are generally performed in tandem, are used to determine the presence of the disorder. In this test a given amount of lactose, usually around 50 grams, is taken and then blood glucose levels are measured. People with normal levels of lactase in their intestines are able to digest the test dose completely, so that their blood glucose levels increase within 15 to 45 minutes. Since the lactose is completely digested, none of it reaches the colon, where it would otherwise ferment and be broken down into hydrogen and excreted in the breath. In the absence or of lactase, where lower-than-normal levels of lactase are present, blood glucose levels either do not increase or increase minimally. Since it is not broken down, lactose enters the colon where it is fermented by bacteria. The fermentation results in formation of hydrogen which is breathed out. The presence of hydrogen in the breath is another indication of the absence of the enzymes.

TREATMENT

There is no treatment for this disorder, although its symptoms are easily prevented.

PREVENTION

Prevention consists of avoiding all dairy foods containing lactose. A number of dairy foods specially formulated for the lactose intolerant, such as Lactaid, have the lactase enzyme added. Yogurt, except for frozen yogurt, can also be consumed because the live cultures in yogurt break down the lactose. Frozen yogurt should be avoided because freezing kills the bacteria.

REFERENCES

Bayless, T.M. Recognition of lactose intolerance. *Hospital Practice* 11 (1976): 97–102.

Bayless, T.M., and Rosensweig, N.S. A racial difference in incidence of lactase deficiency. *JAMA* 197 (1966): 968.

Bujanover, Y., A. Katz, Y. Peled, et al. Lactose malabsorption in Israeli children. *Israel Journal of Medical Sciences* 21 (1985): 32–35.

Charney, M., and R.D. McCracken. Intestinal lactase deficiency in adult non-human primates: Implications for selection pressures in man. *Social Biology* 18 (1971): 416.

Flatz, G., and H.W. Rotthauwe. Lactose nutrition and natural selection. *Lancet* 2 (1973): 76.

Gilat, T., R. Kuhn, E. Gelman. Lactase deficiency in Jewish communities in Israel. *American Journal of Digestive Diseases* 15 (1970): 895.

Goodman, Richard M. *Genetic Disorders among the Jewish People*. Baltimore: Johns Hopkins University Press, 1979, 389–393.

Johnson, R.C., R.E. Cole, and F.M. Ahern. Genetic interpretation of ethnic differences in lactose absorption and tolerance: A review. *Human Biology* 53 (1981): 1–12.

Rosado, J.L., and N.W. Solomons. Sensitivity and specificity of the hydrogen breath-analysis test for detecting malabsorption of physiological doses of lactose. *Clinical Chemistry*, 1983, 545–548.

Simoons, F.J. "Geographic patterns of primary adult lactose malabsorption: A further interpretation of evidence for the Old World." In D.M. Page and T.M. Bayhless, eds. *Lactose Digestion*. Baltimore: Johns Hopkins University Press, 1981, 23–48.

CHAPTER EIGHT

Metabolic and Endocrine Disorders

Metabolism is a general term for the various chemical activities that occur in the body. Many of these activities are regulated by hormones, the chemical messengers produced by endocrine glands. Hormonal balance is closely regulated in the body. When levels of hormones produced by one of the endocrine glands are lower or higher than normal, an area of the brain called the hypothalamus, which is sensitive to such levels, directs the pituitary gland (the "master gland") to send out hormones that cause that endocrine gland to increase or decrease its output. If hormonal balance cannot be restored, too much or too little of a particular hormone will be produced, and this can affect the actions of other glands and organs. Likewise, when biochemicals that are normally removed from a particular organ of the body instead accumulate, they often cause damage to that organ and other organs as well.

Abetalipoproteinemia

Abetalipoproteinemia is the opposite of Familial Hypercholesterolemia, a disorder that will be explained later on in this chapter. Instead of an excess of cholesterol and low-density lipoproteins in the blood, as occurs in Familial Hypercholesterolemia, people with abetalipoproteinemia have cholesterol levels that are much lower than normal.

The disorder is also known as Bassen and Kornzweig Disease, after the two physicians who first described its main symptoms in an 18-year-old Ashkenazi Jewish girl in 1950. Several years later the two doctors described a similar cluster of symptoms in the girl's brother. It was subsequently found that the main defect was an absence of a specific type of lipoprotein.

Lipoproteins are combinations of lipids and specialized proteins called apoproteins. More than 10 different apoproteins have been identified. The main constituents of these lipoproteins that distinguish them from each other in terms of their function are their apoprotein components. As mentioned in conjunction with Familial Hypocholesterolemia, apoproteins enable lipids to move through the blood stream, and they also react with specific receptors on the surface of cells so that the lipoproteins will be absorbed into cells. But these are not their only jobs. They also activate or inhibit enzymes involved in metabolizing cholesterol in the lysosome where the degradation occurs; and they facilitate exchanges from one lipoprotein to another. If one of these apoproteins does not perform its job, the body's cells cannot get their cholesterol; depending on which apoprotein is affected, a recognizable disorder will occur. The apoprotein disorder that disproportionately affects Ashkenazi Jews is caused by the absence of beta-apoprotein, and this disorder is called abetalipoproteinemia.

FREQUENCY

Abetalipoproteinemia has been found in many different ethnic groups, but in most cases marriage between first cousins has been a common feature. Although the frequency of the disorder has not been determined because of its rarity, carrier frequency in the general population has been estimated at 1 in 20,000. Despite its rarity, the disorder has been disproportionately found in Ashkenazi Jews.

SYMPTOMS

The main clinical symptoms of abetalipoproteinemia are poor appetite, vomiting, failure to thrive, foul smelling diarrhea, deteriorating eyesight, progressive deterioration of motor function, absence of deep tendon reflexes, and the presence of star-shaped ("crenated") red blood cells.

The earliest signs of the disorder are vomiting, chronic diarrhea characterized by loose, pale, bulky stools (a condition called "steatorrhea"), and associated growth retardation, beginning in the first year of life. Steatorrhea often decreases in severity by four or five years of age due to dietary changes, usually decreased consumption of fat. At the same time that the symptoms of steatorrhea lessen, symptoms of deteriorating vision due to retinitis pigmentosa and deteriorating neurological function begin to appear or worsen.

Neurological effects include unsteadiness and muscle weakness, which often begin to appear by two years of age. Movements become uncoordinated, and ability to walk and stand without support becomes increasingly difficult by 10 years of age. By 30, patients are confined to a wheel chair. Intellectual ability is impaired in some but not all.

Other effects include fatigue due to anemia, an enlarged heart, cardiac arrythmia and congestive heart failure, as well as night blindness in infancy due to vitamin A deficiency, retinal blindness (often by age 10), drooping eyelids (a condition called "ptosis"), and cataracts.

CAUSE

When dietary lipid (another term for fat) is consumed, it is broken down into triglycerides, cholesterol, phospholipids and free fatty acids. As noted in conjunction with Familial Hypercholesterolemia, triglycerides and cholesterol are transported in the blood by very-low-density lipoprotein (VLDL) and low-density lipoprotein (LDL).

Each lipoprotein contains a specialized protein called a B apolipoprotein that secretes a particle and attracts lipids. The predominant B apoprotein is apoprotein B-100. The absence of B apoproteins, called abetalipoproteinemia, results in an almost total absence of very-low and low-density lipoprotein. The disorder is believed to be caused by abnormalities in the transfer of apoproteins involved in the assembly or secretion of triglyceride-rich B apoproteins; one of these is called microsomal triglyceride transfer protein. When apo B is missing VLDL is not produced and subsequent conversion to LDL cannot occur. This means that triglyceride and cholesterol levels in the blood are very low. Triglyceride levels may be as low a 10 mg/dl; cholesterol levels are often as low as 20 mg/dl. Since LDL is the major lipoprotein that delivers cholesterol to cells and enables them to take cholesterol inside them, their absence can cause serious damage. Their absence also results in decreased absorption of fat-soluble vitamins such as vitamins E and A.

DIAGNOSIS

Diagnosis is based on clinical observations of chronic diarrhea, steatorrhea, failure to thrive, pigmentation of the retina, absent or diminished reflex activity, presence of crenated red blood cells, and very low levels of LDL.

TRANSMISSION

Abetalipoproteinemia is a an autosomal recessive disorder that affects both males and females.

Treatment

During the first years of life, treatment consists of monitoring food intake carefully to restrict certain types of triglycerides, called long-chain fatty acids, such as those in butter, cream, margarine and nuts. Instead of these foods, diets need to contain medium-chain fatty acids such as those contained in food made from coconut or palm oil, which, though not usually sold in supermarkets, can be obtained from stores selling dietary supplements. Vitamin E supplements have been found to reduce and in some cases reverse the neurological deterioration and muscle wasting and may prevent retinopathy if treatment is started very early. Vitamin A supplements have also been found to improve night blindness; Vitamin K has been given to prevent blood coagulation; and iron supplements are given to correct anemia.

For Further Information

Office of Rare Diseases
31 Center Dr.
Bethesda, MD 20892
Telephone: 301-402-4336

References

Bassen, F.A., and A.L. Kornzweig. Malformation of the erythrocytes in a case of atypical retinitis pigmentosa. *Blood* 5 (1950): 381–385.

Kane, John P., and Richard J. Havel. "Disorders of the biogenesis and secretion of lipoproteins containing the B apolipoproteins." In: Scriver, Charles R., Arthur L. Beaudet, William S. Sly, eds. *The Metabolic and Molecular Basis of Inherited Disease*. New York: McGraw-Hill, 1995, 1853–1886.

Sharp, B., L. Blinderman, K.A. Combs, et al. Cloning and gene defects in microsomal triglyceride transferprotein associated with abetalipoproteinemia. *Nature* 365 (1993): 65–69.

Shoulders, C.C., D.J. Brett, J.D. Bayliss, et al. Abetalipoproteinemia is caused by defects of the gene encoding the 97 kDa subunit of a microsomal triglyceride transfer protein. *Human Molecular Genetics* 2 (1993): 2109–2116.

Yang, X.P., A. Inazu, K. Yagi, et al. Abetalipoproteinemia caused by maternal isodisomy of chromosome 41 containing an intron 9 splice acceptor mutation in the microsomal triglyceride transfer protein gene. *Arteriosclerosis, Thrombosis and Vascular Biology* 19 (1999): 1950–1955.

Congenital Adrenal Hyperplasia

Congenital adrenal hyperplasia, also called adrenogenital syndrome, refers to a genetically related disorder in which the adrenal gland is unable to produce sufficient amounts of two hormones, cortisol and aldosterone. To compensate, precursors which are androgenic (male hormones) are overproduced. The combination of androgenic overproduction and under-production of cortisol and aldosterone results in masculinity in girls and shock for both boys and girls, resulting in possible death.

VARIATIONS

There are two main types of the disorder, usually referred to as classic and nonclassic. The classic variation also has two variations, depending on whether salt-wasting is also present.

The classic form of the disorder is the more severe of the two main variations and is observed at birth in girls and involves alterations in the external (but not the internal) genitalia that often require corrective surgery. The external genitalia in boys is not affected. However, both girls and boys are equally affected by the aldosterone deficiency of the classic form, which results in an inability to retain salt. This latter effect can result in dehydration and shock from infection or injuries, resulting in death. Shock is more likely to occur in boys since in girls the abnormal sex organs indicate the more obscure salt problem, whereas in boys the problem may not be evident until a crisis occur.

The nonclassic variation is a much milder form of the disorder, appears in late childhood, and is not life-threatening.

There are also two different variations affecting Ashkenazi and Iranian Jews due to a deficiency in two different adrenal enzymes.

SYMPTOMS

The most important consequences of classic congenital adrenal hyperplasia are neonatal death due to salt-wasting and underproduction of cortisol. For those who are less severely affected, the most common symptoms are masculinity in girls and accelerated puberty and short stature in boys. These may or may not also be accompanied with a salt-wasting syndrome.

Classic congenital adrenal hyperplasia results in an excess production of male hormones and an insufficiency of cortisol and aldosterone, the two main hormones that are also produced by the adrenal. In girls, the abnormal production of male hormones begins to act on a girl's genitals early in fetal life and results in abnormal growth of the clitoris and masculization of genital-urinary structures. In severe cases, the clitoris is so enlarged it resembles a penis, and the labial folds are sometimes joined and wrinkled, so that they look like a scrotum, with the result that girls may be even mistaken for boys. In the case of boys, the effects of the excess androgens are not observed at birth but after birth, they cause accelerated growth and early puberty; the latter has the effect of reducing postpubertal growth and causes short stature.

The other main symptoms result from the absence of cortisol and aldosterone, which can predispose individuals to an "adrenal crisis." In part, this is due to the aldosterone deficiency, which results in an inability to retain salt, a condition more commonly known as "salt-wasting." This causes vomiting and poor feeding in infants, which result in slower growth, drowsiness, and diarrhea and dehydration, which in turn can result in shock and death.

Symptoms of nonclassic congenital adrenal hyperplasia usually do not occur until late childhood or adolescence. In contrast to the classic form of the disorder, the female genitals are normal in appearance. However, androgen production may still be above normal, resulting in increased growth and premature development of public hair in girls. At puberty, girls develop excessive body hair on other parts of the body, including the face (a condition called hirsutism), severe acne, and irregular menstrual periods. Production of aldosterone is normal and cortisol levels are only slightly below normal. In boys, the condition is usually associated with short stature and early puberty. Heterosexual relations are usually normal for both men and women, although some men and women may be infertile. For men, this results from low sperm counts; for women, from infrequent ovulation.

FREQUENCY

The worldwide frequency of the classic variation of the disorder is estimated at about 1 in 14,000. The nonclassic form is much more common, especially among certain ethnic groups such as Ashkenazi Jews, who have an estimated prevalence of almost 4 percent for the disorder; Hispanics, who have an estimated prevalence of almost 2 percent, and Yugoslavs, for whom the frequency is estimated at about 1.6 percent. The frequency in the general population is estimated at between 1 in 100 and 1 in 1,000.

CAUSE

The adrenal glands, which are the endocrine glands involved in congenital adrenal hyperplasia, are small organs located just above each kidney at the level of the waistline and toward the back. Each adrenal gland is composed of two distinct parts, an internal area called the "medulla" and an external part called the "cortex." The medulla secretes adrenaline and noradrenaline, the hormones involved in "fight and flight." The cortex produces three classes of hormones: the glucocorticoids (like cortisol, which regulates the response to stress) that regulate glucose, the body's energy supply; the mineralcorticoids (like aldosterone) that regulate salt balance; and sex steroids like testosterone. Cholesterol is the precursor for these hormones. Cholesterol in the blood binds to low-density lipoproteins, which react with receptors on the adrenal cortex, enabling cholesterol to enter these cells. The cholesterol is then metabolized by a series of five different enzymes to the various adrenal hormones.

Congenital adrenal hyperplasia is caused by mutations in the family of genes that code for the enzymes that the adrenals use to make these hormones. A deficiency in a gene called CYP results in a deficiency in one of these enzymes, and this results in a build-up of an intermediary hormone along the synthesis pathway. Almost all (95 percent) cases of the disorder are due to one of a number of different mutations in the same gene, called CYP21, that results in a deficiency in an enzyme called 21-hydroxylase. As a result of the deficient enzyme, the cholesterol-cortisol pathway is interrupted, resulting in an absence of cortisol and a build-up of intermediary hormones that have male androgenic effects. This has the effect of masculinizing the external genitals of girls before they are born. At birth, these girls have a normal uterus and ovaries, but their clitoris is overly developed and their other external genitalia are underdeveloped. A partial deficiency in this enzyme results in a much milder form of the disorder, called the nonclassic form, which is far more common than the classic form and is considered to be one of the most common human recessive genetic disorders.

While a deficiency in the 21-hydroxylase enzyme is very common among Ashkenazi Jews, it is relatively rare among Sephardic Jews. They also experience the same disorder, although not to the same extent, but the cause is due to a deficiency in a different adrenal enzyme, 11-beta-hydroxylase. This enzyme is primarily involved in the pathway for making aldosterone, and as a result of the mutation in its gene, salt levels in the blood remain high, resulting in high blood pressure and the manifestations of androgen excess.

Although different mutations in the CYP21 gene distinguishing Ashkenazi and Sephardic Jews have not been identified, all Ashkenazi Jews with the disorder are positive for a white blood cell marker called antigen B14, and most have the marker DR1. These markers are found much less frequently among Sephardic and Oriental Jews. There is some speculation that the mutation occurred some time after the Second

Diaspora in C.E. 70 and was consolidated by the time the major Ashkenazi communities were established in Northern and Eastern Europe by C.E. 1100.

FAUSTIAN BARGAIN

A disorder with as high a prevalence as nonclassic congenital adrenal hyperplasia, which is associated with decreased fertility and with a number of different mutations in the same gene, suggests that there may have been some survival advantage to being a carrier. Dr. S.F. Witchel found that carriers in fact had elevated cortisol responses to stress and speculated that the higher response might enable them to return more quickly to normal levels after a reaction to infections, inflammation or other environmental stresses, and might also protect them from deleterious immune responses like those associated with autoimmune diseases.

DIAGNOSIS

Diagnosis is based on the classic signs of the disorder combined with measuring hormonal levels in the blood. Low levels of cortisol and high levels of 17-hydroxyprogesterone, a precursor biochemical out of which it is made, after their release is stimulated by a pituitary hormone called ACTH, are indicative of the disorder. People with the classical form of the disorder have the least increase in cortisol and greatest increase in the precursor.

Diagnosis can also be made by testing for the presence of a marker gene that codes for a white blood cell protein called human leukocyte antigen (HLA). This gene is located on the same chromosome and very close to the gene for congenital adrenal hyperplasia and is always coupled with it.

Diagnosis of congenital adrenal hyperplasia can now be made prenatally by amniocentesis and chorionic villus sampling.

TREATMENT

Treatment for severely affected genital development in girls requires surgical treatment to reconstruct the vagina and reduce the size of the clitoris. Restoring the hormonal balance can result in almost normal growth and puberty. In some extremely rare cases, the adrenals may be surgically removed to reduce the androgen output and to avoid administering high levels of cortisol-mimicking drugs (called glucocorticoids), which can have serious side effects, such as growth retardation and increased susceptibility to infection. Girls with classic CAH may develop psycho-sexual problems as a result of disturbances in gender identity. In some instances, girls with the disorder and their parents may need psychological counseling to help them understand and deal with this disorder.

The nonclassic form does not require any corrective surgery. Irregular menstrual cycles and low sperm counts may be improved by gender-appropriate hormonal replacement.

Treatment for the diminished cortisol activity involves medication with glucocorticoids, such as hydrocortisone (Cortef), which is usually given to children, and prednisone and dexamethasone, which are usually given to adults. Glucocorticoid treatment also suppresses adrenal androgen production, and this in turn results in an improvement in hirsutism and acne and a return to normal menstrual cycles in girls and women.

Aldosterone deficiencies are treated with the drug fludrocortisone (Florinef) which mimics aldosterone's effects, enabling the body to retain salt, in conjunction with sodium supplements. Infants have to have salt added to their formulas.

TRANSMISSION

Congenital adrenal hyperplasia is an autosomal recessive trait, caused by a mutation in the gene coding for a hormonally-related enzyme, 21-hydroxylase. Carriers that do not have classic form of the disorder can still exhibit mild forms. It is also possible for parents with a mild form of the disease to have a child with the classic form of the disease. This can happen if a person's parents each have one mild form and one severe form of the mutation. Whether someone inherits the severe classic form or milder nonclassic form depends upon which forms of mutant gene are passed on. If someone inherits the severe form of the gene from both parents, that individual will develop the classic variation; inheriting the mild form from each will result in development of nonclassic CAH. Inheriting one severe form and one mild form of the gene will result in an intermediate condition. Ashkenazi Jews most commonly have the mild form of the disease.

PREVENTION

Carrier testing for the 21-hydroxylase gene can be performed directly or indirectly by testing for the presence of the specific human leukocyte antigen (HLA) in each parent, since a specific HLA is almost always coupled with the 21-hydroxylase gene. Prenatal testing can likewise be done using any of these methods.

Hormonal testing for congenital adrenal hyperplasia is now included in the newborn tests routinely performed in many states and several other countries. Testing involves a heel-prick and subsequent examination of a blood specimen. The reason for testing at an early age, especially in boys, is that the disorder is not readily recognizable in boys at birth, but the deficiency in aldosterone can result in a life-threatening adrenal crisis.

It is possible to prevent the excessive prenatal exposure to androgens from a fetus' adrenal glands by administering dexamethasone, a potent long-lasting synthetic glucocorticoid, to a pregnant women. This is sometimes done prior to determination of the sex and status of the fetus, which can be determined by amniocentesis or chorionic villus sampling, in the case of a mother who has previously had a child affected by the disorder. However, this treatment is not generally done because the chances of a child inheriting the classic form of the disorder is 1 in 4, and since only half of these children will be girls, the chance of a girl inheriting it is 1 in 8. This means that 7 out of 8 children will be needlessly exposed to the drug, the prenatal effects of which are not yet known.

FOR FURTHER INFORMATION

MAGIC Foundation for Children's Growth
1327 Harlem Ave.
Oak Park, IL 60302
TELEPHONE: 708-383-0808
FAX: 708-383-0899

National Adrenal Diseases Foundation
505 Northern Boulevard
Great Neck, NY 11021
TELEPHONE: 516-487-4992
E-MAIL: nadfmail@aol.com

SCREENING CENTERS

Baylor College of Medicine—Kleberg Cytogenetics Laboratory
All Children's Hospital—Molecular Genetics Clinical Laboratory

Celtek Laboratories
Chapman Institute of Medical Genetics
Children's Mercy Hospital

REFERENCES

Cohen, Tirza, Rachel Thodor, and Ariel Rosler. Selective hypoaldosteronism in Iranian Jews: an autosomal recessive trait. *Clinical Genetics* 11 (1977): 25–30.
Cutler, G.B., and L. Laue. Congenital adrenal hyperplasia due to 21-hydroxylase deficiency. *New England Journal of Medicine* 323 (1990): 1806–1813.

Holler, W., S. Scholz, D. Norr, et al. Genetic differences between the salt-fasting, simple virilizing, and nonclassical types of congenital adrenal hyperplasia. *Journal of Clinical Endocrinology and Metabolism* 60 (1985): 757–763.

Laron, Z., M.S. Pollack, R. Zamir, et al. Late onset 21-hydroxylase deficiency and HLA in the Ashkenazi population: A new allele at the 21-hydroxylase locus. *Human Immunology* 1 (1980): 55–66.

New, Maria I. "Nonclassical 21-hydroxylase deficiency." In: Bonne-Tamir, Batsheva, and Adam Avinoam, eds. *Genetic Diversity Among Jews. Diseases and Markers at the DNA Levels.* New York: Oxford University Press, 1992, 154–169.

Rosler, A., E. Leiberman, and T. Cohen. High frequency of congenital adrenal hyperplasia (classic 11-beta-hydroxylase deficiency) among Jews from Morocco. *American Journal of Medical Genetics* 42 (1992) 827–834.

Rosler, A., D. Rabinowitz, R. Theodor, et al. Nature of defect in salt-wasting disorder in Jews in Iran. *Journal of Clinical Endocrinology and Metabolism* 44 (1977): 279–291.

Speiser, P.W., B. Dupont, P. Rubinstein, et al. High frequency of nonclassical steroid 21-hyroxylase deficiency. *American Journal of Human Genetics* 37 (1985): 650–667.

Urban, M.D., P.A. Lee, and C.J. Migeon. Adult height and fertility in men with congenital virilizing adrenal hyperplasia. *New England Journal of Medicine* 299 (1978): 1392–1396.

White, P.C., M.I. New, and B. Dupont. Congenital adrenal hyperplasia. *New England Journal of Medicine* 316 (1987): 1580–1586.

Witchel, S.F., P.A. Lee, M. Suda-Hartman, et al. Evidence for a heterozygote advantage in congenital adrenal hyperplasia due to 21-hydroxylase deficiency. *Journal of Clinical Endocrinology and Metabolism* 82 (1997): 2097–2101.

Wudy, S.A., J. Homoki, and W.M. Teller. Successful prenatal treatment of congenital adrenal hyperplasia due to 21-hydroxylase deficiency. *European Journal of Pediatrics* 153 (1994): 556–559.

Cystinuria

Anyone who has ever had a kidney stone knows pain. It can be excruciating. To put that pain into perspective, some women who have given birth and have had kidney stones, give the edge to kidney stones when it comes to pain.

The kidneys are two large organs located around the wasteline and toward the back. These organs perform a variety of important functions such as regulating the blood's sodium and potassium content and its acidity and pressure, and they also influence production of red cells in bone marrow. Another of their main jobs is to filter wastes from blood and eliminate those wastes through urine formation and excretion. The filtering occurs through a unit called a nephron; there are about a million nephrons in each kidney. Urine then passes from the kidneys through a tube called the ureter to the bladder.

Kidney stones often become lodged at the junction between the kidneys and the ureter, or within the ureter where it passes over a blood vessel which causes it to narrow somewhat, or at the junction between the ureter and the bladder. Each location is associated with a characteristic pain due to the inflammation they cause. Stones near the kidney are sensed in the groin; those in the ureter are felt in the side; those at the junction of the bladder are felt as bladder pain and feel like you have an urgent need to urinate. When kidney stones become lodged in the ureter, they are not only painful, they are potentially life-threatening. Once they enter the bladder, they generally leave in the urine without discomfort.

Kidney stones are caused by many different factors but one of these is genetically related to a disorder involving an amino acid called cystine, the least soluble of all the amino acids. For reasons as yet unknown, this amino acid is not reabsorbed completely in the kidney and is instead excreted in the urine in higher than normal amounts, a condition called "cystinuria." In some cases it precipitates in the kidneys before excretion, forming crystals and in some instances, "calculi," the medical term for kidney stones. While cystinuria occurs in many different ethnic groups, Libyan Jews suffer from this disorder more frequently than any other ethnic group.

Cystinuria is not the same as cystinosis. Although cystine is involved in both, the latter involves the accumulation of cystine in a number of different areas of the body and its symptoms are much different.

VARIATIONS

Most kidney stones are made of calcium oxalate or calcium phosphate or some combination of the two. Kidney stones due to cystinuria are composed of an entirely different substance, the amino acid cystine.

Three different variations in cystine-related kidney stones have been identified, based on the amounts of cystine found in urine. In type I, the amount of cystine in the urine is normal. In type III, amount of cystine is twice normal levels. In type II, amounts are in between. Libyan Jews tend to fall into the types II and III classification.

SYMPTOMS

Kidney stones usually begin with a dull ache toward the middle of the back which then becomes increasingly painful as it moves to the side and toward the front. In the beginning, it may be mistaken for severe constipation. In some instances, it is accompanied by fever and chills.

Cystinuria may develop in childhood but most often occurs during the 20s and 30s. If untreated, the obstruction can result in infection, hypertension, and kidney failure.

FREQUENCY

The world wide frequency of cystine stones is estimated at about 1 in 15,000 in the United States. Among Libyan Jews, the prevalence is estimated at 1 in 2,500; carrier frequency is estimated at 3 to 4 per 100.

CAUSE

Kidney stones are a form of undissolved waste material. Normally this waste is dissolved in urine and is excreted out of the body during urination. However, when there is too much waste or not enough water for it to dissolve in, or when there is some underlying problem in the reabsorption of compounds from the urine by the kidneys, the waste matter may precipitate out of the fluid and form stones. The basic problem in cystinuria is that because of a genetically related defect, instead of being absorbed back into the blood, too much cystine remains in the urine. Since cystine is not very soluble, after a critical concentration is exceeded, it precipitates out and forms crystals and these crystals combine to form stones. Alternatively, if less urine is being produced because of decreased fluid intake, it could also result in greater concentration and subsequent precipitation.

Even though cystine may precipitate out of the urine, it may only form crystals that pass out of the body without any indication of their presence other than detected under a microscope. If these crystals aggregate, for reasons not yet known, they may become attached to the inside of one of the canals in the kidney and attract more crystals, eventually becoming big enough to form a stone. Under pressure from moving urine, it breaks free from the lining and is carried by the urine until it becomes trapped at some narrow junction. Until they reach these junctions, stones are painless; when they do, their presence cannot be ignored.

DIAGNOSIS

Diagnosis is based on clinical symptoms along with tests indicating the presence of blood in the urine. In the two types of the disorder that affect Libyan Jews, characteristic hexagonal-appearing crystals can be seen when urine is examined under the microscope. An X-ray of the kidney-bladder-ureter area will usually reveal the presence of most kidney stones. Other tests usually performed include a kidney ultrasonography to determine the size and location of the stone.

TRANSMISSION

Cystinuria is an autosomal recessive disorder. Although the actual gene has not been identified, the different variations are presumed to be due to a different mutation in the same gene.

TREATMENT

Most kidney stones are smaller than 5 millimeters and will pass through the kidneys and urinary tract by frequent urination. To facilitate this happening, patients need to drink very large amounts of fluids. In the case of cystine stones, they need to consume foods that make the urine more alkaline because this increases the solubility of cystine, and to take antibiotics to combat any infection that may occur.

Stones too large to pass naturally may be shattered, depending on their location, by electrical shock waves in a procedure called lithotripsy. The procedure is painless and involves lying down while the shock waves are focused on the stone. If the stone can be shattered into smaller pieces, those pieces may then be eliminated uneventfully.

In some cases the stone may be lodged in a part of the ureter where lithotripsy cannot be used. In this case a flexible tube is inserted through the urinary tract and bladder into the ureter. The tube may be fitted with a laser that can be focused on the stone to shatter it or with a basket to capture it.

If neither of these procedures is effective, the stone will have to be removed through surgery.

PREVENTION

The main preventative measure is diet. In the case of cystinuria, the stone is caused by the precipitation of cystine in the urinary tract. Low-sodium diets are recommended to decrease cystine excretion. Increasing urinary volume will also reduce cystine concentration and reduce the chances for precipitation. Solubility is decreased when the urine is acidic. This means that drinks like lemonade should be avoided, whereas bicarbonates should be increased. Drug treatment includes D-penicillamine or thiola, which also reduce cystine excretion and make the urine more soluble for cystine.

For Further Information

Cystinuria Support Network
2100 NE 36th Street
Redmond, WA 98053
Telephone: 425-868-2996
E-Mail: cystinuria@aol.com

References

Books
Cameron, Stewart. *Kidney Disease*. New York: Oxford University Press, 1986.
Kelly, S. Cystinuria genotypes predicted from excretion patterns. *American Journal of Medical Genetics* 2 (1978): 175–190.
Wartenfeld, Robert, Eliahu Golomb, Giora Katz, et al. Molecular analysis of cystinuria in Libyan Jews: Exclusion of the SLC3A1 gene and mapping of a new locus on 19q. *American Journal of Human Genetics* 60 (1997): 617–624.
Weinberger, A., O. Sperling, M. Rabinovitz, et al. High frequency of cystinuria among Jews of Libyan origin. *Human Heredity* 24 (1974): 568–572.

Essential Pentosuria

Essential pentosuria refers to a condition in which a sugar called pentose l-xylose is excreted into the urine each day. Although abnormal, this condition has no damaging effects associated with it. It occurs, however, almost exclusively in Ashkenazi Jews and those of Lebanese ancestry.

Symptoms

There are no physical symptoms associated with the disorder. The main complication is that the presence of pentose may be confused with glucose and result in a mistaken diagnosis of diabetes mellitus.

Frequency

Essential pentosuria occurs almost exclusively in Ashkenazi Jews, especially those from Poland and Russia, although it has also been found among non–Jewish Lebanese. The incidence among American Jews is estimated at between 1 and 2,000 to 2,5000. Carrier frequency is estimated at 2 per 100.

CAUSE

Essential pentosuria is the result of a deficiency in the enzyme l-xylulose reductase in red blood cells. As a result, the sugar l-xylulose is not rapidly broken down to xylitol, so that l-xylulose attains very high concentrations in urine and blood. Since only people of Ashkenazi and Lebanese descent have this anomaly, medical geneticists speculate that the mutation which gave rise to it originated 2,000 years ago, prior to the Diaspora.

DIAGNOSIS

Since urine is routinely tested for the presence of glucose as an indication of diabetes mellitus, the presence of pentose-1-xylose, which belongs to the same family as glucose, may be mistaken for glucose and diabetes and if so, could result in inappropriate dietary and insulin therapy. However, diabetes has a number of easily recognizable features (for example, thirst, hunger, frequent urination, weight loss) that are totally absent from essential pentosuria. If suspected, it can easily be distinguished from glucose if the proper test is performed.

TREATMENT AND PREVENTION

Since this is a totally unproblematic disorder, no treatment is necessary.

REFERENCES

Goodman, Richard. *Genetic Disorders among the Jewish People*. Baltimore: Johns Hopkins University Press, 1979, 378–380.
Hiatt, Howard H. "Pentosuria." In: Scriver, Charles, Arthur L. Beaudet, William S. Sly, et al., eds. *The Metabolic and Molecular Bases of Inherited Disease*. New York: McGraw-Hill, 1995, 1001–1014.
Lane, B., and T. Jenkins. Human l-xylulose reductase variation: family and population studies. *Annals of Human Genetics* 49 (1985): 227–235.

Familial Hypercholesterolemia

Heart disease, also called coronary heart disease, is America's number one killer for people 35 or older. After the age of 45, you are four times more likely to die of a heart attack than you were at 35. At 55, the probability rises to 15 times; at 65, it jumps to 35 times; and if you live to 75 or more, it's 100 times higher. Few children or teenagers die of heart attacks—unless they have Familial Hypercholesterolemia.

Heart disease is a general term for a number of disorders affecting the circulatory system, but in most cases it refers to a disorder, usually a blockage, that develops in the arteries that supply blood and oxygen to the heart. One of the substances that causes or contributes to such blockages is cholesterol.

Cholesterol is a soft, waxy substance that is classified as a lipid, which also refers to fat, but they are actually not the same. The term lipid covers a variety of different compounds that are linked, not by their function, but by the fact that they are not soluble in water. Although cholesterol is a lipid, it is unlike other lipids in that it does act as a source of energy for metabolism; but it is like other lipids in being insoluble in water. Instead of providing energy, the body uses cholesterol as part of its cellular framework and as a precursor for some of its hormones. For instance, cholesterol is an integral part of cell membranes and myelin, the insulating sheaths around many nerves. Cholesterol is also the substance out of which the body makes its sex and adrenal hormones, and it is also a major constituent in the bile acids used in digestion. The human body cannot function without cholesterol. We get some cholesterol from the foods we eat, but most of the body's cholesterol comes from the liver, which manufactures about 1000 milligrams of it every day and releases it into the blood for incorporation into cells elsewhere. What is not used normally returns to the liver and is broken down and eliminated.

Since cholesterol is essential to health, cells in the body make their own cholesterol. How much they make depends on how much they receive from the blood. This in turn depends on diet and liver function. When levels are low, cells increase their cholesterol production. If we eat foods that contain high levels of cholesterol like meat, cheese and butter, cells don't need to produce their own. In people whose regulating mechanism is adversely affected, cholesterol levels may be much higher than normal, not because of increased cholesterol synthesis in the liver, but because of a genetically related inhibition of its absorption by the body's cells. As a result, cholesterol levels build-up in the blood, a condition that increases the risk of a heart attack and stroke. One of the hereditary conditions that results in very high cholesterol levels in blood is called Familial Hypercholesterolemia (FH). The disorder results from a gene mutation which occurs with a higher frequency in Ashkenazi Jews, especially those whose ancestry is Lithuanian, than in the general population.

VARIATIONS

There are two variations of the disorder, usually described as "severe" and "milder." The disorder itself is the same, but as the defining terms indicate, differs in degree.

FREQUENCY

Familial Hypercholesterolemia is one of the most commonly occurring genetic disorders, with a worldwide estimated prevalence for the less severe form of about 1 in every 500. The estimated frequency for the severe form is a much lower 1 per million. This low frequency is due to the fact that people with the severe form often die before they have children. In some populations such as Jewish Ashkenazis, Turks, Christian Lebanese, French Canadians, Puerto Ricans, and Afrikaners, the prevalence is believed to be much higher. About 35 percent of Jewish Ashkenazi patients in Israel with Familial Hypercholesterolemia have one of the gene mutations that results in the disease; Sephardic Jews living in Northern Israel have a unique "Sephardic mutation" in the same gene which differs from the kind affecting Ashkenazi Jews.

SYMPTOMS

The most visible symptoms of Familial Hypercholesterolemia are hard orange-yellowish bumps under the skin, called xanthomas (zanthomas). These bumps (typically in the webbing between the fingers, over the knuckles, on the back and buttocks, on the elbows, around the Achilles tendon in the heel, and even on the eyelids) may be observable at birth and are nearly always observable by four years of age for those with the severest form of the disorder, and usually by the 20s for those with the milder form. However, the reason people with Familial Hypercholesterolemia first seek medical treatment is the arthritic-like symptoms connected with the disease, especially the tenderness and swelling in the hands and feet every 10 to 14 days.

People with severe Familial Hypercholesterolemia develop coronary heart disease between 10 and 20 years of age. The severe form results if someone has two defective genes for the disorder. Those who have only one defective gene have a less severe form, but they too are likely to develop coronary heart disease at an early age and to experience at least one heart attack by age 40 in men and age 50 in women, and nearly all with Familial Hypercholesterolemia have had at least one heart attack by age 65.

CAUSE

Familial Hypocholesterolemia is an autosomal dominant disorder. This means that it is necessary to inherit only one of the defective genes for the disorder to develop its symptoms. People who have only one of these defective genes develop its less severe form. Those who inherit two defective genes develop its more severe form. The consequence of inheriting one or two of these defective genes is a decrease or an absence of a receptor, akin to a passageway on the surface of cells, that enables cholesterol to enter them.

Lipids like cholesterol are oily. That means they don't dissolve in blood. Therefore, to move them through the blood stream they have to be packaged in specialized transporting substances, called lipoproteins. Lipoproteins are large molecules capable of combining lipids and complex proteins called apoproteins. The main lipoprotein transporter that carries cholesterol to the cells of the body and enables it to enter through the receptor passageways is called low-density liporotein (LDL). If the receptor passageway is missing or inoperative, the LDL and its cholesterol cannot enter in the normal manner. People with one defective gene for the disorder have only half the normal amount of receptors. The result is that LDL enters cells at half the normal rate and this results in a doubling of normal levels of LDL cholesterol levels in the blood. Those who have two defective genes for the disorder have no functioning receptors and their LDL cholesterol levels increase fourfold. Although the absence of LDL receptors keeps most of it from entering cells, when LDL levels are very high, some of it is still able to enter cells by an LDL receptor independent pathway, so cells are never completely devoid of cholesterol.

The first stage in cholesterol transport and utilization involves its absorption from the intestine by a class of lipoproteins called chylomicrons. These lipoproteins primarily contain triglycerides, but they also contain some cholesterol. After they deliver their triglycerides to cells throughout the body, where they are used for energy or stored for future energy use, the chylomicrons break down and form a "remnant" which now primarily contains cholesterol. These remnants are removed from the blood by the liver. The cholesterol from the chylomicrons is then repackaged in the liver with more triglycerides in another lipoprotein called very-low-density lipoprotein. When the triglycerides are delivered to their cellular locations and removed, the very-low-density lipoprotein (VLDL) also forms a "remnant" and returns to the liver, where it is broken down and then combined with a specific apolipoprotein called apolipoprotein B, which transforms the very-low-density lipoprotein into a cholesterol-rich low-density lipoprotein. LDL is then sent into the blood to cells and is removed from the blood through the interaction between the apoB portion of the lipoprotein and the LDL receptor on the cell membrane's surface.

After cholesterol is released back into the blood from dying cells or because it is not needed, it is picked up by another lipoprotein called high-density lipoprotein (HDL), which carries it back to the liver where it is either recirculated or sent to the intestine for elimination.

Since LDLs increase the risk of heart disease and HDLs decrease it, the former are sometimes called "lousy" or "bad" cholesterol while the latter are called "healthy" or "good" cholesterol.

In Familial Hypercholesterolemia the receptor on the surface of cells, to which the LDL ordinarily binds, is either missing or nonfunctional. There are several different kinds of mutations responsible for these abnormalities. One mutation causes the cell not to produce the receptor that LDL binds to, thereby preventing LDL from entering the cell. In another mutation the receptor is produced, but it doesn't get to the cell membrane, making it the functional equivalent of not having a receptor at all. A third mutation causes the receptor to be formed incorrectly so that LDL cannot lock onto it. A fourth mutation interferes with the cell's ability to transport the LDL molecule into the cell after it has bound to its receptor. Different ethnic groups have different mutations. One such mutation is responsible for about a third of all cases of the disorder in Ashkenazi Jews and is not found in non–Ashkenazis with the disorder. Interestingly, more than half of the Ashkenazis with the mutation are of Lithuanian origin.

Regardless of the nature of the receptor problem, Familial Hypercholesterolemia results in a very high elevation of LDL and free cholesterol in the blood and its subsequent deposition into various tissues. The characteristic xanthomas (bumps of cholesterol) in the skin and tendons result from these abnormal deposits. More dangerous are the deposits of cholesterol in the arteries ("atheromas") which result in plaques, hardening of the arteries, heart attacks and strokes.

The initial step in the origin of heart attacks is believed to be a tiny break in the interior surface of an artery. This damage is believed to trigger a cascade of events involving LDL and cholesterol that result in the artery becoming blocked.

The reason the initial damage occurs is unknown, but once it does, it attracts the debris from LDL that has been attacked or "oxidized" by highly reactive compounds called free radicals in the blood. A free radical is a molecule that is missing one of its electrons. This makes them very reactive because the molecule will attack any substance to steal an electron to make up its loss.

Free radicals are constantly being produced in the body, so oxidative damage goes on all the time, not only for LDL but for all parts of the body. However, if blood contains an increased amount of LDL, there are more opportunities for free radicals to attack it. When this happens, LDLs become stickier and this increases their tendency to form plaques. At the same time, the immune system is turned on by the presence of oxidized LDL. Whereas nonoxidized LDL is recognized as part of the body, oxidized LDL is not, and to protect the body from this potential invasion, the immune system's scavenger cells, the macrophages (the same cells that are involved in Gaucher Disease), engulf the oxidized LDL. These enlarged macrophages, however, often become trapped in the tiny crevices of damaged arterial walls and in so doing, they also reduce blood flow.

When the macrophages build up in the walls of the arteries that bring blood to the heart and brain, they may also combine with other substances in the blood, like calcium, to form a thick, hard deposit called a plaque. As they grow on the arterial wall, these plaques narrow the arterial passageway and in so doing, further block blood flow. The build up of plaques within an artery's walls is called atherosclerosis, which literally means "hardening of the arteries."

Ordinarily, the walls of our arteries are flexible and strong. This flexibility and strength enables them to expand or contract in response to pressure changes inside them that are produced when the heart contracts and relaxes. By hardening arterial walls, plaques narrow their passageways and reduce their flexibility, thereby increasing the pressure inside the artery. This increase in arterial pressure is called hypertension. When the plaques increase in size to the point that they begin to block blood flow, they may cause a kind of chest pain called angina. If the inside of an artery becomes very narrow, or a break occurs in the lining and blood seeps out, blood is no longer able to flow through it to an organ and it may become damaged. The most common areas where these build-ups and breakages occur is in the coronary arteries, the arteries in the brain and kidneys, and the arteries in the legs. Since the smaller arteries are the weakest, they often break first from the pressure inside them. A clot (called a thrombus) can also break away from these plaques and block the flow of blood somewhere else.

When the blood supply to the heart is cut off, it is called a heart attack or myocardial infarction. When the brain is cut off from its blood supply, it is called a stroke. If the heart can still beat with an orderly rhythm, the chances of recovery are good. Recovery is possible because our bodies are often able to reroute blood through other vessels around blocked arteries. However, if the large branch of the artery supplying the heart becomes blocked, many heart cells will die and then the heart may no longer be able to beat rhythmically. Instead, it beats with an irregular rhythm, a condition called fibrillation. When fibrillation occurs, the heart loses its power to pump blood through the body. Without blood, body organs don't get the oxygen they need. When that happens they stop working and we die.

TRANSMISSION

Familial Hypercholesterolemia is an autosomal dominant disease caused by as many as 200 different mutations in the gene for the low-density lipoprotein receptor. Since it is a dominant disorder, inheriting only one defective gene will result in the disorder; inheriting two defective genes increases its severity. If someone inherits the severe form, both parents will probably have the milder form. In the latter case, when both parents are heterozygotes, their children have a 1 in 4 chance of inheriting the severe form, that is, the defective gene from each parent, and a 1 in 2 chance of inheriting only one defective gene from one of their parents. The fact that this disorder has its highest frequency in countries and communities that have relatively isolated populations like the Afrikaners in South Africa, the French Canadians, the Christian Lebanese, and the Jews, implies it is due to a founder effect which has occurred independently in these groups.

DIAGNOSIS

A doctor may suspect Familial Hypercholesterolemia on the basis of the yellow-orange nodules and a family history of the disease. This suspicion can be confirmed by measuring total blood cholesterol levels, which are often as high as 1000 mg/dl, and LDL levels which are often as high as 900 mg/dl in the severe form of the disorder (normal levels are 200 and 45 mg/dl respectively).

According to the American Heart Association, levels of 250 mg/dl and above increase the risk of a heart attack as much as three times compared to levels below 200 mg/dl. However, the risk is much higher when these high levels occur in younger people.

A definitive test involves determining if the LDL receptors are decreased or nonfunctioning. To do this, a tiny piece of an individual's skin is taken and grown in a special culture that stimulates LDL receptors. LDL cholesterol is then taken from a donor, made radioactive, and then added to the medium containing the suspect cells. If there are no cells, there will be very little binding to the cells.

TREATMENT

Hardening of the arteries begins almost from the moment we are born. Usually the rate of hardening is very slow, but the older we get, the more our arteries become hardened. Once arteries becomes hardened, there is no way to unharden them. While the condition cannot be improved, its progress can be delayed or kept from worsening.

One way of reducing the amount of cholesterol in the blood is by avoiding foods like meat and cheese that contain high levels of cholesterol. But in the case of Familial Hypercholesterolemia, the problem is the absence of receptors for LDL, and treatment is directed not only at reducing cholesterol intake and removing cholesterol from the blood, but also at increasing LDL receptors on cells. Three different types of medication are currently being prescribed to do this. One type called "statins" or HMGCoA reductase inhibitors, such as Lipitor, Mevacor and Zocor, lower cholesterol levels by interfering with its production. A second type are a class of drugs known as bile acid sequestrants such as Questran and Colestid. The third type is not a drug but a vitamin, niacin.

A more radical form of treatment is a liver transplant. Since the liver is the main organ in the body responsible for producing and removing cholesterol, the aim of transplantion is to provide a new organ that contains LDL receptors which will then be able to remove LDL from the blood.

PREVENTION

A heart attack due to increased cholesterol levels may be preventable by medication. All relatives of anyone with Familial Hypercholesterolemia should have their cholesterol levels regularly tested, even in early childhood.

FOR FURTHER INFORMATION

Medped
University of Utah
410 Chipeta Way, Room 167
Salt Lake City, UT 84108
TELEPHONE: 1-800-244-2465
FAX: 1-801-581-5402

References

Books
Kwiterovich, Peter O. *Beyond Cholesterol. The Johns Hopkins Complete Guide for Avoiding Heart Disease.* Baltimore: Johns Hopkins University Press, 1989.

Journal Articles
Goldstein, Joseph L., Helen H. Hobbs, and Michael S. Brown. "Familial Hyper-cholesterolemia." In: Scriver, Charles R., Arthur L. Beaudet, William S. Sly, et al., eds. *The Metabolic Basis of Inherited Disease.* New York: McGraw-Hill, 1995, 1981-2030.

Meiner, Vardiella, Daniel Landsberger, Neville Berkman, et al. A common Lithuanian mutation causing Familial hypercholesterolemia in Ashkenazi Jews. *American Journal of Human Genetics* 49 (1991) 443–449.

Reshef, Ayeleth, Henrik Niesen, Liat Triger, et al. Molecular genetics of Famil-ial Hypercholesterolemia in Israel. *Human Genetics* 98 (1996): 581–586.

Westhuyzen, D. R. A common Lithuanian mutation causing Familial Hyperc-holesterolemia in Ashkenazi Jews. *American Journal of Human Genetics* 49 (1991): 443–449.

Familial Hyperinsulinism

Familial Hyperinsulinism (also called persistent hyperinsulinemic hypoglycemia of infancy and pancreatic nesidioblastosis) is a disorder that is the opposite of diabetes. In diabetes, levels of the blood sugar glucose become very high due to a defect in the pancreas. The pancrease produces and secretes insulin, the hormone that enables glucose to enter cells. When the pancreas does not produce enough insulin, glucose does not enter cells and remains in the blood and is excreted in urine. Since glucose is the fuel cells use to perform their intricate operations, its inability to enter cells undermines their ability to function. As a result, cells die and tis-sues and organs falter.

In hyperinsulinism just the opposite occurs in the pancreas. Instead of producing too little, the pancreas is in overdrive and secretes too much insulin; therefore, blood glucose levels remain very low, causing a condi-tion called hypoglycemia.

Variations

There are two basic variations of the disorder, a "serious" variation that manifests itself soon after birth and a "mild" variation that doesn't make its effects until several weeks or months later.

FREQUENCY

The prevalence of Familial Hyperinsulinism in the general population is estimated at about 1 in 50,000, although in some populations, like Finland, it is 1 in 3,200. The incidence among Jews is still unknown, but carrier frequency among Ashkenazi Jews is a relatively high 1 in 100.

SYMPTOMS

Symptoms of neonatal hypoglycemia become readily observable soon after birth. Babies are born with reserves of glucose, but once those are used up, the babies begin to exhibit signs of low blood glucose such as a high pitched cry, low body temperature, poor feeding, tremors, irritability, lethargy, pallor, difficulty breathing, sweating, chills, seizures, and even death. All of these symptoms are typically seen in hypoglycemia, regardless of its cause. Although about 50 percent of all cases of persistent infantile hypoglycemia are due to Familial Hyperinsulinism, there are many conditions that can cause hypoglycemia, so that a correct diagnosis may not be straightforward. However, hypoglycemia can cause brain damage, so it is important to determine the cause as soon as possible.

CAUSE

The sugar you sweeten coffee with is sucrose. Glucose is another form of sugar. The sugar in blood, which is used by every cell in the body to make energy, is glucose. Blood glucose levels are maintained within a narrow range of between 80 and 120 milligrams per 100 cubic centimeter of blood.

Glucose is unable to enter cells without the help of insulin, a hormone produced by the pancreas. If there is too much insulin, too much glucose enters cells and glucose levels in the blood fall below normal, a condition called hypoglycemia. Too little insulin results in the opposite: not enough glucose enters cells and glucose levels in the blood become excessive, a condition called hyperglycemia. Hyperglycemia is the main correlate of diabetes mellitus.

Because glucose is so essential to cellular function, cells take up excess glucose from the blood and store it as glycogen for future needs, mostly in the liver and muscles. The pathway in the storage process involves a large number of different enzymes.

The cause of Familial Hyperinsulinism is uncontrolled production and secretion of insulin by the pancreas due to a disorder in its sulfonylurea receptors, which regulate glucose levels in the blood. Since the brain cannot be deprived of blood glucose, even for a brief moment, without upsetting its intricate mechanism, symptoms appear almost immediately and require immediate treatment to raise blood glucose.

There are several known causes of hyperinsulinism including cancer, noncancerous tumors, and Familial Hyperinsulinism, the hereditary type which primarily affects Ashkenazi Jews. In the early 1990s, Familial Hyperinsulinism was traced to a particular area on chromosome 11 for Ashkenazi Jews. Subsequently, two genes on this chromosome have been associated with the disorder. A mutation called phe1388del, which is found only in the sulfonylurea SUR1 gene of Ashkenazi Jews, is responsible for 88 percent of all such cases in this group. A second mutation, called 3992-9G-to-A is present in both Ashkenazis and non–Jews. The mutation appears to have originated independently in two different founders.

DIAGNOSIS

Diagnosis is based on testing the blood for glucose and insulin. A high insulin level coupled with low blood glucose is usually diagnostic of the disorder. However, in some cases insulin levels are not as high as might be suspected in the condition, so that diagnosis may be difficult.

TREATMENT

Immediate treatment involves intravenous administration of dextrose, a sugar similar to glucose, followed by drugs such as diazoxide and octreotide which inhibit the release of insulin from the pancreas.

In cases of severe hyperinsulinism, the only alternative is complete or partial removal of the pancreas, as soon as possible in an infant's life. If the operation is delayed, permanent damage to the brain or other organs may occur.

Following surgery, most infants progress well. Most require minimal further treatment, although in some cases additional treatments may be required.

PREVENTION

No prevention is available. Since the newborn brain is very dependent on glucose, keeping glucose levels normal is very important for preventing brain damage.

REFERENCES

Araricio, L., M.W. Carpenter, R. Schwartz, et al. Prenatal diagnosis of familial neonatal hyperinsulinemia. *Acta Pediatrica* 82 (1993): 683–686.

Aynsley-Green, A., J.M. Polak, S.R. Bloom, et al. Nesidioblastosis of the pancreas: definition of the syndrome and the management of the severe neonatal hyperinsulinaemic hypoglycaemia. *Archives of Diseases of Children* 56 (1981) 496–508.

Glaser, B., K.C. Chiu, R. Anker, et al. Familial hyperinsulinism maps to chromosome 11p14-15.1, 30 cM centromeric to the insulin gene. *Nature Genetics* 7 (1994): 185–188.

Glaser, B., K.C. Chiu, L. Liu, et al. Recombinant mapping of the familial hyperinsulinism gene to an 0.8 cM region on chromosome 11p15.1 and demonstration of a founder effect in Ashkenazi Jews. *Human Molecular Genetics* 4 (1995): 879–886.

Glaser, B., J. Furth, C.A. Stanley, et al. Intragenic single nucleotide polymorphism haplotype analysis of SUR1 mutations in familial hyperinsulinism. *Human Mutation* 14 (1999): 23–29.

Glaser, B., P.S. Thornton, K. Herold, et al. Clinical and molecular heterogeneity of familial hyperinsulinism. *Journal of Pediatrics* 133 (1998): 801–802.

Meissner, T., B. Beinbrech, and E. Mayatepek. Congenital hyperinsulinism: molecular basis of atherogeneous disease. *Human Mutation* 13 (1999): 351–361.

Nestorowicz, A., B.A. Wilson, K.P. Schoor, et al. Mutations in the sulfonylurea receptor gene are associated with familial hyperinsulinism in Ashkenazi Jews. *Human Molecular Genetics* 5 (1996): 1813–1822.

Tarui Disease

Tarui Disease (TD), named after Dr. S. Tarui, who described its symptoms in 1965, affects fewer than 200,000 persons; but despite its rarity, it occurs much more often in Ashkenazi Jews than in the general population.

SYMPTOMS

Tarui Disease primarily affects people when they exercise. The main symptom is painful cramping muscle pain. Low intensity activities can often be performed without any symptoms, but more intense activities like pushing or lifting heavy objects, jogging, playing tennis, or swimming often cause tiredness and muscle cramps. Besides these symptoms, people with Tarui Disease also experience nausea and vomiting when they exert themselves.

The symptoms of Tarui Disease usually begin in early childhood during play, when children, for some reason nearly all boys, become easily fatigued; they are especially unable to hold their own in running games. Often their legs feel heavy and ache, and they may feel nauseous and feverish. Arms and hands are affected less often but repetitive activities like practicing piano lessons can cause aching and muscle cramping.

Rough and tumble games can cause severe cramping and muscle deterioration. While these symptoms often begin in childhood, in some cases they may not begin to occur until 60 years of age when climbing stairs or getting out of low chairs.

The severity of symptoms is not the same in every individual, and even within families, one sibling with the disease may experience mild fatigue whereas another may experience severe muscle weakness and hemolysis.

Other common symptoms include bouts of gouty arthritis and gallstones which can be so severe that the gall bladder has to be removed.

FREQUENCY

Tarui Disease affects fewer than 200,000 Americans. Since the symptoms are very mild in some people, they may not even know they have the disease. Although proportionately more Ashkenazi Jews are affected than the general population, there are no estimates of its frequency in either the general population or among Ashkenazi Jews. Most of the Ashkenazi Jews with Tarui Disease, however, have ancestors who came from Russia or Poland. Interestingly, Tarui Disease also occurs much more often in people of Japanese, Swedish, and French Canadian descent as well.

CAUSE

Every living things needs a source of energy to work. For cells, including muscle cells, the usual source of energy is carbohydrates in the form of glucose taken up from the blood or glycogen, which is a stored form of glucose in the cell. When we exercise, our cells first break down their glycogen stores into glucose. Once these are used up, they turn to blood glucose.

The conversion of glucose into energy involves many different chemical reactions which are catalysed by enzymes. A genetic defect leading to a missing enzyme or one whose activity is impeded can shut the energy producing mechanism down. This is what happens in Tarui Disease, which is also called glucogenosis Type VII.

Tarui Disease is due to a mutation in the genes that control the production of an enzyme called phosphofructokinase, usually abbreviated as PFK, which enables cells to break down glucose to get their energy. Fifteen different mutations affecting this gene have now been identified; two of these mutations are especially prevalent in Ashkenazi Jews with the disease. Because of the absence of PKF in muscle cells, they are unable to get the energy they need to function, resulting in cramping and a breakdown in the cell's machinery. This breakdown results in a loss of enzymes and other components, especially myoglobin, a protein that normally transfers oxygen from the cell membrane into the interior. Myoglobin and these other cell components then enter the blood and are excreted in the urine. The presence of myoglobin in urine is called myoglobinuria, and it causes urine to appear pale brown and even black.

In Tarui Disease, PFK is totally absent in muscles but oddly, is only partially missing in red blood cells. This anomaly occurs because there are at least three different genes that determine the structure of the enzyme. Despite the presence of some PFK in red blood cells, however, exercise still causes them to break down. This "hemolysis" can in turn result in an increase in bilirubin, a breakdown product of hemoglobin. The increased bilirubin, called hyperbilirubinemia, causes the yellowish skin associated with jaundice. However, it is not the yellowish skin color that is dangerous, but the brain damage that hyperbilirubinemia causes makes this a medical emergency.

DIAGNOSIS

The diagnosis of Tarui Disease is based on its main symptoms of exercise intolerance, muscle cramping, the absence of lactate (a byproduct of glucose metabolism) after exercise, myoglobinuria, and hemolysis. A conclusive diagnosis can be made by measuring PFK enzyme levels in a biopsy of skeletal muscle. Since there is no PFK, there is also an elevated amount of glycogen in muscle fibers.

TRANSMISSION

Tarui Disease is an autosomal recessive genetic defect. This means that both parents have to be carriers for the disorder to occur in their children. Although men and women are equally susceptible, for reasons yet unknown some symptoms such as marked hemolysis and elevated uric acid have only been seen in men.

TREATMENT

There are no effective treatments to correct the PFK deficiency responsible for Tarui Disease. Most people cope by reducing their exercise levels so that they do not strain themselves.

PREVENTION

Since only two mutations are responsible for nearly all the cases of Tarui Disease in Ashkenazi Jews, Dr. Jeffrey Sherman of the National Institute of Arthritis, a Division of the National Institutes of Health, believes it should be possible to develop a rapid screening procedure for Ashkenazi patients with suspected PFK. This would also enable doctors to diagnose the disease without having to perform a painful muscle biopsy. However, this test has not yet been developed.

SCREENING CENTERS

Athena Diagnostics

Children's Hospital of Buffalo, Biochemical Genetics Laboratory

Columbia-Presbyterian Medical
Center, Mitochrondrial and
Glycogen Disorder Laboratory

Duke University Medical Center,
Glycogen Storage Disease Laboratory

REFERENCES

Raben, N., and J.B. Sherman. Mutations in muscle phosphofructokinase gene. *Human Mutations* 6 (1995): 1–6.

Raben, N., J.B. Sherman, E. Adams, et al. Various classes of mutations in patients with phosphofructokinase deficiency (Tarui's Disease). *Muscle and Nerve* 3 (1995) S35–38.

Sherman, Jeffrey B., Nina Raben, Catherine Nicastri, et al. Common mutations in the phosphofructokinase-M gene in Ashkenazi Jewish patients with glyocogenesis VII—and their population frequency. *American Journal of Human Genetics* 55 (1994): 305–313.

CHAPTER NINE

Respiratory Disorders

When we breathe, we inhale air and exhale carbon dioxide. The part of the body which enables us to do this is the respiratory system, which is roughly divided into two sections, the upper and lower airways. The upper airway consists of the passageways that carry air into and out of the lungs. When we inhale, we take air into either our noses or mouths. From there, it enters the conducting passages, first the throat (called the pharynx), then down the voice box (called the larynx) and into the windpipe (the trachea). The trachea branches into two smaller tubes called the bronchi (singular bronchus) which go to each lung. Inside the lung, each bronchus in turn branches into smaller tubes called secondary bronchi, and these in turn branch into even smaller tubes called bronchioles. The bronchioles again branch out and become even smaller passageways. Eventually the passageways end in tiny air sacs inside the lungs.

The lungs are hollow structures in the chest cavity, where the exchange of oxygen and carbon dioxide actually takes place. Each lung is somewhat different from the other; the right lung has three lobules whereas the left lung only has two. Each lung contains millions of alveoli sacs. When we inhale, air is forced into these sacs and the oxygen in the air passes into capillaries that line the alveoli sacs. When we exhale, we expel carbon dioxide that the cells have formed and which they have passed back into the blood. The blood carries it back to the lungs and then we expel it from our lungs into the air.

The bronchioles and the lungs are more than just tubes. Air is filled with dust, pollen, bacteria, chemicals, etc., that are potentially damaging to the body should they enter the blood. To keep this from happening, these passageways contain dozens of different types of cells that shield the body from disease. Some of these cells, called epithelial, become defective in disorders like cystic fibrosis and do not develop ducts through which chemicals like sodium and potassium are able to pass. The end result is that the thin slippery viscous mucus that also lines the surface of these cells become thicker and clogs the passageways. When this occurs in the airways, breathing becomes more difficult and the bacteria that become trapped result in recurrent infections.

Cystic Fibrosis

Cystic fibrosis is the most common hereditary disorder among Caucasians in America. It is not, therefore, specifically a Jewish disorder, nor is it due to a single mutation. Although a single gene is involved, more than 700 disease-causing mutations in the cystic fibrosis gene have been discovered. However, one of these mutations accounts for almost 50 percent of all Jewish cystic fibrosis cases, and since it along with three others account for almost all such cases, cystic fibrosis is included here as a "Jewish disorder."

VARIATIONS

The most common symptoms of cystic fibrosis are chronic coughing and wheezing, frequent infections, especially pneumonia, foul-smelling stools, and a "salty" sweat. While the same pattern of symptoms is nearly always seen in everyone with cystic fibrosis, since there are hundreds of different mutations affecting the gene responsible for the disease, it is not surprising there are wide variations in terms of how severely different bodily organs are involved, and in life expectancy. In some cases, for instance, the pancreas is unaffected; in others susceptibility to infection is not affected; and in still others, the sweat and lung problems are relatively mild and the pancreas is most severely affected. The type and severity of symptoms depend on which form of the mutation is present.

For some people, symptoms are so mild they are not diagnosed until they reach middle age, although this is relatively uncommon.

FREQUENCY

About 1,000 new cases of cystic fibrosis are diagnosed each year. The frequency of the disorder in the general American population and the Jewish Ashkenazi population are about the same: 1 in 2,500 to 3,300. The carrier status frequency is likewise a similar 1 in 25 for both. This means that about 10 million Americans are symptomless carriers of one of the defective genes for cystic fibrosis. The difference between Jews and non–Jews lies in the different forms of their mutations in these two groups. The mutations most common among Jews are associated with severe pancreatic disturbances whereas breathing difficulties are relatively mild.

Although Ashkenazi Jews have the same prevalence of cystic fibrosis as do non–Jews, the mutations causing the disease among Ashkenazi, Sephardic and Oriental Jews differ, as does the frequency of its occurrence. Ashkenazi Jews and non–Ashkenazi Jews from Tunisia, Libya, Turkey and Georgia have an incidence of 1 in 2,500 to 3,200, whereas Jews from Yemen have a much lower incidence of 1 in 8,800, and Oriental Jews from Iraq have the lowest incidence (1 in 332,000).

SYMPTOMS

The main symptoms of cystic fibrosis are persistent wheezing or chronic coughing which often brings up dark green phlegm; weight loss despite ravenous hunger; growth retardation, digestive disturbances; bulky, foul-smelling stools; repeated episodes of pneumonia; and a skin that tastes very salty.

Although the individual symptoms of the disorder have been recognized for a long time, it was not until 1938 that doctors realized that they were collectively part of a syndrome and began to suspect that this syndrome was due to a single cause. The breakthrough came about as a result of studies by Dr. Dorothy Andersen, a pathologist at Columbia University. After examining the dead bodies of 49 children, some of them as young as three days of age, Dr. Andersen found a common link between them: every one had dark patches of scar tissue in the pancreas (the organ in the body that produces insulin and digestive enzymes). On the basis of this common link, she called the condition "cystic fibrosis of the pancreas."

Although all of the children had this scarring in their pancreases, several of the youngest infants had not died of pancreatic disease but because of lung disease from bacterial infection. At the time Dr. Andersen did not understand how the problem in the pancreas was related to the lung disease, but her seminal discovery led to further study until the common link was finally discovered.

CAUSE

The immediate cause of cystic fibrosis is the absence of a protein that functions as a channel in cell membranes, enabling the transport of particles called ions into and out of these cells. The missing protein is due to an abnormality in a single gene, called the cystic fibrosis transmembrane-conductance regulator gene, whose existence was only discovered in 1989.

Ions are electrically charged particles like chloride that combine with other electrically charged particles like sodium to form chemical compounds like sodium chloride. Better known as table salt, sodium chloride affects the movement of water in and out of cells. The basic problem in cystic fibrosis is that the chloride can't get into cells because its entry channel is impaired. Since chloride can't get into the cell, it remains outside along with sodium and the two combine to form the salty taste on the outside of the skin. The high level of salt in the sweat has little clinical importance except in hot weather or during intense exercise. When an excessive amount of salt is lost from the body, the resulting low levels of sodium and chloride in the blood can cause shock and heart arrhythmias.

The build-up of thick dehydrated mucus in the airways results in two serious problems. One is that the bronchial tubes become clogged so that air can no longer enter and leave easily. Because breathing involves using muscles in our chest, it's possible for someone with cystic fibrosis to get air into the lungs by breathing. The labored breathing is heard as wheezing. The harsh paroxysmal coughing is an attempt to dislodge the mucus, which comes up as thick green phlegm. The greenish color is due to the present of a specific bacteria called *Pseudomonas aeruginosa*. Since there are no comparable muscles for blowing air out of the lungs (when we exhale, we basically relax the muscles we use for breathing in), air inside the lungs can't get out. When it builds up, it causes the lungs to swell with stale air that has no oxygen, and eventually suffocation can occur.

The second problem affecting the respiratory system is infection. Ordinarily, mucus traps bacteria before it can cause problems. In fact, when the airways detect airborne pathogens in mucus, they secrete more mucus. The lungs also secrete immune factors to destroy these pathogens before they can get through the mucus to the underlying cells. But when mucus becomes very thick, as it does in cystic fibrosis, the immune factors also can't get through the mucus to the pathogens. Instead, the thick mucus becomes a good resting and growing place for bacteria and other disease-causing agents in the air, resulting in infectious diseases like pneumonia.

Even though immune factors can't get at the entrenched pathogens, they nevertheless continue trying and these attempts result in inflammation. Unchecked, inflammation can harm healthy cells. This is why inflammation reactions usually last only a short time; the immune cells destroy the infection and then vacate the area, leaving behind other chemicals that help the damaged area to heal. But when inflammation lasts for a long time, healthy cells are damaged. Not only is their function lost, they wind up in the mucus thereby making it even thicker. The thickened mucus adds to the clogging so that eventually no air can get into the lungs.

Similar reactions occur in other duct-bearing glands like the pancreas. The pancreas produces insulin and glucagon, hormones that regulate blood sugar levels, and they also produce enzymes involved in digestion. Although insulin and glucagon are eventually affected, cystic fibrosis first attacks the ducts through which the pancreas secretes its digestive enzymes. As a result, the digestive enzymes can't reach the intestine, and this prevents nutrients from being absorbed into the body.

The characteristic weight loss, hunger, and digestive disturbances are related to the blockage of digestive enzymes from the pancreas. The pancreas lies just below the stomach, near the intestine, and ordinarily secretes enzymes such as trypsin, amylase and lipase that enable fats and protein to be broken down and absorbed from the intestine. When the tiny pancreatic ducts are blocked, these enzymes are kept from entering the intestine. As a result, food passing through the intestine is not completely digested and much of its nutritional value is lost.

As a result of the inability to absorb fats, fat-soluble vitamins like vitamins A, D, E and K are also not absorbed, and this results in delayed bone growth, poor blood clotting, and delayed sexual development. The inability to absorb food accounts for the failure to thrive and also results in the distended abdomen characteristic of the disease. Other effects related to this malabsorption are constant hunger, abdominal pain due to a build-up of gas from incompletely digested food, chronic diarrhea, excretion of bulky, foul smelling stools, and a protrusion (prolapse) of the rectum due to wasting of the supporting tissues in the rectal area.

The accumulating mucus in the pancreas also destroys its internal structure so that it is no longer able to produce insulin. Insulin insufficiency in turn results in the characteristics of diabetes. The build-up of bacteria in the mucus leads to frequent infections, often resulting in pneumonia.

The same accumulation of mucus that destroys the inner structure of the pancreas also destroys the inner structure of the liver, resulting in cirrhosis and portal hypertension.

An early symptom of cystic fibrosis is the failure to excrete meconium, a dark green mucilaginous substance in the intestines of most newborns. The reason for its absence is that the intestinal passage is obstructed. As a result of this obstruction, the child develops a distended abdomen, and frequent vomiting and constipation.

The salty taste of the skin is yet another consequence of clogged passageways. The amount of salt inside our cells is carefully regulated in our bodies. If our cells contain too much salt, they take in water to lower the concentration; too little salt, and cells release water. Cells regulate their water content by pumping chloride ions (usually along with sodium) into or out of their interiors.

Among Ashkenazi Jews, the three most common mutations, accounting for 90 percent of all cases of cystic fibrosis, are G542x (4 percent), Delta F508 (23 percent), and W1282X (60 percent). These mutations primarily affect the pancreas rather than the bronchial tubes. Among Sephardic Jews, the Delta F508 mutation accounts for as much as 35 percent of all cases, whereas the W1282X mutation accounts for only 2 percent. On a worldwide basis, the W1282X mutation is likewise very rare (less than 2 percent).

FAUSTIAN BARGAIN

One of the reasons the cystic fibrosis gene mutation is so common is that it may in some way be involved in a Faustian bargain with Nature. Although cystic fibrosis is a life-threatening disorder, being a carrier confers resistance to a number of diseases like typhoid fever and cholera.

In both typhoid fever and cholera, the resistance comes through the otherwise abnormal channel for transporting chloride ions across cells. Whereas someone with cystic fibrosis has no channels to secrete chloride ions, a carrier for the abnormal gene has either fewer or very small chloride channels. Typhoid fever and cholera are both characterized by chronic diarrhea that can become so severe it can cause death from dehydration. When the bacteria that cause these diseases infect the body, they cause the cells in the intestine to secrete very high levels of chloride and fluid; if unchecked, this fluid loss can cause death. Because of the decreased ability of chloride to leave cells in cystic fibrosis carriers, much less fluid will be secreted in response to typhoid fever and cholera or any other infection that causes chronic diarrhea.

While no longer common in western countries, in the past diseases like typhoid fever and cholera often ran rampant in some communities. So while inheriting two copies of this abnormal gene destined someone to develop cystic fibrosis, inheriting only one protected him or her from contracting typhoid fever. From an evolutionary standpoint, a population carrying around the abnormal gene for cystic fibrosis had a better chance of surviving typhoid fever or cholera than one that didn't. Today, however, being a carrier for this abnormal gene offers no advantage.

DIAGNOSIS

One of the first clues parents have that their baby has cystic fibrosis is that their baby's skin tastes salty when they kiss it. Prior to the advent of modern medicine, midwives would often lick the head of newborn children to see if it had this salty taste; if it had the characteristic salty taste of cystic fibrosis, they would predict that the child would die at an early age because of breathing problems.

If a doctor suspects cystic fibrosis on the basis of the physical symptoms described earlier, he or she will order a "sweat test." For this test, a doctor will administer pilocarpine, a drug that causes sweating, and the salt content of the patient's sweat is measured. An abnormally high level of salt, coupled with the other symptoms of the disease, indicates its presence.

Other tests that may be performed involve testing the fat content in the stools, which is also highly elevated in cystic fibrosis since fat is not absorbed from the intestines. A chest X-ray may also be performed to see if the lungs are obstructed. Other tests may be performed to look for evidence of pancreatic insufficiency.

Following discovery of the cystic fibrosis gene in 1989, it is now possible to detect many of its mutations by means of a blood test. However, there are over 150 known variations of the defective gene that causes cystic fibrosis, so that the current test is capable of detecting only the most common variations.

TREATMENT

Cystic fibrosis is an incurable disease, but improvements in treatment have increased the average life expectancy, from only 14 years in the 1960s to almost 40 years of age in the 1990s. The main treatment depends on the organs that are affected and how seriously they are damaged.

Other than the daily routine treatment needed to keep the lungs clear and to provide missing enzymes and nutrients, children with cystic fibrosis (who have normal intelligence) can lead relatively normal lives with respect to schooling, physical activity, and social interactions for many years. However, as people with cystic fibrosis approach their 20s, they usually develop many more lung infections requiring frequent hospitalization.

The primary concerns in treating cystic fibrosis are keeping the airways clear and alleviating the various other complications of the disease.

The lung obstruction is treated with breathing exercises, postural drainage, and chest physiotherapy which involves striking the back over the area of the lungs with cupped hands to dislodge the mucus inside them. Oxygen therapy also assists breathing.

Drug therapy includes drugs for thinning the mucus in the lungs. One such drug, Pulmozyme, is a genetically engineered form of the human enzyme, Dnase, which is taken by inhalation. Other aerosols taken to loosen secretions may contain TOBI (tobramycin), a drug that also helps thin the mucus secretions and reduces the risk of lung infections. Humidifiers and air conditioners help breathing; oxygen therapy is also used when breathing is difficult.

Infections are treated orally with broad spectrum antibiotics. Serious bouts of infection are treated more aggressively with intravenous administration. Ibuprofen has also been found to decrease the incidence of lung inflammation in children with cystic fibrosis.

Pancreatic enzyme insufficiency in cystic fibrosis is treated by supplements of pancreatic enzymes that provide the missing enzymes.

Since the digestive system is affected, nutritional supplements containing fat soluble vitamins (A, D, E and K) need to be taken to maintain nutritional status. Diets need to be low in fat and high in protein.

Treatment of sweat electrolyte losses involves eating highly salted foods and taking sodium supplements.

Current research is evaluating the feasibility of gene therapy in which an attempt is being made to introduce normal genes to cells in the airways, with the hope that the normal genes will replace the defective ones. The first indication that this is possible occurred in 1990 when research scientists reported that they were able to correct cystic fibrosis cells in test tubes by adding normal copies of the cystic fibrosis gene. In 1993, medical scientists were able to do the same in a human cystic fibrosis patient. Since then, many more with cystic fibrosis in the United States have undergone this as-yet-experimental therapy in which suspensions of normal cystic fibrosis genes were dripped onto the inner nasal surfaces. These experimental tests showed that the treated nasal cells will take up the normal genes, but the improved results last for only a few days. The fact that uptake and improvement occurs at all, however, means that gene replacement therapy for cystic fibrosis is certainly a possibility in the near future.

Transmission

Since people with cystic fibrosis are infertile, they are unable to have children. Since 1 in 25 Americans is a carrier, cystic fibrosis will continue to remain a very common disorder in the United States. However, since cystic fibrosis is an autosomal recessive disease, both parents must be carriers for their child to develop cystic fibrosis; in this case a child has a one in four chance of developing cystic fibrosis. Carriers with only one defective gene will not develop any of the symptoms of the disease.

PREVENTION

Since 97 percent of the cases of cystic fibrosis among Ashkenazi Jews are caused by five mutations, carrier screening is possible. It is also possible to determine the presence of these mutations through prenatal screening. Since screening for these five mutations will detect almost all carriers among Ashkenazi Jews, Dr. Dvorah Abeliovich, a physician at the Hadassah Hebrew University Hospital in Israel, believes that screening for the mutation among Ashkenazi Jews will soon be widespread. However, as noted previously, there are seven additional mutations of this defective gene that cause the disease in Jews, so that it is possible for a child to develop cystic fibrosis even if screening for the most common mutations is negative.

FOR FURTHER INFORMATION

National Jewish Medical and
  Research Center
Lung Line
1400 Jackson Street
Denver, CO 80206
TELEPHONE: 1-800-222-5864
E-MAIL: lungline@njc.org

Cystic Fibrosis Foundation
6931 Arlington Rd.
Bethesda, MD 20814
TELEPHONE: 1-800-344-4823

SCREENING CENTERS

Baylor College of Medicine—DNA
  Diagnostic Laboratory
Boston University School of Medicine—Center for Human Genetics
Celtek Laboratories
H.A. Chapman Institute of Medical
  Genetics
Children's Hospital—Clinical
  Genetics Laboratory
Children's Hospital Oakland
Cornell University Medical College
  and New York Hospital
Dianon Systems, Inc.

Eastern Virginia Medical School
Emory University—Department of
  Pediatrics, Division of Genetics
Henry Ford Hospital
Genetics & IVF Institute
Genzyme Genetics
Hospital for Sick Children—Molecular Genetics Laboratory
IWK—Grace Health Center
Thomas Jefferson University
Johns Hopkins University School of
  Medicine—DNA Diagnostic Laboratory

Keesler Air Force Base
Mayo Clinic
Medical Genetics Institute, S.C.
Mount Sinai School of Medicine
New York University School of
  Medicine—Molecular Genetics
  Laboratory
North Shore University Hospital at
  Manhasset
Quest Diagnostics, Inc.
SmithKline Beecham Clinical
  Laboratories
State University of New York at
  Stony Brook
State University of New York Health
  Science Center
University of California at Davis
  Medical Center
University of California at Los
  Angeles Medical Center
University of California at San
  Diego
University of California at San
  Francisco—Molecular Diagnostics
  Laboratory
University of Colorado School of
  Medicine
University of Pennsylvania Health
  System
University of Pittsburgh Medical
  Center
University of Tennessee Medical
  Center—Developmental and
  Genetic Center
University of Utah
Washington University School of
  Medicine
Wayne State University—Harper
  Hospital

References

Books
Davis, Pamela B. *Cystic Fibrosis*. Marcel Dekker, 1993.
Harris, Ann, and Maurice Super. *Cystic Fibrosis: The Facts*. New York: Oxford University Press, 1995.
Orenstein, David M. *Cystic Fibrosis: A Guide for Patient and Family*. Raven Press, 1989.

Journal Articles
Abeliovich, Dvorah, I.P. Lavon, I. Lerer, T. Cohen, C. Springer, et al. Screening for five mutations detects 97 percent of cystic fibrosis (Cystic fibrosis) chromosomes and predicts carrier frequency of 1:29 in the Jewish Ashkenazi population. *American Journal of Human Genetics* 51 (1992): 951–956.
Borgo, G., G. Cabrini, G. Mastella, P. Ronchetto, M. Devoto, and G. Romeo. Phenotypic intrafamilial heterogeneity in cystic fibrosis. *Clinical Genetics* 44 (1993): 48–49.
Callen, N., et al. Liposome-mediated Cystic fibrosisTR Gene Transfer to the Nasal Epithelium of Patients with Cystic Fibrosis. *Nature Medicine* 1 (1995): 39.
Kerem, B., J.A. Buchanan, P. Durie, M.L. Corey, H. Levison, J.M. Rommens, et al. DNA marker haplotype associated with pancreatic sufficiency in cystic fibrosis. *American Journal of Human Genetics* 44 (1989): 827–834.
Kerem, B., J.M. Rommens, J.A. Buchanan, D. Markiewica, T.K. Cox, et al. Identification of the cystic fibrosis gene: Genetic analysis. *Science* 245 (1989): 1073–1080.

Krem, Eitan, Y.M. Kalman, Y. Yahav, et al. Highly variable incidence of cystic fibrosis and different mutation distributions among different Jewish ethnic groups in Israel. *Human Genetics* 96 (1995): 193–197.

Lerer, I., M. Sagi, G.R. Cutting, et al., Cystic fibrosis mutations delta F508 and G542X in Jewish patients. *Journal of Medical Genetics* 29 (1992): 131–133.

Pier, Gerald B., M. Grout, T. Zaidi, et al. Salmonella typhi uses CFTR to enter intestinal epithelial cells. *Nature* 393 (1998): 79–82.

Sherif, E., K.N. Gabriel, B.H. Brigman, R.C. Koller, et al. Cystic Fibrosis Heterozygote Resistance to Cholera Toxin in the Cystic Fibrosis Mouse Model. *Science* 266 (1994): 107–109.

Shoshani, T., A. Augarten, E. Gazit, et al. Association of a nonsense mutation (W1282X), the most common mutation in the Ashkenazi Jewish Cystic Fibrosis patients in Israel, with Presentation of Severe Disease. *American Journal of Human Genetics* 50 (1992): 222–228.

Welsh, M.J., and R.B. Fick. Cystic fibrosis. *Journal of Clinical Investigation* 80 (1987): 1523–1526.

Wine, J. No CFTR: are Cystic fibrosis symptoms milder? *Nature Genetics* 1 (1992): 10.

Chapter Ten

Sensory Disorders

S ensory disorders refer to disturbances in seeing, hearing, tasting, touch-
ing and feeling pain. These disorders can stem from peripheral or central disturbance. Peripheral disturbances include damage to sensory receptors
or the nerves that transmit sensory impulses to the spinal cord or brain. Central disturbances refer to abnormalities in the brain or spinal cord.

Although several studies have suggested that Jews experience visual
disturbances like myopia and color blindness more commonly than other
groups, the linkages are not strong enough for them to be discussed, other
than mentioning them. Although Familial Dysautonomia affects the tear
ducts, this is not a sensory disturbance and therefore has been included
among the disorders affecting the central nervous system. On the other
hand, several studies have confirmed that hearing loss is more common
among Ashkenazi Jews and this disturbance has now been traced to a
specific genetic anomaly.

Hearing Loss

The ear is composed of three main parts: an outer, a middle, and an
inner section. The outer ear is the visible part of the ear and the canal.
The ear funnels sound to a structure at the end of the canal called the
eardrum, which vibrates in response to sound. On the other side of the
eardrum, in the area of the middle ear, are three tiny bones called ossi-
cles, which transmit the eardrum's vibrations to the "oval window," which
is the outer edge of the inner ear. The inner ear contains the cochlea, the
sensory receptor which converts the sound vibrations into nerve impulses.
These impulses are carried to the brain where they are interpreted.

There are two main types of hearing loss. Conductive hearing loss results from problems in the outer or middle ear and is usually temporary. Sensorineural hearing loss, the kind that affects Ashkenazi Jews, results from either a disturbance in the cochlea, the nerve which transmits impulses from the cochlea to the brain, or the area of the brain involved in hearing. Most hearing loss results from disorders affecting the cochlea.

When hearing loss occurs in the absence of any other medical factors, it is called "nonsyndromic hearing loss." About 80 percent of all nonsyndromic cases are due to hereditary factors, ranging from mild to complete deafness.

FREQUENCY

About 1 in every 2,200 Ashkenazi Jews are born with hearing loss. The hereditary form of hearing loss affecting Ashkenazi Jews has been traced to two mutations. These two mutations are very rare in the general population, but the carrier rate among Ashkenazi Jews is estimated at almost 5 per 100, which is very similar to the carrier rates for Gaucher Disease, Tay-Sachs Disease, and Familial Dysautonomia.

CAUSE

Although as many as 100 genes are believed to be involved in hearing, in 1998 Dr. Robert Morel and his colleagues at the National Institute on Deafness and Communicative Disorders discovered two mutations in one of these genes, GJB2, which are responsible for virtually every instance of the hereditary condition among Ashkenazi Jews.

The GJB2 gene produces a protein called "connexin 26" which is expressed in the inner ear and which affects the way sound is received. Mutations in GJB2 account for most of the cases of hereditary deafness, and two mutant variants, called 30delG and 167delT in particular, account for all cases of hereditary hearing loss among Ashkenazi Jews.

The authors attributed the 167delT mutation, the more common of the two, to a founder effect which occurred about seven generations ago.

DIAGNOSIS

A test for hearing loss can be made at any age, including infancy. The simplest tests are the "Weber" and "Rinne" tests. In the former, a vibrating tuning fork is held against the forehead. People with conductive hearing loss sense that the sound is louder in the affected ear, whereas those with sensorineural hearing loss sense a louder sound in the less affected ear. In the Rinne test, the vibrating turning fork is held near each ear and then against the bone behind that ear. If the sound is louder when the tuning fork is held near the ear, it indicates either normal hearing or sensorineural hearing loss; if louder when it is held against the bone, it indicates conductive hearing loss.

A more sophisticated test, called audiometry, involves wearing headphones that deliver sounds of varying frequencies to one ear at a time. Then the test is repeated with the sound delivered through a speaker positioned against the bones behind each ear. In hearing loss, sound frequencies have to be much higher than normal for them to be heard. More sophisticated still is the tympanometer test in which an instrument is placed into the ear canal to measure the responses of the eardrum and bones of the inner ear.

TREATMENT

While there are no cures for hereditary deafness, in many cases hearing can be improved through hearing aids and cochlear implants. If a hearing loss in very young children is not detected, it can result in a number of related problems, including poor speech and communication abilities, poor reading ability, and impaired cognitive development.

PREVENTION

While hearing loss resulting from hereditary factors cannot be prevented, the consequences of hearing loss described above can be reduced or prevented with early identification and correction. Hearing loss can be identified even in newborns, and early screening for hearing has been recommended by the National Institutes of Health.

FOR FURTHER INFORMATION

American Society for Deaf Children
1820 Tribute Road, Suite A
Sacramento, CA 95815
TELEPHONE: 1-800-942-2732
    916-641-6084
FAX: 916 641 6085
E-MAIL: ASDC1@aol.com

National Association of the Deaf
814 Thayer
Silver Spring, MD 20910
TELEPHONE: 301-587-1788
E-MAIL: NADinfo@nad.org
American Speech-Language-

Hearing Association
10901 Rockville Pike
Rockville, MD 20852
TELEPHONE: 1-800-498-2071
    301-897-5700
E-MAIL: actioncenter@asha.org

Self Help for Hard of Hearing People
7910 Woodmont Ave.
Bethesda, MD 20814
TELEPHONE: 1-800-255-0411
    301-657-2249
E-MAIL: national@shhh.org

SCREENING CENTERS

Boston University
Chapman Institute of Medical
  Genetics

University of Washington

REFERENCES

Cremers, C. W., H. A. M. Marres, and P. M. Van Rijn. Nonsyndromal profound genetic deafness in Childhood. *Academic Science* 630 (1991): 197–202.

Morell, Robert J., Hung Jeff Kim, Linda J. Hood, et al. Mutations in the connexin 26 gene (GBJ2) among Ashkenazi Jews with nonsyndromic recessive deafness. *New England Journal of Medicine* 330 (1998): 1500–1505.

Van Camp, G., P. Willems, and R.J.H. Smith. Nonsyndromic hearing loss: unparalleled heterogeneity. *American Journal of Human Genetics* 60 (1997): 758–764.

Zbar, R.I.S., A. Ramesh, C.R.S. Srisailapathy, et al. Passage to India: The search for genes causing autosomal recessive nonsyndromic hearing loss. *Otolaryngology and Head and Neck Surgery* 118 (1998): 333–337.

Zelante, L., P. Gasparini, X. Estivill, et al. Connexin 26 mutations associated with the most common form of nonsyndromic neurosensory autosomal recessive deafness (DFNB1) in Mediterraneans. *Human Molecular Genetics* 6 (1997): 1605–1609.

CHAPTER ELEVEN

Skin Disorders

Our skin is more than just a container holding us together. Composed of two main layers, the epidermis and the dermis, the skin is actually the body's largest organ, protecting us against infection, injury, heat and light and helping us regulate body temperature. The outer epidermal layer contains several different kinds of cells including the melanocytes, the cells that produce the melanin that give skin its color. The inner dermal layer contains blood and lymph vessels, hair roots and sweat glands. Like other organs in the body, the cells in these layers are also susceptible to various disorders.

Bloom Syndrome

Bloom Syndrome is a relatively uncommon genetic disease named after New York dermatologist Dr. David Bloom, who reported its main characteristics in 1954. Although there are fewer than 200 known cases, it is estimated that about 1 percent of all Ashkenazi Jews have the defective gene. As with most recessive conditions, carriers do not experience its symptoms.

FREQUENCY

Bloom Syndrome is a relatively rare disorder. The frequency of its occurrence in Israel is estimated at 1 in every 48,000 Ashkenazi Jews. Its carrier frequency among an unselected population of American Ashkenazi Jews is about 1 to 2 per 200; among Ashkenazi Jews of Polish descent, its frequency was estimated at 1 in 37. Although the syndrome occurs in both males and females, it occurs disproportionately more often in males.

Males also have more severe skin patches than females. The disparity between occurrence and carrier frequency indicates that the genetic condition responsible for the syndrome has relatively low penetrance.

SYMPTOMS

The main characteristics of Bloom Syndrome are growth retardation, red patches on the face, weakened immune function, and predisposition to cancer.

The earliest symptom of Bloom Syndrome is the birth of a baby who is abnormally small, but otherwise appears perfectly normal. After birth, the baby and then child continues to lag behind his or her peers in growth. In adulthood, the person is rarely taller than five feet. An extra finger (polydactyly) is not uncommon and many have a crooked fifth finger (clinodactyly).

Children with Bloom Syndrome are very thin and have a striking resemblance to one another. They have narrow faces and prominent noses. Although their skin does not appear abnormal at birth, during their first year red patches begin to appear on their faces; in many cases, the patches also appear on other parts of the body. The red facial patches have a "butterfly pattern" with the center on the bridge of the nose and the "wings" on the upper cheek areas next to it, as well as on the lower eyelids and lower lip. These skin problems vary in intensity from very mild in some individuals to disfiguring in others. In many cases, the skin problem improves with age; however, exposure to the sun makes them worse. Photosensitivity becomes less severe with increased age, but during infancy, protective measures have to be taken since sunlight can result in marked disfigurement such as scarring and loss of eyelashes.

Bloom Syndrome is also associated with a number of other problems. Muscle strength is reduced in older children and adults. Sexual development is normal, although males often develop smaller than normal testes and some women have irregular menstrual periods. Upper respiratory tract infections are common and can be life-threatening. The risk of chronic lung disease and cancer, especially leukemia, are all increased. Most people with Bloom Syndrome die from cancer during their second or third decades. Diabetes occurs in about 10 percent of sufferers. Although some individuals may have a slightly less-than-normal intelligence, impaired mental abilities are not a common component of the syndrome. People with Bloom Syndrome tend to be outgoing but remain childlike in maturity and are very easily misled.

CAUSE

Bloom Syndrome results from one or more breaks in the chromosomes, the structures along which genes are arrayed. The breakages are in turn due to an autosomal recessive mutation in the "BLM" gene. Since this mutation occurs almost exclusively in Ashkenazi Jews, it is also called "BLMash." Most Ashkenazi Jews affected by Bloom syndrome are descended from families who lived in Eastern Europe between Warsaw and Crakow in Galacia (southeastern Poland) and Kiev and Chernovtsy in southwestern Ukraine.

The BLM gene produces a protein that belongs to a family of enzymes known as DNA helicases. These enzymes enable the "double helixed" stranded DNA to uncoil so that cells can make new copies of each strand. With the BLM mutation, the enzyme is missing. As a result, the duplication of the DNA code is no longer free of errors as cells divide, resulting in "genomic instability," the medical term for an increased number of breakages or interchanges (called "sister chromatid exchanges") in the chromosomes. This means that some chromosomes lose parts of their structures and therefore many genes, or they become rearranged, thereby changing their genetic code. In this regard, Bloom Syndrome resembles Fanconi Anemia, a disorder that also occur more frequently in Ashkenazi Jews compared to the general population.

Since the gene BLMash is common to all Jews with the disorder, medical geneticists believe it is the result of a founder effect that originated in Eastern Europe some time between the 14th and 17th centuries when the Ashkenazi Jewish population was forming. Since the carrier rate is very high among Polish Jews, the founder was probably Polish.

DIAGNOSIS

A clinical diagnosis can be made on the basis of the syndrome's main features of short stature, narrow face and prominent nose, sun-sensitive facial lesions, pigmented skin lesions, and higher-than-normal occurrence of infections. The clinical diagnosis can now be confirmed by examining blood or skin cells for the presence of the BLMAsh gene.

TRANSMISSION

Bloom Syndrome is a rare autosomal recessive disorder caused by a mutation in a single gene. Carriers can be screened for the presence of the gene. There is no known environmental contribution to the syndrome, so there are no precautions that can be taken to reduce its occurrence from that source.

TREATMENT AND PREVENTION

There is no treatment for the growth retardation component of the syndrome. People with Bloom Syndrome should avoid excessive exposure to sunlight. Since susceptibility to cancer is a characteristic of the syndrome, avoidance of X-rays, sunlight (that is ultraviolet radiation), and chemotherapeutic drugs are advisable. Another precaution is for people with Bloom Syndrome to "bank" their own bone marrow in case they may later need replacement. Infections need to be taken care of immediately and can be kept under control with antibiotics. Regular check-ups are recommended to make sure that if cancer does develop, it is detected at a very early stage.

Carrier testing can be done to identify carriers and prenatal diagnosis is also available.

FOR FURTHER INFORMATION

Bloom's Syndrome Registry
NY Blood Center
310 East 67th St.
New York, NY 10021
TELEPHONE: 212-570-3075
FAX: 212-570-3195

SCREENING CENTERS

All Children's Hospital—Dept. of Pathology and Laboratory Medicine

Baylor College of Medicine, DNA Diagnostic Laboratory

Genzyme Genetics

Hospital for Sick Children—Cytogenetics Laboratory

Memorial Sloan Kettering Cancer Center, Diagnostic Molecular Laboratory

Mount Sinai School of Medicine

New York University School of Medicine—Molecular Genetics Laboratory

REFERENCES

Bloom, D. Congenital telangiectatic erythema resembling lupus erythematosus in dwarfs. *American Journal of Diseases in Children* 88 (1954): 754–757.

German, James. Bloom's Syndrome. *Dermatologic Clinics* 13 (1995): 7–18.

German, James, David Bloom, Eberhard Passarge, et al. Bloom's Syndrome. VI. The disorder in Israel and an estimation of the gene frequency in the Ashkenazim. *American Journal of Human Genetics* (1977): 553–562.

Oddoux, Carole, Carlos M. Clayton, Holly R. Nelson, et al. Prevalence of Bloom Syndrome heterozygotes among Ashkenazi Jews. *American Journal of Human Genetics* 64 (1999): 1241–1243.

Roa, Benjamin B., Carlo V. Savino and C. Sue Richards. Ashkenazi Jewish population frequency of the Bloom Syndrome gene 2281 delta6ins7 mutation. *Genetic Testing* 3 (1999): 219–221.

Shahrabani-Gargir, Limor, Ruth Shomrat, Yuval Yaron, et al. High frequency of a common Bloom Syndrome Ashkenazi mutation among Jews of Polish origin. *Genetic Testing* 2 (1998): 293-296.

Straughen, Joel E., Juliana Johnson, Donna McLaren, et al. A rapid method for detecting the predominant Ashkenazi Jewish mutation in the Bloom's Syndrome gene. *Human Mutation* 11 (1998): 175–178.

Pemphigus Vulgaris

Pemphigus Vulgaris is a disorder that affects the skin and mucous membranes and usually appears relatively late in life. Although seemingly minor, in some individuals it can be life-threatening.

SYMPTOMS

The most characteristic symptoms are blisters on the face, neck, armpits and other areas of the skin, and lesions in the mouth and then in the groin which often do not appear until the 50s and 60s. Men and women are equally affected. Although people with the disorder may be otherwise healthy, there are also some who have died as a result of the disorder or its treatment.

FREQUENCY

Pemphigus Vulgaris is relatively common among Jews. It occurs more often in Ashkenazim than non–Ashkenazim (3 in 10,000 versus 0.6 in 10,000).

CAUSE

Pemphigus Vulgaris is an autoimmune disorder, which means that individuals with the disorder form antibodies against their own tissues. Several studies have found a strong association between a marker (HLA-Dr4) and Pemphigus Vulgaris. When patients were grouped by ethnic origin, the frequency of HlA-Drv was much higher in Ashkenazim (97 percent) than in non–Ashkenazim.

DIAGNOSIS

Diagnosis is based on the presence of characteristic blisters and lesions and the characteristic appearance of skin cells when examined under a microscope.

TREATMENT

The main treatment involves suppression of the immune system. Corticosteroids have been given in conjunction with immunosuppressant agents such as azathioprine. In one study, the disease resolved itself in 18 percent of the patients treated with these drugs; however, the disorder persisted in 87 percent and adverse effects were noted in 78 percent, two of whom died.

REFERENCES

Ahmed, A.R., R. Wagner, K. Khatri, et al. Major histocompatibility complex haplotypes and class II genes in non-Jewish patients with pemphigus vulgaris. *Proceedings of the National Academy of Sciences* 88 (1991): 5056–5060.

Ahmed, A.R., E.J. Yunis, K. Khatri, et al. Major histocompatiblity complex haplotype studies in Ashkenazi Jewish patients with pemphigus vulgaris. *Proceedings of the National Academy of Sciences* 87 (1990): 7658–7662.

Brauthbar, C., M. Moscovitz, T. Livshits, et al. HLA-DrW-4 in pemphigus vulgaris patients in Israel. *Tissue Antigens* 16 (1980): 238–243.

Goodman, Richard. *Genetic Diseases among the Jewish People.* 436–439.

Park, M.S., P.I. Terasaki, A.R. Ahmed, et al. HLA-DRW-9 in 91 percent of Jewish pemphigus vulgaris patients. *Lancet* II, (1979): 441–442.

Scharf, S.J., A. Friedmann, L. Steinman, et al. Specific HLA-DQB and HLA-DRB1 alleles confer susceptibility to pemphigus vulgaris. *Proceedings of the National Academy of Sciences* 86 (1989): 6215–6219.

Scully, C., O. Paes De Álmedia, S.R. Porter, et al. Pemphigus vulgaris: the manifestations and long-term management of 55 patients with oral lesions. *British Journal of Dermatology* 140 (1999): 84–89.

Udey, M.C., and J.R. Stanley. Pemphigus—diseases of antidesmosomal autoimmunity. *JAMA* 282 (1999): 572–576.

CHAPTER TWELVE

Eliminating Jewish Genetic Diseases

Medical science now has the technology to determine if people have genes that make them more likely to develop a disease if they have not already exhibited its symptoms, or equally important, if they carry a gene that they can pass on to their children which may make them more likely to develop a disease. This raises controversial personal and social issues concerning who should be tested for the presence of these genes.

"There are basically two types of people ... when it comes to being tested for a genetic predisposition to diseases that have no real cures and whose date of onset cannot be predicted," says Barbara Biesecker, co-director of the National Institute of Health's genetic counseling programs. These two types she calls the "want-to-knowers" and the "avoiders."

Knowing, or not knowing, that you or your children carry a gene for a particular disease has profound implications. On the positive side, screening reduces uncertainty. Screening enables people who are otherwise healthy to know if they are carriers of a particular disease, and equally if not more important, it enables couples who are both carriers to know that they have a definite risk for conceiving a child with that disease. A negative result can assure a couple that their children will not develop a disease despite a family history for doing so. If a couple learns that they are both carriers and therefore at risk for conceiving a child with a fatal disease, those couples then have to face a number of difficult decisions. The first is, if they are not yet married, whether to avoid marriage at all. For ultraorthodox Jews, the wish for children may be great but the alternatives may be unacceptable; because of religious principles, they may decide to find another partner to marry. The advantage of knowing is that they are prepared for eventualities.

For less orthodox Jews who wish to marry but not take the risk of conceiving a child with a fatal disease, there are other options. One is to adopt a child. Another is to have a pregnancy through artificial insemination or by egg donation, in which case the donor will have been previously screened to make sure he or she is not a carrier. If the couple decides to have children of their own, they know the risks of conceiving a child with the disease ahead of time. They also have the opportunity of screening any child they conceive to see if in fact he or she is affected. If that child is affected, however, they would then have to face the difficult decision of aborting that pregnancy.

Another benefit is that early diagnosis and related presymptomatic treatment may improve their chances of preventing the disease from occurring. As noted in conjunction with colon cancer, a mutation for colon cancer occurs in about six percent of Ashkenazi Jews. However, regular colonoscopies and associated removal of the slow-growing polyps out of which the cancer develops can reduce the likelihood of developing colon cancer to almost zero. In this instance, knowing you have the gene for colon cancer can save your life if you use that information wisely.

Likewise, if a woman knows she carries the gene mutation predisposing her to breast cancer, she may be able to catch the disease at a very early stage by performing monthly self-exams and taking annual mammograms. By catching it at an early stage, she too can increase her chances of a cure.

There may be definite advantages for screening children as well. While early screening may in some way interfere with early parent-child bonding, medical researchers in England compared 57 children with cystic fibrosis who were born before neonatal screening for the disease was introduced in that country between 1978 and 1981, with 60 children born after screening was introduced in mid–1981. The children screened for cystic fibrosis were consistently taller and heavier than those who weren't screened and had fewer infections.

On the other hand, there are adverse consequences of screening that cannot be ignored. While genetic science offers the possibility of a life relatively free of disease, at present there are many genetically related disorders that do not have any cure. Knowing that you do or do not have a positive test for a genetic disease can be traumatizing. The news that someone is positive can be debilitating; we may become so fixated on eventual decline that we grow depressed to the point we require psychiatric hospitalization or become suicidal. Knowing you have a genetic risk for a disease also doesn't tell you when or if you will in fact develop that disease or whether you will respond to treatment. Having a gene that is linked to some disorder only means that a person has a predisposition for developing that disorder; it is not a certainty. For a disorder like Tay-Sachs, a child who inherits the defective gene for the disease from each parent will develop the disorder. On the other hand, a woman who has the BRCA1 gene linked to breast cancer may not develop that disease. In other words, genetic risk is not the same as certainty. At the same time, not having the mutation is no guarantee that a woman will not develop breast cancer. If a woman tests positive for BRCA1 or BRCA2 gene mutations, she knows that she has an added risk for breast cancer. What she should do about it is an altogether different question.

Knowing you do *not* have a particular disease-causing gene is also no nirvana. You may not develop the disease, but is your good luck shared by your brother or sister? Some people worry about what their families may say if they tell them they are going to be tested. They may not want to tell family members who already have the disease that they too have it because they worry that such news will increase a parent or a sibling's guilt or anxiety. Close relatives who were only slightly concerned or were totally unaware of their genetic risks would suddenly have to confront their own increased risk. Someone who suffers from a medical problem known to be genetically linked, but does not have the gene that causes it, may not be able to deal with that newly discovered information, since now he or she wouldn't be able to explain why they have come down with the disease.

There is also the related possibility that someone may test negative and yet still have the mutation for which the test was performed. This is because there are different testing procedures and some are more accurate than others. It is also possible that someone who tests negative for one gene mutation may have a mutation in an as-yet-undiscovered gene that predisposes that person to the same disorder. Alternatively, someone may have a mutation in another gene whose main effect is not the one he or she is being tested for, but which nevertheless increases the risk for developing that disorder.

Apart from issues concerning our individual health, gene testing has raised important social issues as well. Knowing someone's genetic makeup may be used to discriminate against that person. Jews are understandably concerned about being stigmatized because they are genetically prone to a particular disease. They and other ethnic minorities are justifiably concerned that research projects which target them because they are identifiable and or descended from relatively small, closely-knit populations may result in genetic discrimination. As more and more information indicates that Jews suffer from certain genetically related diseases more than other people, there is a concern that such news will contribute to anti–Semitic rhetoric about genetic inferiority.

Some bioethicists believe researchers ought to consult community leaders before beginning a study that might identify a particular gene peculiar to that group. They note that the genetic mutation that predisposes Ashkenazi Jews for colon cancer was made on samples that were originally obtained during screening for Tay-Sachs. The BRCA2 gene mutation for breast cancer was likewise discovered using archived samples for Tay-Sachs. In both instances, the people who provided the samples were told that their personal identities would not be linked to the samples they provided and the results were widely disseminated to various Jewish organizations. However, there are literally millions of archived genetic samples and there are no guidelines as to their usage. If a community is being particularly targeted, regardless of the reasons, bioethical considerations begin to emerge. On the other hand, if access to these samples is denied, then many genetically linked diseases may go undiscovered. Even if the Jewish community is consulted beforehand, who speaks for the Jewish community?

Another reason to be concerned about screening is that it could affect medical insurance coverage and job discrimination. Life insurance premiums are based on probabilities that someone will die. Some people will die at an early age, some when they are quite old. The insurance company doesn't know who the lucky ones are and it bases its premiums on estimated risks. If you smoke, your premiums are higher because smoking causes diseases that shorten your life. The better an insurance company is at calculating risks, the more money it stands to make. Since insurance companies are naturally less inclined to insure people who have a higher-than-normal chance of dying at an early age, knowing a potential client's genetic makeup would be particularly helpful in securing profits.

The results of a survey conducted at Georgetown University concerning insurance are therefore not surprising. That study found that 22 percent of a group of 32 people with known genetic predispositions had been denied insurance coverage. Another survey conducted by the federal Office of Technology Assessment found that 17 of the 29 insurance companies that were contacted said they would not cover people whose genetic testing indicated they were carriers of a chronic disease. In other words, insurance companies could create a genetic underclass. Many Jews with Jewish-sounding last names are becoming concerned that they could be forced to take a test and then, if they do have a particular gene mutation, be denied insurance or be turned down for a job because concerns about health care costs may keep those companies from insuring or employing them. Genetic stigmatization is a real concern for Jews.

The possibility that the results of a test will result in their being denied employment or insurance also raises possibilities that many people may not tell their doctors their full medical histories because such information would make their doctors advise testing. This could result in their receiving a mistaken diagnosis or result in a test or treatment not being given that might otherwise be life-saving. In other words, because they are afraid their coverage would be canceled or their premiums increased, many people with colorectal cancer may avoiding testing even when it might enable them to prevent its occurrence through periodic colonoscopies. Even when there is no reason to believe that someone is a carrier for a particular disease, the fear that some otherwise unsuspected condition may be revealed by experimental testing could keep many people from participating in medical research that could in the long run result in the cure of a disease.

On the other hand, many people, like Jews of Ashkenazi descent, who are potentially at high risk for having children with diseases like Tay-Sachs, will want to know if they are carriers. Thanks to medical science, many of the tests to find out who is a carrier are very inexpensive. This in turn has resulted, in the case of Tay-Sachs Disease, in community education programs, carrier screening and genetic counseling programs in many parts of the world aimed at preventing this disease. The first of these community-based programs began in 1970 in Baltimore and Washington, D.C. Since then, they have spread to other cities throughout the United States and Canada, and comparable programs can now be found in Israel and in Jewish communities in Europe, Australia, South Africa, and South America.

These community programs aimed at eliminating Tay-Sachs have been enormously successful. Prior to 1970 there were about 60 new cases of Tay-Sachs Disease every year in the United States among Ashkenazi Jews. Since 1983, 3 to 5 cases are born each year in either the United States or Canada, a decrease of over 90 percent in the incidence of this disease. By contrast, the incidence of Tay-Sachs among non–Jews in the United States has not changed, underscoring the importance of testing.

While it is now possible to do the same kind of widespread testing for other diseases, Dr. Michael Kaback and his colleagues at the International Tay-Sachs Data Collection Network point out in an article in the *Journal of the American Medical Association* in 1993 that whether it is feasible to do so depends on several important considerations. The first is if a particular disease occurs primarily in a defined population. The second is whether the tests that are available are relatively inexpensive and are highly accurate.

Worldwide screening for Tay-Sachs Disease is now almost routine for Jewish couples because it satisfies the essential requirements of any successful screening program: the disease occurs with a relatively high frequency among Jewish people; the test is very accurate; and it is inexpensive (about $20 to $75). Screening for certain other diseases like Gaucher's Type I Disease, Canavan Disease, and cystic fibrosis among Jews is equally possible now for the same reasons.

In this regard, however, a new wrinkle concerning cost has recently emerged. The test for Canavan Disease was developed by Dr. Reuben Matalon in 1993 at the Miami Children's Hospital. The hospital owns the patent, and although previously it allowed genetic laboratories to use the test for free, it is now requiring facilities that use it to pay the hospital a royalty fee amounting to between 6 percent and 15 percent of the cost, which varies from $50 to $300 depending on where it is performed. The Canavan Screening Consortium has been the most vocal opponent of these royalty payments because it fears that if the test is too expensive, many potential users and insurers would be unable or unwilling to pay, and this would reduce testing. The wider implication is that if Miami Children's Hospital starts collecting royalties, hospitals that own similar patents for carrier testing of "Jewish genes" might start asking for royalties as well. This could set a precedent, making the costs so high that it could seriously impact on the entire genetic screening programs that have been developed over the last several decades. A related disturbing issue is that hospitals like Miami Children's might give exclusive licensing to a particular laboratory, so that testing might not be as widely available.

The decision to undergo genetic testing is something more and more people are beginning to consider, but at the same time there are questions that need to be thought about. The opportunity to know if you or some member of your family has a disease-causing gene before any symptoms appear is something we have not had to consider fully. Knowledge is a two-edged sword. If results are negative, the uncertainty that you are going to develop a disease linked to a particular gene is lessened, but that doesn't necessarily mean you will not develop it. If you find out you do have the gene, you and your family may become so traumatized you may no longer be able to live a normal life even if you do not develop symptoms of the disease.

Genetic discrimination is no longer science fiction. Denial of insurance and employment because someone's genome contains a particular gene has become a reality. Although insurance companies and employers are not yet demanding genetic testing as a prerequisite for coverage or employment, the possibility is not far-fetched. Although several states have now passed legislation that restricts such testing, it is far from universal and loopholes can always be found where the profit motive is involved. For Jews and other minorities, these are real concerns since discrimination is as much a part of their history as are their genetic endowments.

References

Beckwith, Jon, and Joseph S. Alper. Reconsidering genetic antidiscrimination legislation. *Journal of Law, Medicine and Ethics* 26 (1998): 205–210.

Biesecker, Barbara. Quoted in Siebert, Charles. "The DNA We've Been Dealt." *New York Times Magazine*, Sept. 17, 1995, 50, 52.

Brown, Jeremy. Prenatal screening in Jewish law. *Journal of Medical Ethics* 16 (1990): 75–80.

Cordori, A., P. Slavney, C. Young, et al. Predictors of psychological adjustments to genetic testing for Huntington's disease. *Health Psychology* 16 (1997): 36–50.

Huggins, M., M. Bloch, S. Wiggins, et al. Predictive testing for Huntington disease in Canada: Adverse effects and unexpected results in those receiving a decreased risk. *American Journal of Medical Genetics* 42 (1992): 508–515.

Rothstein, Mark A. Genetic privacy and confidentiality: Why they are so hard to protect. *Journal of Law, Medicine and Ethics* 26 (1998): 198–204.

Schneider, Katherine A. Genetic counseling for BRCA1/BRCA2 testing. *Genetic Testing* 1 (1997): 91–98.

Waters, Donna L., Bridget Wilcken, Les Irwig, et al. Clinical outcomes of newborn screening for cystic fibrosis. *Archives of Diseases of Children* 80 (1999): F1–F8.

Williams, Janet K., Debra L. Schute, Catherine A. Evers, et al. Adults seeking presymptomatic gene testing for Huntington Disease. *Image: Journal of Nursing Scholarship* 31 (1999): 109–114.

Glossary

Abscess: A build-up of pus in an area, usually due to bacterial infection.

Absorption: The process whereby nutrients are passed into the blood stream from the intestine, or into cells from the blood.

Acute: Of brief duration, as opposed to chronic.

Adrenals: Two small glands located above the kidneys, which produce a number of different hormones such as corticosteroids.

Allele: Variant form of the same gene. The alleles can be identical, in which case they are homozygous, or different, in which case they are heterozygous.

Allergy: Hypersensitivity of immune system to certain substances which do not cause symptoms in most people. The allergic reaction may take the form of inflammation, labored breathing, headache, etc.

Alpha-fetoprotein: Protein excreted by fetus into amniotic fluid and from there into mother's blood.

Amino acid: One of 20 chemical compounds that are combined to form proteins. Some proteins are composed of as many as 100,000 amino acids.

Amniocentesis: A procedure performed between 16 and 18 weeks of pregnancy in which a needle is inserted through the mother's abdomen into the fluid in the amniotic sac surrounding the fetus. A sample of fluid is removed and the cells it contains are examined for enzyme levels or gene or chromosomal defects.

Amyloidosis: A condition in which blood cells produce an abnormal protein that settles in tissues and can interfere with their functioning.

Amyotrophic lateral sclerosis: "Lou Gehrig's Disease," a disease in which the nerve cells in the brain and spine are damaged resulting in muscle wasting.

Androgens: Male hormones.

217

Anemia: A condition in which the number of red blood cells, hemoglobin, or amount of blood in the body is reduced.

Antibiotic: A drug that kills bacteria.

Antibody: A protein in blood and tissue fluids, produced by cells of the immune system called B-lymphocytes, that recognizes and binds to proteins called antigens on the surface of bacteria and viruses, and neutralizes them.

Antigen: A protein present on the surface of cells that triggers an immune response, provoking the formation of antibodies.

Anus: The part of the digestive system, specifically the outlet of the rectum, through which undigested food is eliminated from the body.

Aplastic anemia: A condition in which the bone marrow does not produce red and white blood cells or platelets.

Artery: The tube-like structures that carry blood from the heart to the various parts of the body.

Asthma: Inflammatory lung disorder resulting in narrowing of air passages and difficult breathing.

Ataxia: Absence of balance control.

Atherosclerosis: A condition in which fatty deposits build up in the lining of the arteries, making them less flexible and restricting the flow of blood through them.

Atherosclerotic plaque: Area on the inner side of an artery where the flow of blood is restricted.

Autoimmune: Condition in which the body's own surface proteins are considered antigens and are attacked as foreign substances.

Autosomal dominant: An allele that overrides its opposite.

Autosomal dominant genetic disease: A disease resulting from the presence of an abnormality in one of the alleles in the gene pair.

Autosomal recessive: An allele whose possible effects are obscured by its opposite allele.

Autosomal recessive genetic disease: A disease resulting from the presence of an abnormality on both alleles of the same gene pair.

Autosome: Any chromosome not involved in determining gender. The human genome consists of 23 pairs of chromosomes; 22 of these pairs are autosomes; the other pair are the sex chromosomes (X and Y chromosomes).

Barium enema: An X-ray of the colon and rectum following an enema containing a white chalky material.

Base: Any one of the four chemical substances (adenine, thymine, guanine, or cytosine) in a DNA molecule. The sequence in which they are located on a DNA molecule determines which proteins are assembled. Bases on one DNA strand are always paired with those on the opposite strand, adenine with thymine and guanine with cytosine.

Base pairs: The complementary pairs of bases (adenine with thymine, and guanine with cytosine) in DNA held together by weak chemical bonds. The complementary strands of DNA are held together in the form of a double helix by the bonds between the base pairs.

Base sequence: The order of nucleotide bases making up the DNA molecule.

Benign: Not cancer-causing.

Bilirubin: An orange-yellowish pigment produced as a result of the breakdown of red blood cells. Excessive production or bilirubin produces jaundice.

Biopsy: Removal of a small sample of tissue from the body to be examined under a microscope for presence of abnormalities.

Blood sugar: Glucose sugar in blood. Normal levels are 80 to 120 mg of glucose per 100 ml of blood.

Bone marrow: The cells in the center of most bones, where blood cells are made. Bone marrow cells produce both the red blood cells that carry oxygen to all parts of the body and the white cells that help the body fight infection.

Bowel: The small intestine. The small intestine is sometimes called the small bowel; the large intestine is sometimes called the colon.

Bronchitis: Inflammation of bronchi lung passages, characterized by persistent coughing and production of sputum.

Bronchus: Part of air passages that connect windpipe and lungs.

Cafe-au-lait spots: Light brownish spots found on parts of the body.

Cancer: A general term for a number of different conditions characterized by abnormal multiplication of cells forming a malignant tumor in some part of the body.

Carbohydrate: A chemical substance made up of starches and sugars.

Carcinogen: A substance that induces cancer.

Carrier: Someone who possesses a flawed gene and can pass it on to his or her child, although he or she may be unaffected by the effects of that flaw. An individual who is homozygous has two flawed genes and will definitely pass one of them on to a child; an individual who is heterozygous has only one copy of a defective gene and has a 50:50 chance of passing the flawed gene on to a child. In some instances, a heterozygous carrier may be resistant to other unrelated diseases. For example, being a carrier for Tay-Sachs may confer resistance to tuberculosis.

Cell: The smallest and most basic unit of life. A cell is composed of an outer membrane that establishes its borders and separates it from other cells, and internal structures called "organelles" (little organs) that perform its specialized functions.

Chemotherapy: Treatment with drugs, usually used in reference to cancer.

Cholesterol: A fat-like substance, also called a lipid, that is taken into the body by diet or is made in the body. Cholesterol is a substance out of which important parts of the body are made, such as steroid hormones and cell membranes.

Chorionic villus sampling (CVS): A procedure performed between eight and 12 weeks of pregnancy, in which a thin tube is inserted through the mother's vagina and cervix, or a needle is inserted through the mother's abdomen, into the placenta where it joins the uterus, and a small sample of cells are removed and examined for enzyme levels or abnormal genes or chromosomes.

Chromosomal disease: A disease due to either one too many or one too few chromosomes, or to damage in the structure of a chromosome.

Chromosome: A rodlike structure in the nucleus of each cell on which the genes are located. Chromosomes are long strands of DNA.

Chronic: Long lasting, as opposed to acute, which means of short duration.

Clinical: Information obtained from observing or questioning a patient, as opposed to information obtained from laboratory tests.

Clone: A cell derived from and genetically identical to a single ancestral cell.

Cloning: Producing clones asexually from other cells.

Clot: Coagulated blood.

Coagulation: Forming a solid clotlike substance from a liquid, as in blood clotting.

Colon: The large intestine; the area of the digestive system from the small intestine to the anus. It is in this area that water is removed from undigested food. The dehydrated food is subsequently removed from the body by defecation.

Colonoscopy: Examination of the interior of the colon through a flexible viewing instrument called a colonoscope.

Colostomy: A surgical procedure in which an opening is made in the colon and the opening is attached to the abdominal wall so that feces can be eliminated.

Congenital: Present at birth.

Corticosteroids: Hormones produced by the outer area of the adrenal glands; also anti-inflammatory drugs similar to naturally occurring hormones.

Crohn's Disease: A chronic disease in which the digestive system, especially the small intestine, becomes inflamed.

Cystic fibrosis: A genetic disorder affecting the respiratory and digestive systems.

Cystocine: One of the base pairs in DNA.

Deletion: An abnormal chromosomal defect resulting from the loss of part of its structure.

Deoxyribonucleic acid: The chemical in which the genetic code is written. The code is written in sequences of chemical bases (see Bases) that direct different kinds of protein.

Deoxyribonucleotide: The building block or "base" for making DNA.

Diabetes: Bodily disorder arising from faulty utilization of glucose. Characterized by higher-than-normal levels of glucose in blood and urine.

Diagnosis: The process by which a medical condition is identified.

Digestion: Breakdown of food in the body by mechanical and chemical processes so that its nutrients can be absorbed through the intestinal wall into the blood and then used by cells.

Digital rectal exam: A medical exam in which a doctor inserts a lubricated gloved finger into the rectum to feel for abnormal tissues.

Diploid: The full set of chromosomes; the diploid set in humans consists of two pairs of 23 chromosomes.

Diverticulitis: Small sacs in the colon that have become infected and inflamed.

Diverticulosis: Small sacs in the colon that are not inflamed.

DNA: The abbreviation for deoxyribonucleic acid, the chemical substance of which genes are made.

DNA sequence: The order of base pairs on a gene or chromosome.

Dominant: An allele in a gene pair that overrides its counterpart. If a parent has this gene, his or her child has a 1 in 2 chance of inheriting it.

Dominant disorder: A genetic disorder in which a single allele overrides a normally functional gene.

Dominant gene: The gene (allele) in the pair of genes that determines which gene product will be produced even if it differs from the other allele.

Double helix: Form assumed by complementary DNA strands when bonded together. The arrangement that the two linear strands assume when they are bonded together in terms of their gene pairs.

Endocrine glands: Glands that secrete hormones into the blood.

Endoscope: An instrument for looking into the inside of a cavity such as the intestine.

Enzyme: A type of protein that speeds up a chemical reaction. A protein that acts as a catalyst; a chemical substance that causes other chemical substances to react faster than they otherwise would. Most enzymes are very specific and catalyze only one kind of chemical reaction.

Erythrocyte: Red blood cell.

Esophagus: The part of the digestive system between the throat and the stomach.

Estrogen: A female hormone.

Familial Polyposis Coli: An inherited condition in which hundreds of polyps develop in the colon and rectum.

Fat: A class of molecules that does not dissolve in water; synonymous with "lipid." Fat is stored in the adipose tissues of the body for future use as a source of energy if needed.

Fecal occult blood test: A test to determine if there is blood in the stool.

Founder effect: A mutation that develops in a single person which is passed on to future generations in an isolated group because the members only marry within that group.

Gamete: A mature male or female reproductive cell (a sperm or an ovum) with a single set (23) of chromosomes.

Ganglioside: A class of molecule, containing both lipid and carbohydrate molecules, and a component of cell membranes.

Gastrointestinal tract: The stomach and intestines.

Gene: The basic unit of heredity. An ordered array of nucleotides which constitutes the code for making a particular protein. Every gene, with the exception of genes on the X chromosome in males, come in pairs.

Gene expression: The means by which a gene's code is converted into a protein.

Gene product: The biochemical material resulting from the expression of a gene. The amount of gene product can be used to determine if the gene is active or dysfunctional.

Gene therapy: A procedure for correcting a genetic defect by inserting normal genes into cells to replace those that are defective.

Genetic: Relating to the genes or heredity.

Genetic code: The genetic "dictionary" containing all the hereditary information. The dictionary specifies which amino acids are to be linked to form a protein.

Genetic disease: A disease primarily resulting from a defect in a gene or chromosome.

Genetics: The study of patterns of inheritance.

Genome: An individual's entire genetic makeup (a contraction of gene and chromosome).

Glucagon: Hormone secreted by the pancreas that increases glucose levels in the blood.

Glucose: A sugar molecule; the "fuel" for normal cell functioning; blood sugar.

Glycogen: Molecule made up of several glucose molecules; the form in which glucose is stored in the body when it is not immediately needed.

Glycosidase: An enzyme that breaks the linkages between sugar molecules.

Guanine: One of the chemicals making up the base pairs in DNA.

Haploid: A single set of chromosomes. The 23 chromosomes in a sperm or ovum cell that will unite with the other set to form a diploid set.

Haplotype: A specific combination of related genes. A contraction of haploid and genotype.

Hemoglobin: Part of red blood cells made up of iron and protein.

Hemorrhoids: Dilated veins in the anus or rectum.

Heredity: Transmission of traits from parent to child through genes.

Heterozygous: The condition in which the two alleles for a given characteristic that are located at the same place on the same chromosome are not identical.

Histamine: Chemical present in cells released during allergic reaction like runny nose, sneezing, itching, and narrowing of airways.

Homozygous: The condition in which the two alleles for a given characteristic that are located at the same place on the same chromosome are identical.

Hormone: Chemical substances produced by endocrine glands secreted into the blood that act on other endocrine glands or cells.

Hyperinsulinism: Excess levels of insulin in the blood.

Hypoglycemia: Lower-than-normal levels of glucose in the blood.

Ileostomy: A surgical procedure in which an opening is made in the small intestine and then attached to the abdominal wall, creating a passage so that waste can be eliminated. (See also Colostomy.)

Ileum: The terminal area of the small intestine.

Immune system: The cells and proteins that protect the body from infection; involved in allergic reactions, hypersensitivities, and rejection of transplanted organs.

Immunosuppressive drugs: Medications that suppress the immune system.

Inborn error of metabolism: An inherited disease involving some chemical reaction in the body.

Inflammation: Reaction of cells to infection or injury, characterized by redness, swelling, and pain.

Inflammatory Bowel Disease: An inflammation of the lining of the digestive system associated with Ulcerative Colitis and Crohn's Disease.

Insulin: Hormone secreted by the pancreas that regulates entry of glucose into cells.

Intestine: Area of the digestive system from the stomach to the anus.

Jaundice: A yellowing of the skin caused by bilirubin.

Jejunum: A part of the small intestine located between the duodenum and the ileum.

Karyotype: A picture of an individual's chromosomes arranged formally with respect to number, size, and shape of each chromosome.

Lactase: Enzyme secreted by intestine that breaks down the milk sugar, lactose.

Lactose: A type of sugar found in milk; composed of glucose and galactose.

LDL: Low-density lipoprotein. The molecule that carries cholesterol into cells. Too much LDL accumulating in artery walls can constrict blood flow.

Leukocyte: White blood cell.

Leukopenia: Low white cell count.

Linkage test: An indirect means of genetic testing in which a known area of DNA near a gene for a disorder is used as a marker for that gene. Linkage tests are used when a flawed gene has not as yet been identified or when direct testing is not feasible because the mutation has not as yet been characterized.

Lipase: An enzyme that breaks the linkage between two lipid molecules.

Lipid: Another term for fat. (See also Fat.)

Lipoprotein: Compounds made up of lipids and proteins.

Lymph: A fluid that derives from and drains into blood; it acts as a conduit for destroying bacterial and cancer cells. On the way to reentry into blood, it is filtered through nodes located primarily in the neck, armpits and groin, abdomen and chest. Lymph nodes contain cells from the immune system that attempt to neutralize foreign cells.

Lymphoctye: Type of white blood cell that produces antibodies.

Lymphoma: A cancer affecting the lymph system.

Lysosomal storage disease: An inherited metabolic disease in which an enzyme normally present in the lysosome is missing. As a result, the cellular debris that would normally be degraded accumulates inside the lysosome, causing it to expand until it fills the entire cell, thereby killing the cell.

Lysosome: A component within the cell that contains enzymes which break down cellular debris.

Macrophage: A type of cell in the circulation and in various tissues, especially the spleen, that is part of the immune system. It "ingests" old blood cells and foreign substances and brings them to the lysosome where they are broken down into harmless substances.

Magnetic Resonance Imaging (MRI): A technique that uses magnetic fields and radio waves to visualize internal structures of the body.

Malignant: Cancerous; uncontrollable growth of cells that can spread from one site of the body to another.

Marker: A region of DNA that can be identified and tracked from one generation to the next.

Meiosis: The process by which haploid gametes are produced. Initially a sex cell divides into two diploid cells, then each of these divides into two haploid cells.

Messenger RNA: The intermediate chemical that converts the DNA code into a protein.

Metabolism: The chemical processes that occur within a cell; the process by which food is transformed into chemicals that the body can use, and conversely the process by which chemicals are broken down into more simple substances.

Metastasis: The spread of cancer cells from one part of the body to another.

Mineral: Nutrients that are inorganic substances.

Mitosis: The process of cell division in which one cell divides into two identical cells.

Molecule: The smallest unit that a substance can be broken down into and still retain its identity.

Mucus: A liquid substance that keeps membranes moist.

Mutation: An alteration in the chemical composition of DNA.

Myelin: A white, fatty sheath found around some nerves which enables them to conduct nerve impulses more rapidly.

Nucleotide: The subunit by which the "bases" in DNA are held together. The nucleotide consists of a base, a phosphate molecule, and a sugar molecule called deoxyribose.

Nutrient: Substance found in food and needed by the body to maintain integrity and function.

Obligate: Relating to a specific set of circumstances, for example, a child whose parents are both carriers of a particular gene.

Occult: Hidden.

Oncologist: A doctor who specializes in treatment of cancer.

Pancreas: Gland located below the stomach which releases digestive juices into the small intestine and insulin and glucagon into the blood to regulate glucose metabolism.

Pancytopenia: Same as aplastic anemia.

Penetrance: Expression of a gene's effects. When a disease-causing gene is not "completely penetrant," only some people with the abnormal gene will develop symptoms of the disease.

Peritonitis: An infection of the membrane lining the abdominal wall.

Phagocytosis: Engulfment of cells or cellular debris by other cells.

Phenotype: The physical characteristics produced by one's genes.

Pituitary: Endocrine gland located in base of brain, which secretes hormones that regulate glands in other part of the body.

Platelets: Blood components that prevent bleeding and bruising.

Polygenic disorder: A genetic disease resulting from the presence of more than one defective allele.

Polymorphism: A genetic variation in which people from the same inter-breeding population can be grouped into two or more distinctive types based on relatively common alternative forms of an allele at a specific locus. Common polymorphic types include blood groups (A,B,O), blood types (Rh-positive and Rh-negative) and certain enzymes. Classes associated with a particular geographical area are known as geographic polymorphism.

Polyp: An abnormal growth on the inside of the colon or rectum.

Presymptomatic testing: Identification of people who have a known disease-causing gene who have not yet developed any symptoms.

Protein: A molecule composed of a sequence of amino acids linked in a specific order which is determined by a gene. Proteins are the basic materials out of which cells are made and cells operate. Each protein has a unique function; some are enzymes, some are hormones, etc.

Radiation therapy: Treatment with X-rays to kill cancer cells.

Recessive gene: An allele that is not normally expressed unless the other allele in the gene pair is also recessive.

Respiration: Breathing. The process by which oxygen is taken into the lungs and the cellular waste products of water and carbon dioxide leave the lungs.

Respiratory system: Group of organs that carry oxygen from air to the blood and expel cellular waste product carbon dioxide.

Retina: Area at back of eye upon which light is focused and where images are formed.

Risk factor: Something that increases someone's chance of developing a disease.

Sex chromosomes: The pair of chromosomes that determine an individual's gender: two X chromosomes for a female, one X and one Y for a male.

Sigmoidoscopy: A exam in which a hollow tube is passed into the rectum and lower colon to look for inflammation, polyps and tumors.

Starch: Complex carbohydrate which is broken down into glucose.

Symptom: Indications of bodily disorders.

Thrombocyte: Platelet.

Thrombocytopenia: Low platelet count.

Tumor: An abnormal clump of cells.

Tumor suppressor gene: A gene that regulates cell division. If both alleles are defective, the "brakes" on cell division are removed and tumors may develop.

White blood cell: Same as leukocyte.

X-linked genetic disease: A disease resulting from a defective gene located on the X chromosome.

Screening Centers

All Children's Hospital of St. Petersburg
801 Sixth Street South
St. Petersburg, FL 33701
    Cytogenetic Laboratory
       (813) 892-8835
    Molecular Genetics Clinical Laboratory
       (813) 892-8985

Allegheny General Hospital
320 East North Avenue
Pittsburgh, PA 15212
    Molecular Diagnostic Laboratory
       (412) 359-6388

Allegheny University of the Health Sciences
Center for Gene Therapy
245 North 15th Street
Philadelphia, PA 19102
(215) 762-7234

Allegheny University of the Health Sciences
Center for Genomic Sciences
3343 Forbes Avenue
Pittsburgh, PA 15212
(412) 330-4645

Applied Genetics, Inc.
1524 South IH 35, #200
Austin, TX 78704
(512) 443-4363

Athena Diagnostics, Inc.
377 Plantation Street
Worcester, MA 01605
(800) 394-4493
(508) 753-5601

Baylor College of Medicine
One Baylor Plaza—T536
Houston, TX 77030
    DNA Diagnostic Laboratory
       (713) 798-6536
    Kleberg Cytogenetics Laboratory
       (713) 798-5919

Blood Center of Southeastern Wisconsin
638 North 18th Street
P.O. Box 2178
Milwaukee, WI 53201
(414) 937-6120

Boston University—HFI Laboratory
5 Cummington Street
Boston, MA 02215
(617) 353-5310

Boston University School of Medicine
Center for Human Genetics
80 E. Concord Street
Boston, MA 02118
(617) 638-7083

Boys Town National Research Hospital
Gene Marker Laboratory
555 North 30th Street
Omaha, NE 68131
(402) 498-6713

Cardinal Glennon Children's Hospital
Molecular Cytogenetics Lab
1465 South Grand Boulevard
St. Louis, MO 63104
(314) 577-5393

Case Western Reserve University
Center for Human Genetics Laboratory
10524 Euclid Avenue
Cleveland, OH 44106-2206
(216) 983-1134

Cedars-Sinai Medical Center
8700 Beverly Boulevard
Los Angeles, CA 90048
(310) 855-7627
(310) 423-9913 (Cancer)
(310) 423-9914 (Pediatric Disorders)

Celtek Laboratories
2323 North Mayfair Road
Milwaukee, WI 53226
(414) 475-7984

Chapman Institute of Medical Genetics
5300 East Shelly Drive
Tulsa, OK 74135
(918) 628-6363

Children's Hospital Los Angeles
Molecular Genetics
4650 Sunset Boulevard
MS #11
Los Angeles, CA 90027
(213) 669-2271

Children's Hospital National Medical
  Center
Biochemical and Molecular Genetics
111 Michigan Avenue NW
Washington, DC 20010-2970
(202) 884-3996

Children's Hospital Oakland
DNA Laboratory
747 52nd Street
Oakland, CA 94609
(510) 428-3623

Children's Hospital of Akron
Molecular Pathology
One Perkins Square
Akron, OH 44308
(330) 379-8722

Children's Hospital of Boston
300 Longwood Avenue
Boston, MA 02115
    Clinical Genetics Laboratory
    (617) 355-7582
    Beggs Lab
    (617) 355-7574

Children's Hospital of Buffalo
Genetics Laboratory
936 Delaware Avenue
Buffalo, NY 14209
(716) 878-7513

Children's Hospital of Dayton
Medical Genetics
One Children's Plaza
Dayton, OH 45404
(937) 226-8408

Children's Hospital of Philadelphia
34th and Civic Center Boulevard
Philadelphia, PA 19104-4399
(215) 590-3856

Children's Hospital of Pittsburgh
Medical Genetics Laboratory
4222 Rangos Research Building
3705 Fifth Avenue
Pittsburgh, PA 15213-2583
(412) 692-5070

Children's Hospital of Seattle
Molecular Diagnostic Laboratory
4800 Sand Point Way NE
Seattle, WA 98105
(206) 526-2216

Children's Hospital San Diego
Molecular Genetics Laboratory
3020 Children's Way—#5031
San Diego, CA 92123
(619) 495-4911

Children's Medical Center at Stony
  Brook
Department of Pediatrics
Stony Brook, NY 11794-8111
(516) 444-2700

Children's Mercy Hospital
Molecular Genetics
2401 Gillham Road
Kansas City, MO 64108
(816) 931-8080

Cincinnati Children's Hospital Medical Center
CHMC Molecular Diagnostic Laboratory
3333 Burnet Avenue
Cincinnati, OH 45229-3039
(513) 836-8430

City of Hope National Medical Center
Clinical Molecular Diagnostic Laboratory
1500 East Duarte Road
Duarte, CA 91010-3000
(888) 826-4362

Columbia Medical Center
630 West 168th Street
New York, NY 10032
(212) 305-7701

Cornell University Medical College
DNA Diagnosis Laboratory
515 East 71st Street
New York, NY 10021
(212) 746-3475

Dartmouth Hitchcock Medical Center
Molecular Genetics Diagnostic Laboratory
One Medical Center Drive
Lebanon, NH 03756
(603) 650-7171

Dianon Systems, Inc.
200 Watson Boulevard
Stratford, CT 06497
(800) 328-2666
(203) 381-4000

Duke University Medical Center
99 Alexander Drive
P.O. Box 14991
Research Triangle Park, NC 27709
 Pediatric Medical Genetics
  (919) 549-0445

Duke University Medical Center
Center for Human Genetics
Box 3445
Durham, NC 27710
(800) 283-4316

Dynacare Laboratory of Pathology
1229 Madison, Suite 500

Seattle, WA 98104
(206) 386-2672

Eastern Virginia Medical School
Jones Institute for Reproductive Medicine
601 Colley Avenue
Norfolk, VA 23507
(757) 446-7168

Emory Genetics Laboratory
2711 Irvin Way, Suite 111
Decatur, GA 30030
(800) 366-1502
(404) 297-1500

Emory University
Department of Pediatrics
2040 Ridgewood Drive
Atlanta, GA 30322
(404) 727-5845

Emory University School of Medicine
Howard Hughes Medical Institute
1510 Clifton Road
Atlanta, GA 30322
(404) 727-5979

Evanston Northwestern HealthCare
2650 Ridge Avenue
Evanston, IL
(847) 570-1029

Fairview University Medical Center
Molecular Diagnostics Laboratory
420 Delaware Street SE
Box 198 Mayo
Minneapolis, MN 55455
(612) 624-8445

Henry Ford Hospital
DNA Diagnostic Laboratory
2799 West Grand Boulevard
Detroit, MI 48202-2689
(800) 888-4340
(800) 999-4340
(313) 876-7681

Genelex
2203 Airport Way South, Suite 130
Seattle, WA 98134
(800) 523-6487

Genetics & IVF Institute
3022 Javier Road

Fairfax, VA 22031
(800) 654-4363

Genzyme Genetics
One Mountain Road
Framingham, MA 01701-9322
(800) 252-7357

Georgetown University Children's Medical Center
Molecular Genetic Diagnostic Laboratory
3800 Reservoir Road, NW
Washington, DC 20007
(202) 687-8996

Greenwood Genetic Center
Molecular Diagnostic Laboratory
1 Gregor Mendel Circle
Greenwood, SC 29646
(864) 941-8177

Huntington Medical Research Institutes
Molecular Oncology Laboratory
99 North El Molino Avenue
Pasadena, CA 91101
(626) 795-4343

Idna Laboratory Inc.
1312 Shermer Road
Northbrook, IL 60062
(847) 362-8378

Indiana University Medical Center
Molecular Genetics
541 Clinical Drive
Indianapolis, IN 46202-5111
(317) 274-7597

Jefferson Medical College
Jefferson Alumni Hall, Room 394
1020 Locust Street
Philadelphia, PA 19107
(215) 955-4923

Johns Hopkins Medical Institute
Kennedy Krieger Institute
Clinical Mass Spectrometry Laboratory
707 North Broadway
Baltimore, MD 21205

(410) 502-9444
Fax: (410) 502-8279
E-Mail: CMSL@KennedyKrieger.org

Johns Hopkins University
Center for Medical Genetics
600 North Wolfe Street
Baltimore, MD 21287-4922
(410) 955-7948

Johns Hopkins University School of Hygiene
Division of Reproductive Biology
615 North Wolfe Street
Baltimore, MD 21205-2103
(410) 955-1055

Johns Hopkins University School of Medicine
Center for Craniofacial Development
600 North Wolfe Street
Baltimore, MD 21287-3914
    Center for Craniofacial Development
    (410) 955-4160
    DNA Diagnostic Laboratory
    (410) 955-1773

Kapiolani Health Research Institute
1946 Young Street
Honolulu, HI 96826-2150
(808) 973-8349

Kimball Genetics, Inc.
Molecular Diagnostic Laboratory
101 University Boulevard
Denver, CO 80206
(800) 320-1807
(303) 320-1807

Lifecodes Corporation
550 West Avenue
Stamford, CT 06902
(203) 328-9500

Massachusetts General Hospital
Neurochemistry/Amino Acid Laboratory
149 13th Street
Boston, MA 02129
    Neurochemistry Laboratory
    (617) 726-3884
    Neurogenetics DNA Diagnostic Lab
    (617) 726-5721

Mayo Clinic
Molecular Genetics Laboratory
200 First Street SW
Rochester, MN 55905
(507) 284-4169

Medical College of Georgia
Neurology Gene Probe Laboratory
15th Street
Augusta, GA 30912
(706) 721-3170

Medical Genetic Consultants, Inc.
910 Washington Avenue
Ocean Springs, MS 39564
(228) 872-3680

Medical Genetics Institute, S.C.
Molecular Genetics Laboratory
4555 West Schroeder Drive
Milwaukee, WI 53223-1470
(414) 357-6555

Montefiore Medical Center
1695 E. Chesterow
Bronx, NY 10461
(718) 405 8210

Mount Sinai School of Medicine
Genetic Testing Laboratory
1184 Fifth Avenue
New York, NY 10029
(212) 241-6043

Myriad Genetic Laboratories
320 Wakara Way
Salt Lake City, UT 84108
(800) 469-7423

National Cancer Institute
8901 Rockville Pike
Bethesda, MD 20889-5105
(301) 469-0901

National Institutes of Health
Medical Genetics
10 Center Drive
Bethesda, MD 20892-1267
(301) 402-8255

New York State Institute for Basic
   Research in Developmental Disabili-
   ties
Clinical Cytogenetics

1050 Forest Hill Road
Staten Island, NY 10314-6399
   Clinical Cytogenetics
   (718) 494-5236
   Genetic Testing
   (718) 494-5239

New York University School of Medicine
Molecular Genetics Laboratory of NYU
   Medical Center
550 First Avenue, MSB 136
New York, NY 10016
(212) 263-7635

North Shore University Hospital at
   Manhasset—Medical Genetics
444 Community Drive, Suite 201
Manhasset, NY 11030
516 365-3996

Ohio State University
Molecular Pathology
121 Hamilton Hall
1645 Neil Avenue
Columbus, OH 43210
(614) 292-5484

Oncormed, Inc.
215 Perry Parkway
Gaithersburg, MD 20877
(800) 662-6763
(301) 208-1888

Oregon Health Sciences University
DNA Diagnostic Laboratory
707 SW Gaines Road
Portland, OR 97201
(503) 494-7821

Oregon Health Sciences University
Hayflick Lab
3181 SW Sam Jackson Park Road
Portland, OR 97201
(503) 494-6866

Puget Sound Blood Center
Coagulation Reference Laboratory
921 Terry Avenue
Seattle, WA 98104-1256
(206) 292-6570
(206) 292-6594

Puget Sound Blood Center

Hemostasis Genetic Diagnostic Laboratory
921 Terry Avenue
Seattle, WA 98104-1256
(206) 292-6570

Quest Diagnostics, Inc.
33608 Ortega Highway
San Juan Capistrano, CA 92690
(800) 642-4657

Roswell Park Cancer Institute
Cancer Genetics
Elm and Carlton Streets
Buffalo, NY 14068-0001
(716) 845-8059

Rush-Presbyterian-St. Luke's Medical Center
Genetics Laboratory
1750 West Harrison
Chicago, IL 60612-3824
(312) 942-6298

Saint Louis University Medical School
DNA Diagnostic Laboratory
1402 South Grand Boulevard
St. Louis, MO 63104
(314) 577-8482

San Francisco General Hospital
1001 Potrero Avenue
San Francisco, CA 94110
(415) 647-3992

Shodair Hospital
Genetics Laboratory
840 Helena Avenue
P.O. Box 5539
Helena, MT 59604
(800) 447-6614
(406) 444-7532

SmithKline Beecham Clinical Laboratories
Genetic Testing Center
7600 Tyrone Avenue
Van Nuys, CA 91405
(800) 877-2520, ext 2424

State University of New York at Stony Brook
Molecular Diagnostics Laboratory
University Hospital

Stony Brook, NY 11794-7300
(516) 444-3747

State University of New York Health Science Center
Molecular Diagnostics Laboratory
750 East Adams Street
Syracuse, NY 13210
(315) 464-6806

Thomas Jefferson University
Lysosomal Diseases Testing Laboratory
1020 Locust Street
Philadelphia, PA 19107
(215) 955-9666

Thomas Jefferson University
Molecular Diagnostic Laboratory
1100 Walnut Street
Philadelphia, PA 19107
(215) 955-8320

University of Alabama at Birmingham
Laboratory of Medical Genetics
908 20th Street South
Birmingham, AL 35294-2050
(205) 934-4983

University of Alabama Health Services Foundation
Immunogenetics Laboratory
1025 18th Street South
Birmingham, AL 35294-4440
(205) 934-2362

University of Arkansas for Medical Sciences
DNA Laboratory
4301 West Markham
Little Rock, AR 72205-71799
(501) 686-7668

University of California at Davis Medical Center
Molecular and Cytogenetics Laboratory
4625 Second Avenue
Sacramento, CA 95817
(916) 734-1670

University of California at Los Angeles
Jules Stein Eye Institute

200 Stein Plaza
Los Angeles, CA 90095
(310) 206-7475

University of California at Los Angeles
  Medical Center
Diagnostic Molecular Pathology Laboratory
10833 Le Conte Avenue
Los Angeles, CA 90095-1713
(310) 206-5294

University of California at San Diego
Molecular Genetics Laboratory
9500 Gilman Drive
La Jolla, CA 92093-0639
(619) 534-1353

University of California at San Francisco
Molecular Diagnostics Laboratory
505 Parnassus Avenue
San Francisco, CA 94143
(415) 476-1525

University of Chicago
Genetic Services
5841 South Maryland
Chicago, IL 60637
(888) 824-3637

University of Colorado School of Medicine
UCHSC DNA Diagnostic Laboratory
4200 East Ninth Avenue
Denver, CO 80262
(303) 315-8415

University of Connecticut Health Center
Surgical Research Center
263 Farmington Avenue
Farmington, CT 06030-1110
(860) 679-4503

University of Iowa
Department of Pediatrics
Iowa City, IA 52242
(319) 335-6946

University of Iowa Hospitals and Clinics
Department of Pathology
200 Hawkins Drive
Iowa City, IA 52242-1078
  Department of Pathology

(319) 356-2129
Molecular Otolaryngology
Research Laboratories
(319) 356-2177

University of Miami School of Medicine
Pediatrics Neurogenetic Laboratory
1601 NW 12th Avenue
Miami, FL 33136
(305) 243-3997

University of Minnesota
Department of Pediatrics
Biochemical Genetics and Metabolism
  Laboratory
516 Delaware Street SE
Minneapolis, MN 55455
(612) 624-5923

University of Minnesota
Pigment Laboratory—International
  Albinism Center
420 Delaware Street SE
Minneapolis, MN 55455
(612) 624-0144

University of Nevada
DNA Analysis Laboratory
Department of Microbiology
Reno, NV 89557-0046
(702) 784-4494

University of Pennsylvania
Department of Genetics
415 Curie Boulevard
Philadelphia, PA 19104-6145
(800) 669-2172
(215) 573-9161

University of Pennsylvania Health System
Molecular Pathology
3400 Spruce Street
Philadelphia, PA 19104
(215) 662-6550

University of Pittsburgh Medical Center
Division of Molecular Diagnostics
3550 Terrace Street
Pittsburgh, PA 15213-2500
(412) 648-8519

University of South Dakota School of
  Medicine

Genetics Laboratory
1100 South Euclid Avenue
Sioux Falls, SD 57105
(605) 333-5202

University of Southern California
School of Medicine
Biochemistry Laboratory
2250 Alcazar Street
Los Angeles, CA 90033-1004
(213) 442-1144

University of Tennessee Medical Center
Biochemical and Molecular Genetics
  Laboratory
1924 Alcoa Highway
Knoxville, TN 37920
(423) 544-9449

University of Tennessee Medical Center
Developmental and Genetic Center
1930 Alcoa Highway
Knoxville, TN 37920-6999
(423)544-9030

University of Texas Health
  Science Center at Houston
Medical Genetics Laboratory
6431 Fannin
Houston, TX 77030
(713) 500-6727

University of Texas Health Science Center at San Antonio
Molecular Diagnostics Laboratory
7703 Floyd Curl Drive
San Antonio, TX 78284-7750
(210) 567-4102

University of Utah
DNA Diagnostic Laboratory
10 North 2030 East
Salt Lake City, UT 84112
(888) 362-6277
(801) 581-8334

University of Vermont
Department of Pathology

Burlington, VT 05405
(802) 656-4553

University of Washington
Department of Pathology
1959 NE Pacific Street
Seattle, WA 98195-7720
(206) 543-8285

Vanderbilt University Medical Center
Department of Pathology
1301 22nd Avenue South
Nashville, TN 37232
(615) 343-8121

Washington University Barnes-
  Jewish Hospital
Molecular Diagnostic Laboratory
216 South Kingshighway
St. Louis, MO 63110
(314) 454-7053

Wayne State University
Biochemical and Molecular Genetics
  Laboratory
Scott Hall
Detroit, MI 48201
(313) 577-8504

Wayne State University
Harper Hospital
Molecular Genetics Diagnostic Laboratory
Detroit, MI 48201
(313) 993-2631

William Beaumont Hospital
Molecular Pathology
3601 W. 13 Mile Road
Royal Oak, MI 48073
(248) 551-7261

Yale University School of Medicine
DNA Diagnostics Laboratory
333 Cedar Street
New Haven, CT 06520-8005
(203) 785-5745

Index

abetalipoproteinemia 159–162; age of onset 160; cause 161; diagnosis 161; discovery 159–160; frequency 160; symptoms 160; transmission 161–132; treatment 162

adrenals 164–165; *see also* Congenital Adrenal Hyperplasia

Adrenogenital Syndrome *see* Congenital Adrenal Hyperplasia

alcohol 6

aldosterone 163; *see also* Congenital Adrenal Hyperplasia

allele *see* gene

amniocentesis 22, 41, 50, 63, 115, 135

androgens 164

anemia 36–37, 48, 54, 150; *see also* Factor XI Deficiency; Fanconi Anemia; Gaucher Disease; Glucose-6-Phosphate Dehydrogenase Deficiency; Thalassemia

angina 179

apoprotein 160, 177

arthritis 138

Ashkenazi 3, 22, 31–32, 34; lysosomal disorders 90; migration to American 29, 34; numbers 29; origins 6, 24, 28, 30; divisions 29; *see also* Abetalipoproteinemia; Bloom Syndrome; breast cancer; Canavan Disease; colorectal cancer; Congenital Adrenal Hyperplasia; essential pentosuria; Factor XI Deficiency; Familial Dysautonomia; Familial Hypercholesterolemia; Familial Hyperinsulinism; Familial Mediterranean Fever; Fanconi Anemia; Gaucher Disease; hearing loss; Hunter Syndrome; Inflammatory Bowel Disease; lactose intolerance; Mucolipidosis Type IV; Niemann-Pick Disease; Pemphigus Vulgaris; Tarui Disease; Tay-Sachs Disease; Torsion Dystonia; ulcerative colitis

asthma 1

Ataxia-telangiectasia 90–94; age of onset 92; cause 92; diagnosis 92–93; frequency 91; prevention 93; screening 94; Sephardic 91; symtoms 91–92; transmission 93; variations 90–91

autonomic nervous system 89, 103; *see also* Familial Dysautonomia

autosomal disorders 18, 20; *see also* Abetalipoproteinemia; Ataxia-telangiectasia; Bloom Syndrome; Canavan Disease; carrier; Congenital Adrenal Hyperplasia; cystic fibrosis; Factor XI Deficiency; Familial Dysautonomia; Familial Mediterranean Fever; Gaucher Disease; Metachromatic Leukodystrophy; Mucolipidosis Type IV; Neimann-Pick Disease; Tarui Disease

autosomal dominant disorders *see* Creutzfeldt-Jakob Disease; Familial Hypercholesterolemia; Torsion Dystonia

balanced translocation 21; *see also* chromosome abnormalities